# FIELD GUIDE TO

# BIRDS

## OF BRITAIN

## & EUROPE

# FIELD GUIDE TO
# BIRDS
## OF BRITAIN
## & EUROPE

CONSULTANT EDITOR
## PAUL STERRY

Published by AA Publishing (a trading name of AA Media Limited, whose registered office is Fanum House, Basing View, Basingstoke RG21 4EA; registered number 06112600).

Packaged for AA Media by D & N Publishing, Baydon, Wiltshire.

© Copyright AA Media Limited 2010
Reprinted November 2010

Text additions and amendments by Paul Sterry and the BTO 2010
Digital imaging and manipulation by Paul Sterry 2010

theAA.com/shop

A04575

ISBNs: 978-0-7495-6251-9 & 978-0-7495-6408-7 (SS)

A CIP catalogue record for this book is available from the British Library.

The contents of this publication are believed correct at the time of printing. Nevertheless, the publishers cannot be held responsible for any errors or omissions or for changes in the details given in this guide or for the consequences of any reliance on the information provided by the same. This does not affect your statutory rights.

The paper is TCF – totally chlorine free. It is also PEFC and FSC and comes from totally renewable forests that are well managed.

Printed and bound in Dubai by Oriental Press.

Contributing authors: Dr Paul Sterry (consultant editor); Andrew Cleave MBE, Dr Andy Clements, Peter Goodfellow and Mike Toms
Designer: Shane O'Dwyer
Managing Editor at AA Publishing: Paul Mitchell
Production at AA Publishing: Stephanie Allen
Maps created by Gulmohur Press Pvt Ltd, New Delhi, India

The Publishers would like to thank Paul Sterry, Shane O'Dwyer, David and Namrita Price-Goodfellow (D & N Publishing), Mike Toms and the staff of the BTO, particularly Chas Holt (for checking the maps) and John Marchant (for checking the text), for all their hard work on this book and dedication to the project. A special thanks to Paul Sterry, without whom none of this would have happened.

Photograph previous page: male Stonechat.

Photograph below: adult winter Ross's Gull.

Photographs opposite page: adult Hobby (*above*) and adult summer female Grey Phalarope (*below*).

# CONTENTS

# HOW TO USE THIS BOOK

The *Field Guide to Birds of Britain and Europe* contains detailed and accurate descriptions for every bird species found on a regular basis in Europe. Stunning photography and artwork underpin the book's function as a field guide and also serve as a visual celebration of the region's wonderful birdlife.

The FIELD GUIDE TO BIRDS OF BRITAIN AND EUROPE's *lavish **illustrations** have been created by some of Britain and Ireland's finest artists. Some of the illustrations portray interesting behaviour while others focus on accurate detail for identification purposes.

**ARTWORK**

*Provides the species's **common English name**, scientific name, **length**, **wingspan** and a **summary** paragraph introducing the bird in question.*

**SPECIES INTRODUCTION**

## MAPS

*Maps of the region show the distribution for every regularly encountered species. Different colours depict differing seasonal status:*

■ = PRESENT IN THE DEPICTED AREA YEAR-ROUND
■ = PRESENT IN SPRING AND SUMMER
■ = PRESENT IN WINTER

## FURTHER INFORMATION

*Unusual and unexpected facts about European birds are presented in boxes that are distributed throughout the book; some relate to the species in question's plumage, others to behaviour or distribution.*

## PHOTOGRAPHS

*Superb **colour photographs** illustrate as wide a range of plumages, poses and behaviours as space permits, for every species found in Europe. Some of the images were taken especially for the book.*

DUCKS

### MALLARD
*ANAS PLATYRHYNCHOS*

LENGTH 50–65cm
WINGSPAN 80–100cm

Mallards can be found in almost any freshwater habitat and are occasionally seen around the coast as well. Mallards are often tame.

The Mallard is probably one of the most familiar wildfowl species in western Europe, often seen being fed by humans in urban parks and on ponds; ducklings are capable swimmers almost immediately after hatching.

*female*

*male*

Male (BELOW) and female (BOTTOM) Mallards are easily distinguished, but the bright orange legs are common to both sexes.

**IDENTIFICATION** Male has yellow bill, green head showing sheen in good light, chestnut breast and otherwise mostly grey-brown plumage; shows black stern and white tail. Female has orange-yellow bill and rather uniform brown plumage. Eclipse male similar to female but more reddish on breast. In flight both sexes show white-bordered blue speculum. **HABITAT** Almost anywhere with water. **VOICE** Female gives familiar quack; male a weak nasal note.

26

## IDENTIFICATION SECTION

*Detailed descriptions are given allowing for easy recognition and separation from superficially similar or closely related species. Every recognisably distinct plumage is covered and, where appropriate, these include male, female, juvenile, summer and winter; sexes are assumed to be similar if not stated otherwise.*

*To complement the main text and identification section, **extended captions** are intended to provide additional information that will aid recognition and identification, or details that will help with the determination of gender or plumage.*

**EXTENDED CAPTIONS**

# WHAT ARE BIRDS?

*BLACKBIRD*

Birds are arguably the most familiar of all animal groups. While they show tremendous variation in colour, plumage and bill shape and size, the shared feature of having a body covered in feathers underlines their common ancestry. Almost all bird species can undertake powered flight and a feature shared by all is that they reproduce by laying eggs.

*WOODPIGEON Contour feather*

*WOODPIGEON primary feather*

*WOODPIGEON tail feather*

*ADULT WOODPIGEON*

*GRIFFON VULTURE*

## FEATHERS AND PLUMAGE

The plumage of a bird creates its external appearance and can either be an indication of gender and social status or provide camouflage from potential predators. Feathers are made from keratin (the same substance that forms our nails and hair) and are good insulators, trapping a layer of air between the body feathers and the skin. Each bird has a number of different feather types, serving different functions within the overall plumage. These include the flight feathers, which are stiff and elongated, held together along the line of the feather shaft by a series of barbules that effectively 'zip' the feather together. There are also contour feathers, which cover the body, comprising a 'zipped' outer section and an 'unzipped' fluffy inner section; the outer section provides protection, the looser inner section serves as insulation.

## FLIGHT

Various tracts of feathers are adapted for flight, particularly those along the rear edge of the wing and on the tail. These feathers are elongated (when compared to other body feathers), strengthened and shaped so that, collectively, they can provide the thrust, lift and manoeuvrability needed in the air. The most energetically costly component of flight is take-off. Once airborne, the process of flying becomes more efficient and many birds can cover a considerable distance with relatively little expenditure of energy. Some species further enhance their energetic effectiveness by soaring on thermals.

# GLOSSARY OF BIRD TOPOGRAPHY

Some of the words and phrases that are used to describe bird body parts and feathers sound a bit technical, so here are simple explanations of the meanings of the words used to label the bird topography illustrations.

**Axillaries** Feathers on the inner part of the underwing, corresponding to what might be called the 'armpit'.

**Belly** The area of underparts roughly between the legs of a bird.

**Breast** The area of underparts above the belly.

**Coverts** The name given to a group of feathers covering a particular part of a bird's body. Thus ear coverts cover the ear, undertail coverts are found on the undertail area and underwing coverts are found lining the inner part of the underwing. Those feathers on the upperwing not concerned with flight are also referred to as coverts; they are arranged in zones, which are, from the leading edge backwards, referred to as greater, median and lesser coverts; those covering the bases of the primary feathers are called primary coverts.

**Crown** Top of the head.

**Eyestripe** Stripe running through the eye.

**Flank** Area of feathers on the side of the underparts.

**Lore** Region of feathers between the eye and the bill.

**Malar stripe** Marking originating at the base of the lower mandible of the bill.

**Mandible** One half of the bill.

**Mantle** Area of feathers on the upper back.

**Nostril** Opening on the bill that allows breathing.

**Primaries** Outer flight feathers.

**Secondaries** Flight feathers in the middle of the wing.

**Supercilium** Stripe above the eye.

**Tarsus** What most people take to be a bird's leg, although anatomically it is part of the foot.

**Tertials** Inner flight feathers.

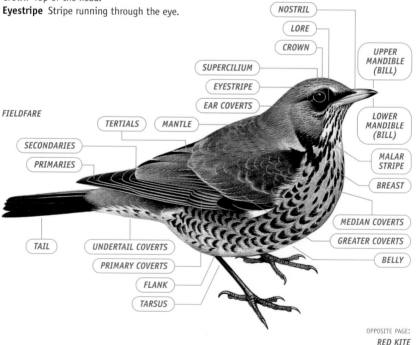

FIELDFARE

NOSTRIL
LORE
CROWN
SUPERCILIUM
EYESTRIPE
EAR COVERTS
TERTIALS
MANTLE
SECONDARIES
PRIMARIES
UPPER MANDIBLE (BILL)
LOWER MANDIBLE (BILL)
MALAR STRIPE
BREAST
MEDIAN COVERTS
GREATER COVERTS
BELLY
TAIL
UNDERTAIL COVERTS
PRIMARY COVERTS
FLANK
TARSUS

OPPOSITE PAGE:
*RED KITE*

AXILLARIES (ARMPIT)

TERTIALS

UNDERWING COVERTS

SECONDARIES

PRIMARIES

# LIFESTYLES AND ADAPTATIONS

Across Europe there are birds in every conceivable habitat, from the highest mountain to the open oceans, and everywhere in between. And one species or another has evolved to exploit almost every available source of food. The range of bill and leg structures amongst European birds is astonishing but, once you know what to look for, each is perfectly adapted for the food the bird eats and the habitat in which it lives. Birds' behaviour also plays a crucial role in ensuring the best possible chances of feeding, reproduction and survival.

## *BILLS*

A bird's bill (or beak) is an extension of its jaw. It has two parts – the upper and lower mandibles – both covered in a horny protective layer of skin. Like a human's, the lower jaw can move while the upper mandible is fixed to the skull. Nostrils are found on the upper mandible.

The main purpose of the bill is to aid feeding. Many sizes and shapes allow different birds to feed in different places and on a wide range of food. In addition to their usefulness in feeding, bills are used for preening, nest-building, and even as weapons of defence or attack. Some have special shapes or colours that are used in display.

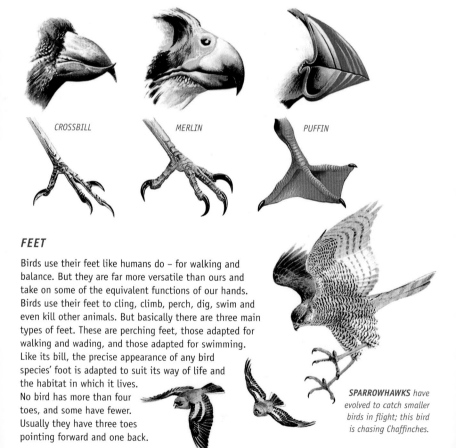

*CROSSBILL*

*MERLIN*

*PUFFIN*

## *FEET*

Birds use their feet like humans do – for walking and balance. But they are far more versatile than ours and take on some of the equivalent functions of our hands. Birds use their feet to cling, climb, perch, dig, swim and even kill other animals. But basically there are three main types of feet. These are perching feet, those adapted for walking and wading, and those adapted for swimming. Like its bill, the precise appearance of any bird species' foot is adapted to suit its way of life and the habitat in which it lives. No bird has more than four toes, and some have fewer. Usually they have three toes pointing forward and one back.

*SPARROWHAWKS* have evolved to catch smaller birds in flight; this bird is chasing Chaffinches.

## DIET

Although there are a few generalist feeders, happy to snatch an opportunistic meal or exploit any food source, most birds are specialist feeders with rather specific diets. On occasions, the diet of a species may change with the seasons (some finches and buntings consume insects in summer, but feed almost exclusively on seeds in winter when invertebrates are scarce). But most birds have bills and bodies adapted to a fairly precise habitat and food source. Some birds are purely vegetarian, feeding perhaps on seeds or fruits, while many more specialise in catching invertebrates; the relative absence of insects in winter means that many species that feed on them migrate south. Other species are predators and specialist diets include fish as well as other bird species.

ABOVE: *Like many other warbler species, this **GRASSHOPPER WARBLER** feeds on invertebrates, primarily insects; this one has spotted a caddisfly.*

BELOW: ***AVOCETS** are specialist feeders: they sweep their long, upcurved bills through the shallows.*

# BIRD BEHAVIOUR

Birds are highly evolved animals with a sophisticated array of behaviour patterns that allow them to increase their chances of survival. Some of these allow them to rub along with members of the same species while others improve their chances of feeding successfully or finding a mate.

## SOCIAL BEHAVIOUR

*Birds establish and maintain pair bonds using an array of behaviours between two individuals. To us, behaviour such as this intimate moment between these **ROOKS**, can look sometimes like a display of affection.*

Getting along with neighbours of the same species is an important part of many birds' lives. Complex behaviour patterns allow, for example, colonially nesting birds to nest in relative peace within bill-stabbing distance of one another. It allows pair bonds to be developed and maintained in species that pair for life. And it enables the complex processes of courtship, mating, nesting and the rearing of offspring to take place.

### MIGRATION

*Although some bird species are essentially sedentary, most take advantage of their ability to fly to move around the environment, often in search of food. Some simply disperse outside the breeding season in a seemingly random fashion. But others migrate; this predictable and typically annual flight takes them from one distinct area used for breeding to another used for wintering. The distances between the two can be continents apart. Migration is a response to the fact that most avian food resources, notably insects, are strongly seasonal in abundance. Most European summer migrants are insectivorous and breed during the long daylight hours that our northern summers provide. Insect abundance declines with the approach of winter and the insect eaters are forced to retreat south to latitudes where insects remain readily available. Other migrants move within Europe and are typically moving south and west to avoid colder weather further north and east.*

*Thanks to the efforts of British Trust for Ornithology ringers (trained volunteers who catch and put small identification rings on birds' legs), we now have a good understanding of **SWALLOW** migration. British Swallows migrate south through western Europe, cross the Sahara and winter in South Africa.*

## VOCALISATION

A few bird species are almost silent but most are vocal to varying degrees and under different circumstances. The apogee of bird vocalisation is song and it is amongst passerines that the finest examples are found. Typically it is males that sing and do so to advertise ownership of a breeding territory, and to attract and retain mates.

Most bird species have a repertoire of calls that serve a variety of behavioural functions. Amongst other things, these serve as alarm warnings to others (for example, at the discovery of a predator) and allow contact with other members of the species, for example when feeding or migrating.

## FLOCKS

Outside the breeding season, many wader species, most ducks and geese, and several passerine species gather in huge flocks that feed and roost together. The principle of safety in numbers operates and with so many eyes on the lookout for danger, potential predators are usually spotted.

*For many, the song of the **NIGHTINGALE** is the finest of all European birds. Rich, liquid and melodious, it often continues throughout the night.*

*During the breeding season, **SNOW BUNTINGS** are usually found in isolated pairs. But in winter (SEEN HERE) they form sizeable flocks that favour coastal grassland.*

# FIELDCRAFT

It takes time, effort and experience to become a skilled birdwatcher, but an awareness of environmental factors and possession of good equipment will speed up the process greatly, as will ownership of a good identification guide, such as the *Field Guide to Birds of Britain and Europe.*

LEFT: *Migrants, such as this* **WOOD WARBLER,** *are at the mercy of Europe's fickle weather, and their appearance in spring is often hindered by bad weather that prevents them from completing their journey from African wintering grounds.*

BELOW: *Severe westerly gales in autumn offer birdwatchers the only realistic prospect of seeing ocean-going seabirds, such as this juvenile* **SABINE'S GULL,** *close to land.*

## WHEN AND WHERE TO WATCH BIRDS

The weather has a profound influence on bird behaviour and hence on our ability to observe them. For example, on dull days raptors that require sun-generated thermals will not be seen soaring, and the same conditions will force swallows, martins and swifts to feed in lower airspaces than usual, making observation of them easier. Wind speed and direction can have an effect on birds' daily behaviour but affects migrating birds too. Northerly winds across Europe in spring will prevent most migrants from heading northwards from wintering grounds in Africa. But as soon as the wind changes direction a flood of migrants will head north to reach their breeding territories. In autumn, easterly winds bring migrants and rarities from Siberia to Europe, while westerly gales force migrating seabirds close to shore.

Use the time of day to get the best from your birdwatching: woodland songbirds are best listened for during the two-hour period after dawn; soaring birds of prey are best between 10am and noon, since they have just taken to the air but not achieved any great height; Starling roosts are best observed at dusk, and this is when nocturnal birds, such as nightjars, are just becoming active.

With a few exceptions, most European birds are adapted to particular environments and habitats. Dippers, for example, are found almost exclusively on fast-flowing rivers while woodpeckers are invariably associated with woodland. Learn these habitat associations and you will improve your chances of finding target species as well as aiding identification of a mystery bird you come across.

## BINOCULARS AND TELESCOPES

It really does pay to invest well in optical equipment. Binoculars come in all shapes, sizes and prices. Look at the numbers stamped on each pair of binoculars: typical examples might be 7×30, 8×40 or 10×40. The first number denotes the magnification and the second the diameter of the objective lens; this latter figure gives an indication of image brightness of the binoculars in question (the larger the number, the brighter the image). An ideal pair for most people would be 8×40 but tastes vary. Try a range of different makes before you purchase a pair and opt for a waterproof model with internal focusing. As your interest in birdwatching grows, sooner or later you will probably require a telescope. Before you buy one, talk to as many telescope owners as you can and visit a specialist shop to try models out side-by-side.

*With the aid of a good pair of binoculars, intimate feather detail*
*can be observed in the field on birds as tiny as this **FIRECREST**.*

## CONSERVATION

We all know the problems that beset our planet: global warming and greenhouse gas emission; insidious pollution of the terrestrial environment; agricultural intensification; housing development; pollution of the sea and the rape of its resources. This list goes on. As members of society, and consumers within it, we all contribute in one way or another to these problems. But potentially we are also the solution. All of us can make decisions that affect the environment for better or for worse.

Being a member or supporter of conservation and birdwatching organisations across Europe is also a really positive thing to do. Give as much money as possible to conservation bodies for the purchase of land, thereby removing areas from threats, such as development and intensive farming. But perhaps the most significant thing you can do is to become a member of, and information contributor to, the British Trust for Ornithology (BTO) if you live in Britain, or one of its sister organisations if you come from mainland Europe. Striving to understand what is happening to our birdlife through rigorous and detached science, organisations such as the BTO have real power to influence important environmental decisions made by governments – and ultimately, that's a good thing for all wildlife, not just birds. Nobody can ignore or dispute rigorous science and watertight analysis. You have obviously dug into your pocket to buy this book. So dig a little deeper and become a BTO member and paid-up citizen scientist!

# MUTE SWAN
*CYGNUS OLOR*

**LENGTH** 145–160cm
**WINGSPAN** 210–235cm

Northwest Europe's most familiar swan, present year-round in the region. Particularly widespread in Britain and Ireland. Males perform spectacular courtship displays in spring, with arched, raised wings.

**IDENTIFICATION** Adult has all-white plumage although neck sometimes stained buffish. Bill is orange-red with large black knob at base. Juvenile buffish-brown with grubby-pink bill; acquires adult feathering during first winter. When swimming, adult and juvenile hold neck in a more graceful 'S' shape than other swans. Sometimes flies in 'V' formation or diagonal lines. **HABITAT** Lakes, slow-flowing rivers, wet meadows and sheltered coasts. **VOICE** Hoarse trumpeting, snorting and hissing calls; non-vocal wing noise in flight.

*adult*

Male swans are aggressive in the breeding season, chasing off intruders by flying, and then swimming quickly towards them; this is known as 'busking'.

ABOVE: **adult**
RIGHT: **juvenile**

*The Mute Swan's long neck allows it to exploit deeper water than geese or dabbling ducks.*

16

# WHOOPER SWAN
*CYGNUS CYGNUS*

145–160cm **LENGTH**
220–240cm **WINGSPAN**

*adult*

*adult*

The sight and sound of wintering Whooper Swan flocks is a memorable one. Swimming through rising mists on a part-frozen loch, they appear more at ease with wintry conditions than most human observers.

LEFT: *The adult's pure white plumage is sometimes stained on the head and neck from feeding.*

*juvenile*

**IDENTIFICATION**  Much larger than superficially similar Bewick's Swan and with proportionately longer neck. Adult has all-white plumage, black legs and black bill with yellow patch at base; area of yellow larger than on Bewick's; wedge-shaped and extends beyond nostrils. Juvenile is pinkish-buff with black-tipped, pinkish bill, grading to white at base. Similar to juvenile Bewick's: best identified by larger size and association with adult birds. **HABITAT** Breeds on northern lakes and marshes; winters on flood meadows, stubble fields and lochs. **VOICE** Loud, trumpeting or bugling calls.

# BEWICK'S SWAN
*CYGNUS COLUMBIANUS*

115–125cm **LENGTH**
180–210cm **WINGSPAN**

*adult*

From October to March Bewick's Swans occur at traditional sites – coastal or lowland wetlands – from Denmark to Britain and Ireland. Family parties can sometimes be discerned among flocks.

**IDENTIFICATION**  Smallest swan in Europe. Adult has all-white plumage. Legs black and bill black with irregularly shaped yellow patch at base; yellow does not extend beyond nostrils. Juvenile is buffish-grey and has black-tipped pink bill, fading to white at base; distinguished from juvenile Whooper Swan by its smaller size, and bill size and shape, but more importantly by association with adult birds. **HABITAT** Breeds on remote tundra areas outside region; overwinters on flood meadows, saltmarsh and shallow lakes. **VOICE** Varied, soft or loud musical, bugling calls; far-carrying.

ABOVE: *adult*
LEFT: *juvenile*

# GREYLAG GOOSE
*ANSER ANSER*

**LENGTH** 75–90cm
**WINGSPAN** 150–180cm

The precise natural distribution of Greylag Geese in Europe is now difficult to determine, since introductions and feral populations have confused the situation. Some feral populations are approachable, but most are wary.

**IDENTIFICATION** Large, stoutly built goose with mainly grey-brown plumage. Most adult birds seen in western Europe have orange bills; eastern birds have pinkish bills. Legs pink in all adult birds. Shows pale margins to feathers on back. Lower belly and undertail white. Some birds have a few dark feathers on belly. In flight, shows grey on forewing, lower back and tail. **HABITAT** Arable land, marshes, lakes. **VOICE** Clattering clamour in flight, less bugling than other grey geese.

*adult*

*Family groups of Greylag Geese, comprising both **adult birds** and accompanying **chicks** (goslings), are a familiar sight on many European lowland lakes in spring and summer.*

BELOW: *The Greylag Goose is the typical grey goose seen in much of Europe, especially during the summer months; this bird is an **adult**.*

60–75cm **LENGTH**
135–170cm **WINGSPAN**

# PINK-FOOTED GOOSE

*ANSER BRACHYRHYNCHUS*

The Pink-footed Goose is essentially an Arctic breeding species, with the entire world population migrating to northwest Europe in September and October.

**IDENTIFICATION** Smaller than superficially similar Bean Goose and with proportionately shorter neck and smaller bill. Bill dark with variable patch of pink, usually in the form of a band, near tip. Head and neck usually dark brown, breast and flanks paler brown and back greyish. Legs pink, although much duller in juvenile. In flight, wings look pale grey except for darker flight feathers; back and tail also paler than on Bean Goose. **HABITAT** Breeds on uplands or tundra; in winter, on fields, roosting on estuaries or lakes. **VOICE** Musical disyllabic or trisyllabic honking; also high-pitched, sharp 'wink-wink'.

*adult*

LEFT: *adult*

RIGHT: *The characteristic pink legs of this species are much duller in the juvenile; the variable pink patch on the bill makes this goose very similar in appearance to the Bean Goose in poor light.*

65–80cm **LENGTH**
150–175cm **WINGSPAN**

# BEAN GOOSE

*ANSER FABALIS*

In Europe, there are two races of Bean Goose: *rossicus*, which nests at more northerly latitudes on open tundra, and *fabalis*, which favours taiga or boreal forest at slightly lower latitudes. Both races are migratory, moving south and west in autumn.

**IDENTIFICATION** Can generally be identified by chocolate-brown appearance, particularly on head and neck, and proportionately long neck. Bill dark with variable orange markings: in race *rossicus* orange limited to near bill tip, but in race *fabalis* orange much more extensive. Legs of both races orange. In flight, upperwings look all dark. Lower back is brown, separated from white-edged brown tail by white band at base. **HABITAT** Breeds on tundra and in northern forests; in winter, on arable and stubble fields. **VOICE** Calls include a nasal cackle.

*adult* fabalis

*adult* fabalis

# WHITE-FRONTED GOOSE

*ANSER ALBIFRONS*

The White-fronted Goose occurs in two races: the Siberian race *albifrons* and the Greenland race *flavirostris*. All adult birds have the same, diagnostic white forehead.

**IDENTIFICATION**  Large goose, which, as adult, has white forehead not extending above eye. Siberian race *albifrons* has pinkish bill, while Greenland race *flavirostris* has orange-yellow bill. Plumage generally grey-brown, with underparts paler, but with variable black bands and crescents on belly; undertail white. Juvenile similar to adult but lacks white forehead. In flight, looks comparatively long-winged and more agile than Greylag. **HABITAT** Breeds on boggy tundra; overwinters on water meadows and near estuaries. **VOICE** Flocks utter musical ringing, laughing and yodelling calls; hissing and yapping calls on ground and non-vocal 'creaking' wings on taking to air.

*adult*
albifrons

White-fronted Geese are very wary of intruders and take to the air in huge, noisy flocks if alarmed.

The Siberian race *albifrons* overwinters in east and southeast Europe and also occurs along the coast of northwest Europe and southern England; the Greenland race *flavirostris*, numbering some 30,000 birds, overwinters in Ireland, Scotland and Wales.

*juvenile* albifrons

*adult* albifrons

20

55–65cm **LENGTH**
120–135cm **WINGSPAN**

# LESSER WHITE-FRONTED GOOSE

*ANSER ERYTHROPUS*

Although small flocks of Lesser White-fronts are found in southeast Europe in the winter, stray individuals are sometimes found in flocks of White-fronted Geese in Northwest Europe.

**IDENTIFICATION** Superficially similar to White-fronted Goose, but more compact and appreciably smaller when seen side by side. Bill on adult relatively small and pinkish-orange. White forehead extends above eye, which has conspicuous yellow eyering; white forehead absent in juvenile and eyering dull. Plumage on all birds mostly grey-brown, darker than White-front, with dark markings on paler belly. Undertail white. In flight, has fast wingbeats and is hard to distinguish from White-front.
**HABITAT** Breeds on tundra; overwinters on meadows and fields.
**VOICE** High-pitched yelping calls.

*adult*

*adult*

53–56cm **LENGTH**
115–135cm **WINGSPAN**

# RED-BREASTED GOOSE

*BRANTA RUFICOLLIS*

A scarce and declining species, the Red-breasted Goose usually nests in accessible sites, often near nesting Peregrines, presumably gaining some protection from the falcon's vigorous defence of its own family.

**IDENTIFICATION** A small but beautifully marked goose. Adult has complicated pattern of red, white and black on head, neck and breast. Back, wings and belly mostly black but shows conspicuous white stripe on flanks. Rear end white except for tail; white is most striking in flight. Juvenile similar to, but duller than, adult. **HABITAT** Breeds on tundra; in winter, on steppe or sometimes arable land. **VOICE** High-pitched, disyllabic call.

*The striking looking Red-breasted Goose is a rare but regular straggler to parts of western Europe; individual birds are invariably found among flocks of Brent, Barnacle or White-fronted Geese.*

*adult*

*adult*

# BRENT GOOSE
## *BRANTA BERNICLA*

**LENGTH** 55–60cm
**WINGSPAN** 110–120cm

Visit almost any sizeable estuary on Europe's North Sea coast between October and February and you are likely to find large flocks of Brent Geese. Flocks increasingly visit nearby arable land and grassland prior to the long migration back to their high Arctic breeding grounds.

**IDENTIFICATION**   A small, dark goose. Adult has all-black head and neck except for white neck patch. Back and wings dark grey-brown except for black flight feathers. Rear end white, most noticeable in flight, but tail dark. Legs and feet black. Race *bernicla* has dark belly; race *hrota* has pale-grey belly. Juvenile has pale-edged feathers on back and lacks white neck; adult characteristics acquired during winter. **HABITAT** Breeds on tundra; in winter, on saltmarsh and coastal grassland. **VOICE** Deep, rolling bark.

*adult dark-bellied*

*The white rear of the Brent Goose is best seen in flight; the white neck patch is more of a stripe, and far less prominent than that on the Canada Goose.*

ABOVE: **adult** *dark-bellied* (bernicla); BELOW: **adult** *light-bellied* (hrota)

**60–70cm** LENGTH
**135–145cm** WINGSPAN

# BARNACLE GOOSE
*BRANTA LEUCOPSIS*

*Barnacle Geese are the subjects of some controversy at their winter grounds on Islay, where they prefer the meadow grasses in fields 'improved' for sheep rearing.*

In Europe, the attractive Barnacle Goose is seen as a winter visitor, arriving in October and departing in March. Their flights at dawn and dusk are remarkable.

**IDENTIFICATION** A small, compact goose. Bill and eye black. Adults have white face and black neck. Back barred black and grey; underparts white. Legs and feet black. Juvenile has more blotched face and greyer chest. In flight, looks very black and white; flight feathers black, and shows conspicuous white rump when seen from above.

*adults*

*adults*

**90–100cm** LENGTH
**150–180cm** WINGSPAN

# CANADA GOOSE
*BRANTA CANADENSIS*

*adults*

Introduced to Europe in the 17th century, Canada Geese seem to favour semi-urban or even man-made habitats and most birds are residents.

**IDENTIFICATION** Europe's largest goose. Head and neck black, except for contrasting white patch on face. Plumage on back and underparts brown, except for white on undertail and black flight

BELOW: *adult* feathers; upperparts can look rather barred. Yellow-buff goslings follow parents. Juvenile birds duller than adults but soon indistinguishable. **HABITAT** Ornamental lakes, flooded gravel pits and nearby meadows. **VOICE** Loud, resonant honking calls, usually two notes 'gor-rronk'; also a variety of other trumpeting notes.

# EGYPTIAN GOOSE
*ALOPOCHEN AEGYPTIACUS*

**LENGTH** 65–73cm
**WINGSPAN** 135–155cm

In Europe, the Egyptian Goose has a long-established feral population in East Anglia and the Thames Valley, in England.

*adult*

**IDENTIFICATION** Superficially similar to Ruddy Shelduck but with distinctive markings. Adult has pinkish bill and legs. Head and neck pale except for dark patch through eye and dark collar. Breast and underparts buffish-brown but with dark chestnut patch on belly. Back usually rufous-brown but sometimes greyish-brown. Juvenile is more uniformly buffish-brown, without clear markings on head or belly; legs and bill dull brown. In flight, adults show striking white forewing patches on both upper and underwing surfaces, green speculum and black flight feathers. **HABITAT** Seldom far from water, usually in fields and marshes. **VOICE** Distinctive loud braying calls.

*adults*

# RUDDY SHELDUCK
*TADORNA FERRUGINEA*

**LENGTH** 61–67cm
**WINGSPAN** 120–145cm

Like its cousin, the Shelduck, the Ruddy Shelduck is a hole-nesting species. Underground burrows are favoured, although birds are not averse to using holes in trees.

*adults*

ABOVE: *male*; BELOW: *female*

**IDENTIFICATION** An attractive and distinctive duck. Sexes similar. Adult has dark bill, eyes and legs. Head and upper neck buffish with clear demarcation from orange-brown body. In breeding season, only the male has black collar separating buff and orange plumage; sexes similar in other plumage respects. At rest, black wingtips can be seen. In flight, wings are strikingly black and white, the black being confined to the flight feathers. Juvenile similar to adult but duller. **HABITAT** Variety of wetland habitats including river deltas. **VOICE** Noisy; flight call 'ang' or rolling 'aarl'.

60–70cm **LENGTH**
110–130cm **WINGSPAN**

# SHELDUCK
## *TADORNA TADORNA*

BELOW: *juvenile*
RIGHT: *adults*

Throughout much of its European range, the Shelduck is essentially a coastal bird. It breeds along much of the northwest European coast, from northern France to Norway, and is common around Britain and Ireland.

**IDENTIFICATION** Adult has bright red bill and legs. Head and upper neck dark green; can look all dark in some lights. Rest of plumage comprises patches of white and black with conspicuous orange-chestnut breast band. Male has red knob at base of bill, while female shows pale feathering at bill base instead; sexes similar in other plumage respects. Juvenile is mottled and marbled brown and white; shows dull pink legs and bill. In flight, adult looks conspicuously black and white. **HABITAT** Mostly coastal on sandy and muddy shores; also inland on flooded gravel pits and marshes. **VOICE** Male whistles; female utters deep, quick quacks.

*The bright colours of this striking species can be seen to great effect in flight.*

*An old Rabbit burrow is a good nesting site for the Shelduck.*

ABOVE: *male*; BELOW: *the smaller female lacks the bill knob of the male.*

25

# MALLARD
### ANAS PLATYRHYNCHOS

**LENGTH** 50–65cm
**WINGSPAN** 80–100cm

Mallards can be found in almost any freshwater habitat and are occasionally seen around the coast as well. Mallards are often tame.

The Mallard is probably one of the most familiar wildfowl species in western Europe, often seen being fed by humans in urban parks and on ponds; ducklings are capable swimmers almost immediately after hatching.

female

male

*Male* (BELOW) *and* *female* (BOTTOM) *Mallards are easily distinguished, but the bright orange legs are common to both sexes.*

**IDENTIFICATION** Male has yellow bill, green head showing sheen in good light, chestnut breast and otherwise mostly grey-brown plumage; shows black stern and white tail. Female has orange-yellow bill and rather uniform brown plumage. Eclipse male similar to female but more reddish on breast. In flight both sexes show white-bordered blue speculum. **HABITAT** Almost anywhere with water. **VOICE** Female gives familiar quack; male a weak nasal note.

45–55cm **LENGTH**
85–95cm **WINGSPAN**

# GADWALL
### ANAS STREPERA

As a breeding bird, the Gadwall occurs rather locally in western Europe, with perhaps a few tens of thousands of pairs breeding at latitudes from northern Britain south to southern Spain.

adult
female

*Outside the breeding season, from August to April, Gadwall are invariably found in flocks and identification of the females is far easier when male and female ducks are seen within the same flock than when females are alone; the species often associates freely with Coots.*

adult male

**adult male** (BELOW) and **adult female** (BOTTOM)

**IDENTIFICATION** At first glance, a rather drab duck. Close views of male in good light reveal grey plumage comprising intricate vermiculation. Female recalls female Mallard with yellow bill and brown plumage. Juvenile resembles dull adult female. Both sexes are easily identified when swimming if flash of white speculum is revealed. This latter feature very obvious in flight, when white underwing also noticeable. **HABITAT** Breeds on wetlands with open water; in winter, on lakes and marshes. **VOICE** Male utters nasal 'mair'; female gives quiet quack.

# WIGEON
*ANAS PENELOPE*

**LENGTH** 45–51cm
**WINGSPAN** 75–85cm

From late August until April flocks of Wigeon move south from breeding grounds to spend the winter on coastal marshes and estuary saltmarshes.

*male*

**IDENTIFICATION** An attractive dabbling duck. Male can look drab in dull light. In good light, reveals orange head with yellow forecrown. Breast pinkish, and back and flanks covered with soft, grey vermiculation. Underparts white and stern black. In water, appears to have black and white rear end. Female has mainly brown plumage with white belly and dark feathering around eye. In flight male shows conspicuous white patch on upper surface of innerwing. **HABITAT** Breeds on northern lakes and wetlands; in winter, on saltmarshes and coastal grassland. **VOICE** Male utters whistling 'whee-OO'; female gives grating purr.

*female*

The Wigeon is one of the most attractive European ducks, the plumage of the male being subtle rather than gaudy.

ABOVE: *male*; BELOW: *female*

34–38cm **LENGTH**
58–65cm **WINGSPAN**

# TEAL
*ANAS CRECCA*

Despite being widely hunted in much of its range, the Teal is still one of Europe's commonest ducks. Except in areas where they are protected from hunting pressures, Teal are wary of man and quick to take to the air.

**IDENTIFICATION** The region's smallest duck. Male has attractive orange-brown head with large green patch from eye to nape, bordered with creamy yellow stripe. Back and flanks show grey vermiculation and underparts white. Black-bordered, creamy-yellow patches on sides of stern. Female and juvenile have grey-brown plumage; best identified by size and association with male. In flight, all birds show green speculum and white underwing.

**HABITAT** Shallow fresh water when nesting; in winter, on flood meadows or saltmarshes.

**VOICE** Distinctive, high-pitched, chirping 'krick'.

*The Teal breeds throughout much of northern Europe; in North America it is replaced by a similar species – Green-winged Teal – which occurs as a vagrant (see p.416).*

*male*

*male*

*female*

*The Teal's winter range extends south of its breeding range and includes most of western and southern Europe; some populations in northwestern Europe are year-round residents.*

ABOVE: *male in flight;* BELOW: *male*

# SHOVELER
### ANAS CLYPEATA

**LENGTH** 44–52cm
**WINGSPAN** 70–85cm

Shovelers are difficult birds to observe during the breeding season, although pairs are sometimes seen performing aerobatic display flights above suitable territories. They are easier to watch at wetland reserves in winter.

**IDENTIFICATION** An unusual duck, the most distinctive feature of both sexes being the broad, flattened bill. Male has green head with sheen in good light. Bright orange belly provides striking contrast with otherwise white breast and flanks.

*female*

*male*

Back and stern dark and bill black. Female has mottled brown plumage. Bill dark but with lower edges orange. In flight, both sexes show blue forewing separated by white band from green speculum. **HABITAT** Shallow water. **VOICE** Quiet 'tuc' uttered by male; female quacks.

Shovelers are often seen in pairs, even outside the breeding season; both share the same bill shape but the **female** (BELOW) is noticeably duller than the more colourful **male** (ABOVE).

51–66cm **LENGTH**

80–95cm **WINGSPAN**

# PINTAIL
*ANAS ACUTA*

In western Europe, the Pintail is a local and rather scarce breeder. In winter it is a different story, with some 60,000 birds present in northwest Europe, mostly in coastal districts, and 250,000 in the Mediterranean region.

**IDENTIFICATION** Male is an elegant duck with chocolate-brown head and white on underparts and on front of neck, forming narrow stripe up side of face. Flanks are grey and black with elongated feathers. Stern is buff and black, with long, upcurved tail. Female has dark-grey bill and largely brown plumage with long-bodied appearance. Juvenile resembles dull adult female. **HABITAT** Open areas with shallow water. **VOICE** Male utters quiet whistle; female gives short quacks.

*male*

In winter, coastal Pintails feed on a tiny mollusc called the Laver Spire Shell, found on mudflats.

*female*

*male*

*In flight, both sexes look particularly long-bodied.*

*male*

*female*

31

# GARGANEY
*ANAS QUERQUEDULA*

The Garganey is unique among European ducks, being a summer visitor to the region; most breeding Garganey from Europe overwinter in tropical Africa. The first migrants start to appear on wetlands in southern Europe in February and March.

**IDENTIFICATION** Male is distinctive with broad, white crescent-shaped stripe over eye leading back to nape. Cap dark but head and neck otherwise reddish-brown. Breast brown, flanks grey and shows long, trailing black, blue-grey and white feathers on back. Female similar to female Teal and best distinguished by association with male. In flight, blue forewing and green speculum of both sexes can be seen. **HABITAT** Shallow wetlands and flooded meadows. **VOICE** Male utters characteristic mechanical-sounding rattle; female gives quiet quack.

*When alarmed, Garganey rise steeply from the water; their flight is direct and fast, without the swerves and twists that characterise Teal flight.*

*The arrival of small parties of Garganey on marshes in the region is a sure sign that spring is on the way.*

*female*

*male*

ABOVE: **male**; BELOW: **Female**; *confusingly similar to female Teal but greyer overall with pale spot at base of bill often noticeable and obviously different wing markings when seen in flight.*

41–49cm **LENGTH**
68–75cm **WINGSPAN**

# MANDARIN
### *AIX GALERICULATA*

The strange-looking Mandarin has its true range in eastern Asia, as its oriental name implies. In Europe, it is a popular bird in captivity and many sightings are in fact escapes.

*male*

**IDENTIFICATION** Male is very distinctive with long mane of dark feathers on cap and nape; broad, pale stripe above eye and radiating orange feathers on neck and breast. Underparts and back dark but flanks orange and shows sail-like feathers at rear end; undertail white. Female mainly grey-brown with white belly and larger white spots on neck and breast. Shows conspicuous white 'spectacle' around eye, and white throat and base to bill. **HABITAT** Wooded rivers and lakes. **VOICE** Mostly silent.

*female*

ABOVE: *male*; BELOW: *female*

# RUDDY DUCK
## *OXYURA JAMAICENSIS*

In poor light and at a distance, a feeding Ruddy Duck
might be mistaken for a Little Grebe. It tends to dive
frequently and bob up to the surface
a few seconds later.

ABOVE: *male*; BELOW: *female*

**IDENTIFICATION** A so-called 'stifftail' duck, which
often lives up to its name by raising its relatively
long tail in the air. Male has mainly orange-brown
plumage but with black cap, white face and bright-
blue bill; stern white. Female has mainly grey-brown
plumage but similar, distinctive outline. Often shows
pale cheeks broken by dark line from base
of bill. Seldom seen in flight.

**HABITAT** Well-vegetated
ponds, lakes
and reservoirs.

**VOICE** Mostly silent.

*This species appeared in
Europe in the 1950s: birds
escaped from Slimbridge
Wildfowl and Wetland Trust
reserve, England; they
have increased ever since.*

male

female

43–48cm **LENGTH**
62–70cm **WINGSPAN**

# WHITE-HEADED DUCK

## *OXYURA LEUCOCEPHALA*

The White-headed Duck is one of Europe's rarest waterbirds, having its last strongholds in Turkey and the south of Spain. Even here, not many more than a few hundred pairs are thought to breed.

**IDENTIFICATION** A 'stifftail' duck, superficially similar to, but larger than, Ruddy Duck. Male is distinctive with white head, black cap and eye and disproportionately large blue bill with strangely swollen base. Body plumage mainly brown. Female has brown body plumage and bill similar in shape to male's but dark grey in colour. Head shows dark brown cap down to level of eye and white face with dark line running from base of bill. **HABITAT** Shallow, well-vegetated lakes and pools; both freshwater and brackish. **VOICE** Mostly silent.

*male*

*female*

40–42cm **LENGTH**
63–67cm **WINGSPAN**

# MARBLED DUCK

## *MARMARONETTA ANGUSTIROSTRIS*

With a decreasing range and population, the Marbled Duck is now a rare bird in Europe, found mainly in southern Spain, where fewer than 200 pairs breed each year.

*male*

*female*

**IDENTIFICATION** Despite subdued colouring, an attractive duck. Sexes similar. Plumage ground colour is grey-brown but covered with pale buff spots; these are particularly large and striking on breast, belly and back. Bill dark and shows dark smudge through eye. In flight has rather uniform brown wings. **HABITAT** Shallow, well-vegetated pools and lakes; freshwater and saline. **VOICE** Mostly silent.

# TUFTED DUCK

*AYTHYA FULIGULA*

**LENGTH** 40–47cm
**WINGSPAN** 68–73cm

Tufted Ducks dive frequently and often for considerable lengths of time, also covering a considerable distance while swimming underwater. In many parts of their range, they have benefited from the increase of reservoirs and flooded gravel pits.

**IDENTIFICATION** Male is very distinctive, looking black and white at a distance. In good light, dark feathering has sheen. Bill is grey with white band towards end, and has black tip. Iris yellow and head bears crest feathers, which can be raised. Female has mostly brown plumage, slightly paler on belly and flanks. Bill pattern similar to that of male and iris yellow. Head bears short tuft of feathers, giving it a rather square outline. Some females have white patch at base of bill; this never as extensive as on female Scaup. Eclipse male similar to female. In flight, both sexes show white wingbar. **HABITAT** Open water, including rivers. **VOICE** Various harsh, growling notes.

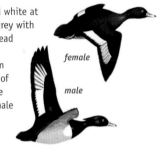

*female*

*male*

The increase in suitable habitats for the Tufted Duck explains its success; winter is spent in large flocks on open water.

ABOVE: *male*; BELOW: *Female could be confused with female Greater Scaup but note the peaked crown and different bill pattern; usually seen in association with male.*

42–51cm **LENGTH**
72–83cm **WINGSPAN**

# GREATER SCAUP
*AYTHYA MARILA*

The Greater Scaup's breeding range in Europe includes northern Scandinavia and its Baltic coasts. Although harsh winter weather may force small parties of Greater Scaup to visit coastal gravel pits and lagoons, they are primarily sea ducks.

**IDENTIFICATION** Male is superficially similar to male Tufted Duck. Can look black, grey and white at a distance, but rounded head has green gloss in good light. Bill grey with black nail at tip and yellow iris. Neck, breast and stern black, belly and flanks white and back soft grey with fine vermiculations. Female has mainly brown plumage but with yellow iris and conspicuous white patches at base of bill and on forehead and cheek. In flight, both sexes show white wingbars. **HABITAT** Breeds on coastal tundra; in winter in shallow, coastal waters. **VOICE** Harsh, grating 'karr-karr' while flying.

*female*

*male*

ABOVE: *male*; BELOW: *female*

*In winter, Greater Scaup are local in the eastern Mediterranean, coastal northwest Europe and the Black Sea as well as on ice-free lakes in central Europe.*

# FERRUGINOUS DUCK

*AYTHYA NYROCA*

**LENGTH** 38–42cm
**WINGSPAN** 63–67cm

During the breeding season and winter, Ferruginous Ducks usually prove more difficult to find than most other diving ducks. The main reason for this is their liking for the cover of marginal vegetation.

ABOVE: *male*; BELOW: *female*

**IDENTIFICATION** Male has rather uniform chocolate-brown plumage with dark back and very conspicuous white stern. Bill grey with dark tip; eye has white iris. Female similar to male but duller and with brown iris. Juvenile similar to female but lacks white stern. In flight, looks slimmer than Tufted Duck and shows striking white wingbar; underwings pale. **HABITAT** Shallow, well-vegetated lakes and pools. **VOICE** Female utters high-pitched, repeated 'karri'.

42–49cm **LENGTH**
72–82cm **WINGSPAN**

# POCHARD
*AYTHYA FERINA*

Outside the breeding season, Pochards are invariably seen in flocks, some of which can be quite sizeable. Birds of this species mix freely with Tufted Ducks and spend much of their time diving for food. A large proportion of their diet comprises plant material.

**IDENTIFICATION** Male is attractive and distinctive. Bill relatively long and black with broad, grey band across middle. Rounded head is reddish-orange and neck and breast are black. Underparts and back grey with intricate vermiculations. Stern black. Female has mottled brown and grey-brown plumage, mostly grey on back. Bill pattern and head shape as male. Usually shows pale 'spectacle' around eye. In flight, wings of both sexes appear rather uniform; belly of female looks pale. **HABITAT** Well-vegetated pools in summer but open water in winter. **VOICE** Harsh, growling notes.

*female*

*male*

ABOVE: *Male showing the distinct and diagnostic bill pattern and head shape;*
BELOW: *Female showing the characteristic white 'spectacle' around the eye.*

From September to March perhaps as many as 250,000 Pochards are found in northwest Europe, some 80,000 of which occur in Britain alone.

# RED-CRESTED POCHARD

*NETTA RUFINA*

**LENGTH** 53–57cm
**WINGSPAN** 85–88cm

This species is a diving duck, an activity that it performs with great ease. Red-crested Pochards also feed in the shallows, however, and frequently up-end to feed in the manner of a Pintail or Mallard.

**IDENTIFICATION** Male is attractive and distinctive. Bill bright red. Head orange-brown and neck and body feathers mostly black except for grey-brown back and white flanks. Female has pink-tipped dark bill. Cap and nape dark brown but cheeks and throat conspicuously pale. Plumage otherwise brown. Eclipse male resembles female but retains red bill. In flight, both sexes show pale underwing and broad, white stripes on upperwing. **HABITAT** Fresh water with extensive cover; in winter, on lakes and flooded gravel pits. **VOICE** Mostly silent.

*male*

*The pale underwing and broad white stripes on the upperwing are obvious in flight.*

As a European breeding bird, the Red-crested Pochard has a very local and patchy distribution, centred mainly on eastern and southeastern Europe and the Iberian peninsula.

ABOVE: *male*; BELOW: *female*

38–45cm **LENGTH**
63–69cm **WINGSPAN**

# HARLEQUIN DUCK
### *HISTRIONICUS HISTRIONICUS*

In Europe, just 3–5,000 pairs of Harlequin Ducks are found in Iceland, and they do not move far in winter. In summer, they favour white-water areas where rivers crash and tumble over boulders and rocks. In the winter, the coastal waters they favour can be no less challenging.

**IDENTIFICATION** Male is attractive and distinctive. Plumage mainly a mixture of blue and deep red with bold white stripes and spots on head and body. Female has more subdued, dark-brown plumage with white patch between base of bill and eye, and white spot behind eye. Eclipse male similar to female. All birds fly low over the water with fast, whirring wingbeats. **HABITAT** In summer, on fast-flowing rivers; in winter, around coasts. **VOICE** Occasionally utters high-pitched squeals but otherwise mostly silent.

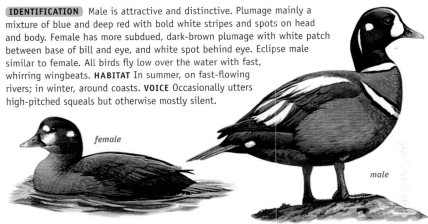

*female*

*male*

*male*

*Harlequin Ducks dive frequently in search of food. While they mainly feed on aquatic insect larvae in summer, they switch to molluscs come winter.*

# EIDER
### *SOMATERIA MOLLISSIMA*

**LENGTH** 50–71cm
**WINGSPAN** 80–105cm

Eiders are engaging birds to watch during the breeding season. Early on, the males perform crooning and cooing calls, throwing their heads and necks back in the process. Having mated, the females move ashore to nest on undisturbed beaches and grassland.

**IDENTIFICATION** A distinctive coastal duck with dumpy body and wedge-shaped bill following line of forehead. Mature male is unmistakable, with black and white markings on body; also shows lime-green markings on head and pink flush to breast. Full plumage not acquired until fourth year. Female has mottled brown plumage, looking rather barred on flanks. In flight, both sexes look heavy and ponderous with slightly drooping neck. Flies low over the water in lines. **HABITAT** Coastal waters, usually close to shore. **VOICE** Male utters humorous 'ah-whooo' during breeding season; otherwise silent.

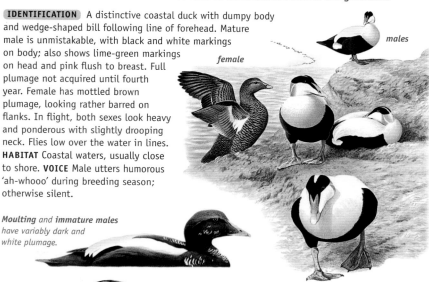

*males*

*female*

*Moulting and immature males have variably dark and white plumage.*

ABOVE: *male*; BELOW: *female*

48–63cm **LENGTH**
85–100cm **WINGSPAN**

# KING EIDER
*SOMATERIA SPECTABILIS*

**King Eiders breed in the high Arctic, but overwinter further south; they are found at this time around the coasts of northern Norway. A few turn up every winter among Eider flocks off the Scottish coast.**

ABOVE: ***Mature male*** has two sickle-shaped 'sails' on back.
BELOW: ***Female*** similar to female Eider but smaller with proportionately shorter bill.

**IDENTIFICATION** Mature adult male has red bill expanded at base into basal knob. Head proportionately large with square outline; marked with pale blue-grey and green, the areas of colour outlined in black. Rest of body plumage black and white. Female similar to female Eider with mottled and barred brown plumage; pale on cheeks and around eye. **HABITAT** Breeds on Arctic tundra; in winter, on northern coasts. **VOICE** Male utters cooing calls during courtship; otherwise mostly silent.

*male*

# COMMON SCOTER
## *MELANITTA NIGRA*

**LENGTH** 44–54cm
**WINGSPAN** 80–90cm

In the winter months, the Common Scoter becomes widespread in European coastal waters, with more than 600,000 birds occurring in the region. In areas where they are common in the winter, Common Scoters form large flocks.

**IDENTIFICATION** A classic sea duck that can look all dark at a distance. Male has black plumage with black and yellow bill. Female has dark-brown plumage but much paler cheeks that show up well even at a distance or in flight. Invariably seen in flocks outside breeding season. Migrating flocks seen flying low over water, sometimes in lines but also in more tightly bunched packs with trailing stragglers. **HABITAT** Breeds on upland moors and tundra; in winter, around coasts. **VOICE** Mostly silent but male utters quiet whistles in breeding season.

*female*

*male*

ABOVE: *male*; BELOW: *female*

51–58cm **LENGTH**
90–100cm **WINGSPAN**

# VELVET SCOTER
### *MELANITTA FUSCA*

Seen in good light, Velvet Scoters are stunning birds. Although they sometimes form small, one-species flocks of 20 or 30 birds, they are also seen during the winter in the company of Common Scoters. Seen side by side, Velvet Scoters are appreciably larger.

*male*

**IDENTIFICATION** Male has all-black plumage but is readily identified, even when among Common Scoters, by conspicuous white eye and white patch below eye. Bill black and yellow. Female has brown plumage with white patches between eye and base of bill and behind eye. In flight, both sexes show extremely conspicuous white wing patches; these are occasionally visible on swimming birds. **HABITAT** Breeds on coastal moors and tundra; in winter, in coastal waters. **VOICE** Male utters whistling call in breeding season and female has grating call; silent at other times.

ABOVE: *male*; BELOW: *Female, which lacks male's white eye patch and has little yellow on bill.*

# BARROW'S GOLDENEYE

*BUCEPHALA ISLANDICA*

**In Europe, the species is represented by the 500–600 or so pairs that breed in Iceland and nowhere else. These are mostly resident and only move to the coast when forced to do so by freezing conditions.**

**IDENTIFICATION** Similar to Goldeneye but distinguished, even in silhouette, by steep, rounded forehead and relatively short, broad bill. Male has dark head with purple gloss and white crescent shape in front of yellow eye. Underparts mainly white and upperparts and stern dark; back shows small patches of white. Female has dark-brown head with yellow eye. Body plumage mainly grey-brown and underparts paler. In flight, both sexes show less white on inner wing than Goldeneye does. **HABITAT** Breeds on Arctic lakes and rivers; in winter, on more coastal Arctic lakes and rivers and sometimes actually in coastal waters. **VOICE** Grunting calls accompany courting male's display; otherwise silent.

*female*

Note characteristic head shape and
relatively small bill of both sexes.

*male*

Like its cousin, Barrow's Goldeneye dives frequently and is at home in turbulent waters

42–50cm **LENGTH**
65–80cm **WINGSPAN**

# GOLDENEYE
### *BUCEPHALA CLANGULA*

In northwest Europe the Goldeneye is best known as a winter visitor, with more than 200,000 birds visiting the region between October and March. Within their usual overwintering range, Goldeneye are usually seen in flocks.

**IDENTIFICATION** Superb diving duck with peaked-cap profile to head, readily seen even in silhouette. Male has dark head with greenish sheen, white circular patch at base of bill and yellow eye. Body plumage mostly white except for dark back and stern. Female has reddish-brown head and dark grey bill with pink patch near tip. Body plumage grey-brown except for paler underparts and white neck. **HABITAT** Breeds beside northern, wooded lakes; in winter on lakes and reservoirs, occasionally on coasts. **VOICE** Creaking display call but otherwise silent.

*male*

*In flight both sexes show white patches on inner upperwing.*

ABOVE: *male*; BELOW: *female*

# RED-BREASTED MERGANSER
## MERGUS SERRATOR

**LENGTH** 52–58cm
**WINGSPAN** 70–85cm

From April to July Red-breasted Mergansers are found on suitable water bodies throughout Scandinavia and locally in northern Britain, Ireland and Iceland. Thereafter they move to coastal seas.

**IDENTIFICATION** Slim-bodied duck with long, narrow sawbill. Male has red bill, legs and eyes. Underparts grey and finely marked, and back black and white. Female body plumage mainly grey-brown, although underparts paler. In flight, both sexes show white on innerwing; less extensive on female and divided by black bar. **HABITAT** Breeds on clear, northern lakes and rivers; in winter, mainly in coastal waters. **VOICE** Mostly silent.

*male*

ABOVE: *male*; BELOW: *female*

58–66cm **LENGTH**
82–96cm **WINGSPAN**

# GOOSANDER
*MERGUS MERGANSER*

In Europe Goosanders nest mainly in the north, although
isolated populations also breed in Britain and the Alps; their
winter range is rather wider. Goosanders swim buoyantly
and winter groups often cruise in unison with great ease.

**IDENTIFICATION** A large, attractive sawbill duck. At a distance, male can look black and white.
At closer range and in good light, head has greenish gloss and white on body plumage suffused
with pink. Bill red; lower back and tail grey. Female similar to female Red-breasted Merganser
but has more elegant, reddish-brown head. Throat and neck white; body plumage mainly
grey-brown with underparts paler. **HABITAT** Breeds beside northern lakes and rivers; in winter,
favours lakes, reservoirs, flooded gravel pits and sheltered coasts.
**VOICE** Ringing calls uttered by displaying male; otherwise silent.

ABOVE: *male*; BELOW: *female*

*In flight, **female**
(CENTRE) shows
undivided white
speculum and
**male** shows
entire white
innerwing.*

# SMEW
### *MERGELLUS ALBELLUS*

Outside the breeding season, Smew favour coastal lagoons or reservoirs, although they also occur on large, ice-free lakes from central Europe south to the Balkans. They are hardy birds and it takes severe conditions in mainland Europe to force them to move.

**IDENTIFICATION** Small sawbill duck with narrow, serrated-edged bill. Male is distinctive and attractive with mainly white plumage but with black lines on body, around eye and on back; at close range, fine grey markings visible on flank. Female has grey-brown plumage, reddish-brown cap and white cheeks and chin. Immature drake resembles female. In flight, both sexes show white bars on wings. **HABITAT** In breeding season, favours wooded lakes; in winter, on lakes, reservoirs and sheltered coasts and estuaries. **VOICE** Mainly silent.

LEFT: *male*

ABOVE: *male*; BELOW: *female*

40–47cm + male tail length **LENGTH**
73–79cm **WINGSPAN**

# LONG-TAILED DUCK
### *CLANGULA HYEMALIS*

Long-tailed Ducks are usually seen in flocks outside the breeding season, favouring the roughest of waters and easily riding breakers in windswept bays. They dive with ease and for long periods, members of a flock sometimes diving and surfacing together.

**IDENTIFICATION** An attractive sea duck with a distinctive outline. Plumage a mixture of black, white and brown but varies throughout year. Male has dark bill with pink band and long central tail feathers, often cocked upwards. In summer, head, neck and breast dark except for white patch around eye. Shows brown back and white underparts. In winter, male has much more white in plumage, face having buff flush and dark cheeks. Female lacks male's long tail and has grey bill. In summer, upperparts mostly brown and underparts white. In winter, body brown but head white with variable dark markings. **HABITAT** Breeds on tundra; overwinters on sea coasts. **VOICE** Very vocal, males having musical calls.

*Displaying **male**.*

*female*

*female*

*male*

*female*

*male*

51

# GREAT NORTHERN DIVER

*GAVIA IMMER*

**LENGTH** 69–91cm
**WINGSPAN** 135cm

**During the breeding season its eerie wails seem to capture the spirit of the large, still lakes on which it breeds. In contrast, winter often finds this species on some of the roughest waters in Europe.**

**IDENTIFICATION** Size and markings make breeding-plumage bird distinctive; sexes are similar. Bill, head and neck black except for bands of narrow, white stripes on side of neck and under chin. Eyes red. Underparts white. Upperparts black except for tiny white spots and white chequerboard pattern on back; also black and white stripes on side of breast. Bill is large and grey with black tip, and neck often shows dark band on sides. Winter adult has dark upperparts and pale underparts. Juvenile similar but with grubbier underparts and pale fringes to upperpart feathers. In flight all birds show large wingspan and trailing feet. **HABITAT** Breeds on large lakes; overwinters in sandy bays and around rocky coasts. **VOICE** Only heard during breeding season: loud, eerie wailing calls.

*winter adult*

ABOVE: ***1st winter***
BELOW: ***Summer adult*** *has spangled appearance and black head.*

53–69cm **LENGTH**
110cm **WINGSPAN**

# RED-THROATED DIVER
*GAVIA STELLATA*

In much of its European habitat, breeding is limited to small lakes and pools within flying distance of the sea, where it feeds. In winter, Red-throated Divers generally favour inshore waters.

**IDENTIFICATION** Sexes similar. Dagger-like bill and red eyes. In breeding season both sexes have red throat, black and white striping on nape and otherwise grey head and neck. Dark-brown back and white underparts. In winter, upperparts grey-brown with white speckling on back and white underparts. Juvenile similar to winter adult but with grubbier appearance to underparts. Swims low in water with superficially Shag-like appearance but head and bill have characteristic upward tilt. Looks goose-like in flight with neck outstretched; in winter, looks very pale in flight. **HABITAT** Breeds on northern coastal pools; overwinters around coasts.

*summer adult*

**VOICE** Only heard during breeding season: goose-like calls; deep, rhythmic quacking in flight; song rapidly repeated 'kwuk-uk-uk'.

*summer adult*

*Except in very good light the red throat patch appears dark, almost black; it is the last part of summer plumage lost in autumn.*

*winter adult*

# BLACK-THROATED DIVER

*GAVIA ARCTICA*

**LENGTH** 58–73cm
**WINGSPAN** 120cm

The Black-throated Diver swims buoyantly and dives smoothly. It breeds from May to August and favours large lakes, where it can both nest and feed. After nesting, they move mainly to the coast.

**IDENTIFICATION** Sexes similar: grey head and neck with black throat and black and white stripes on side of neck and under chin. Sides of breast have black and white stripes that grade into black on back and uppperparts; distinctive white chequerboard pattern on back. In winter, bill grey with black tip; plumage dark on upperparts and pale on underparts. Throat and cheeks often look conspicuously white; white patch on flanks at waterline. Juvenile similar to winter adult, but with neat scaly pattern on upperparts. **HABITAT** Breeds on large lakes; overwinters around coasts. **VOICE** Only heard during breeding season: Raven-like croaks and wailing calls.

*winter adult*

ABOVE: *summer adult*; BELOW: *winter immature*

75–91cm **LENGTH**
150cm **WINGSPAN**

# WHITE-BILLED DIVER

### *GAVIA ADAMSII*

**The White-billed Diver is a breeding bird of the high Arctic. In Europe it is mainly a winter visitor; reasonable numbers winter off the coast of Norway and smaller numbers penetrate the northern North Sea.**

**IDENTIFICATION** Superficially similar to Great Northern Diver except for bill, which is large, dagger-like and pale yellow. Head and bill characteristically held with upward tilt. In breeding plumage, head and neck are black except for bands of narrow, white stripes on sides of neck and under chin. Upperparts mostly black except for white chequerboard effect on back and scattering of small white spots. Underparts white except for black and white stripes on side of breast. Juvenile similar to winter adult. **HABITAT** Breeds on high Arctic coastal lakes; overwinters in coastal waters. **VOICE** Wailing calls on breeding ground, similar to Great Northern Diver; otherwise silent.

ABOVE: *summer adult*

*In **winter adult**, upperparts mostly dark brown and underparts white; head and neck grubby brown with dark smudge on side of neck and behind eye; face whitish.*

# LITTLE GREBE
*TACHYBAPTUS RUFICOLLIS*

**LENGTH** 25–29cm
**WINGSPAN** 40–44cm

The Little Grebe is mainly resident, but birds from eastern Europe and southern Scandinavia are migratory. Within their resident range, Little Grebes often move in the autumn from small areas of water to larger lakes less likely to freeze; some move to the coast.

**IDENTIFICATION** Small, dumpy bird with powder-puff appearance to body feathers. Yellow-green legs and lobed feet sometimes visible. Dark bill shows lime-green patch at base and pale tip. In summer, looks mainly dark brown except for bright chestnut on neck and face. In winter, appears paler brown but darker on cap, nape and back. Tail end is whitish; pale patch at base of bill. **HABITAT** Shallow-edged lakes, ponds, slow-flowing rivers and canals. **VOICE** High-pitched, whinnying trill.

*summer adult*          *winter adult*

# BLACK-NECKED GREBE
*PODICEPS NIGRICOLLIS*

**LENGTH** 28–34cm
**WINGSPAN** 55–60cm

Larger lakes in western Europe sometimes hold breeding colonies of Black-necked Grebes. In winter, its range is similar to that of the Slavonian Grebe.

**IDENTIFICATION** Superficially similar to Slavonian Grebe but with steep forecrown, upturned bill and upward-tilted head and bill. Sexes similar. Adult in summer plumage has black head, neck and back. Underparts brick red. Eyes red with orange-yellow feather tufts behind them. In winter has mostly dark upperparts and white underparts. Black cap looks more extensive than it does on Slavonian Grebe, while neck appears greyer and generally more grubby. In flight, shows white wedge on trailing edge of innerwing only. **HABITAT** Breeds on shallow, well-vegetated ponds; overwinters on coastal waters. **VOICE** Chittering trill.

*winter adult*

*summer adult*          *winter adult*

31–38cm **LENGTH**
60–65cm **WINGSPAN**

# SLAVONIAN GREBE

*PODICEPS AURITUS*

Slavonian Grebes nest in loose colonies on shallow, reedy lakes. A visit to a colony in May is well worthwhile, with plenty of bird activity to see. In northwest Europe Slavonian Grebes are most familiar as coastal winter visitors to sheltered bays and estuaries.

**IDENTIFICATION** A beautiful bird in breeding plumage, when neck, underparts and flanks are brick red and head black except for striking orange-yellow feathering from eye to ear tufts. Bill black with white tip, and eyes red. Back black, with small white tuft of feathers at rear end. In winter, appears mainly black and white and most easily confused with Black-necked Grebe. Cap is black, leading to narrow black line on nape, which widens on back of neck. Black back and white underparts. In flight, shows white patches on leading and trailing edges of innerwing; patch on leading edge is small.

*winter adult*

**HABITAT** Breeds on well-vegetated lakes and pools; overwinters on coastal waters. **VOICE** Various screams and cries heard at nest.

ABOVE: *The spectacular orange-yellow eyestripe and tufts of* **breeding plumage** *birds are prominent in mating displays.* BELOW: **winter adult**

# RED-NECKED GREBE

*PODICEPS GRISEGENA*

**LENGTH** 40–50cm
**WINGSPAN** 80–85cm

For many birdwatchers in western Europe, the Red-necked Grebe is most familiar as a winter visitor, seen from October to March. They often breed in loose colonies, favouring well-vegetated lakes.

ABOVE: *Summer adult with chick*; BELOW: *summer adult preening.*

*winter adult*

**IDENTIFICATION** Most easily confused with Great Crested Grebe, but smaller and more compact. Sexes similar. During breeding season, adult very distinctive with black-tipped yellow bill, silver-grey face, black cap and brick-red neck. In winter loses red neck, although a hint may remain in autumn birds. Black cap extends down to level of eye. Silver-grey cheeks look conspicuous and black-tipped yellow bill still a good feature. Juveniles have stripy heads but soon resemble winter adults. In flight, shows white wedges on leading and trailing edges of innerwing; less extensive than in Great Crested Grebe. **HABITAT** Breeds on shallow lakes with abundant water plants; overwinters mainly on coastal waters. **VOICE** During breeding season utters cackling and ticking sounds, and loud wails; otherwise silent.

46–51cm **LENGTH**
85–89cm **WINGSPAN**

# GREAT CRESTED GREBE
### PODICEPS CRISTATUS

Great Crested Grebes occur patchily across central and southern Europe. In freezing conditions the birds are forced to abandon their chosen lakes and some move to coasts of western Europe.

**IDENTIFICATION** Elegant waterbird with slender neck. Sexes similar. At a distance can look black and white. In breeding season has pink bill, white face, black cap and large, showy, orange-chestnut and brown ear tufts. Nape and back brown but underparts white. In winter, loses ear tufts and has mainly brownish upperparts and white underparts; black cap appears above level of eye and contrasts with white face. Bill pink. Juvenile in early autumn is stripy but resembles winter adult by late autumn. In flight, shows white wedges on leading and trailing edges of innerwing in all plumages. **HABITAT** Breeds on lakes, gravel pits and slow-flowing rivers; occasionally on the sea in winter. **VOICE** Barking 'rah-rah-rah' and a clicking 'kek'; most vocal in spring.

*During the head-shaking display (RIGHT) the crest is raised to make the bright colouring as obvious as possible.*

*Adult birds perform ritualised displays in spring, prior to nesting; these displays continue, sporadically, throughout the breeding season, reinforcing pair-bonds.*

LEFT: *Ear tufts are lost in winter; bird always appears paler than Red-necked Grebe.*

ABOVE: *juvenile*; BELOW: *summer adult*

# FULMAR
## *FULMARUS GLACIALIS*

**LENGTH** 45–50cm
**WINGSPAN** 102–112cm

Over the last 100 years the Fulmar's range has expanded dramatically and today it occurs across much of the North Atlantic. Fulmars usually nest on sea cliffs. Non-breeding birds often range far out to sea, especially in winter months.

**IDENTIFICATION** Sexes similar. Superficially gull-like but distinguished by stiff-winged flight and large tube-nostrils. Adults have white head with dark smudge through eye. Bill comprises horny plates and has hooked tip and tube-nostrils. Wings relatively narrow and pointed; upperwing blue-grey and underwing white. Back and rump grey. Underparts white. Rarely seen northern birds may be all grey. **HABITAT** Coastal waters, especially near cliffs. **VOICE** Loud cackling and crooning at nest, grunts and cackles in feeding flocks; otherwise silent.

*Rapid wingbeats alternate with low gliding over water.*

*adult*

*Nests on sea cliffs, invariably in the company of other seabird species.*

BELOW: *Displaying **adult** calling to its mate.*

30–38cm **LENGTH**
76–89cm **WINGSPAN**

# MANX SHEARWATER
*PUFFINUS PUFFINUS*

**In summer it is quite easy to see Manx Shearwaters from ferries and headlands in northwest Europe. But their burrowing, nocturnal nesting habits mean they are hard to see on land.**

**IDENTIFICATION** Usually seen flying low over water. Sexes similar. At a distance, appears all black above and all white below. Body cigar-shaped and wings comparatively narrow and pointed. Tube-nostrils only visible at very close range. Upperparts almost black. Underparts white, including undertail feathering. Underwing white except for dark margin. Flies on stiffly held wings except in very calm conditions, when rapid wingbeats interspersed with long glides are used. **HABITAT** Breeds on offshore islands; otherwise seen at sea. **VOICE** Excited cackling noises at breeding colonies; otherwise silent.

*Adults in flight.*

*During the day, Manx Shearwaters are seen out to sea in long lines, banking from side to side and revealing alternately their dark upperwings and pale underwings.*

ABOVE: **Adult** *at entrance to nest burrow.*
BELOW: **Adult** *swimming.*

*Manx Shearwaters are well-adapted seabirds, but are barely able to shuffle along on land.*

BALEARIC

YELKOUAN

*main breeding range*

*core breeding range circled*

# BALEARIC SHEARWATER
*PUFFINUS MAURETANICUS*

# YELKOUAN SHEARWATER
*PUFFINUS YELKOUAN*

**LENGTH** 33–38cm
**WINGSPAN** 80–89cm

Formerly considered to be races of Mediterranean Shearwater, the main range for both species is the Mediterranean where birders are only likely to see them at sea. They nest in burrows on remote islands, and only return to land after dark. Yelkouan Shearwaters occur mainly in the eastern Mediterranean while Balearics favour the west.

**IDENTIFICATION** Usually seen flying in long lines, low over water. Note short, cigar-shaped body and narrow, stiffly held wings. In flight, legs project slightly beyond tail. Yelkouan Shearwater has dark sooty brown upperparts and whitish underparts overall but with grubby undertail coverts. Balearic has warmer brown upperparts and buffish or dusky underparts, especially dark on undertail coverts. **HABITAT** Breeds on inaccessible islands and cliffs; otherwise seen at sea. **VOICE** Raucous cackles at breeding colonies; otherwise silent.

YELKOUAN
SHEARWATER

BALEARIC
SHEARWATER

40–51cm **LENGTH**
94–109cm **WINGSPAN**

# SOOTY
# SHEARWATER
*PUFFINUS GRISEUS*

**The Sooty Shearwater breeds on islands in the southern oceans, then embarks on a daunting clockwise journey around the North Atlantic, reaching Europe by late summer.**

**IDENTIFICATION** Invariably seen in flight; appears all dark except at close range or in very good light; however, identification is straightforward. Larger and longer-winged than Manx Shearwater. Body is cigar-shaped and bill long and thin compared with other shearwater species. Sexes similar. Body and upperwing are dark sooty brown. Underwings are mostly dark but show a pale, silvery stripe along their length, which can be conspicuous in good light. **HABITAT** Open oceans; seen close to land only during severe onshore gales. **VOICE** Silent within its European range.

*adult*

45–50cm **LENGTH**
100–115cm **WINGSPAN**

# GREAT
# SHEARWATER
*PUFFINUS GRAVIS*

**Like its cousin, the Sooty Shearwater, the Great Shearwater breeds in the southern hemisphere during the northern winter, and only passes through coastal waters of northwest Europe from July to September.**

**IDENTIFICATION** Noticeably larger than Manx Shearwater. Invariably seen in flight on stiffly held wings. Sexes similar. Seen from above, dark cap is clearly separated from grey-brown mantle by white nape band. Upperwings and back dark, but pale feather edging to mantle and wing coverts visible in good light. White-tipped uppertail coverts produce white-rumped effect. Underparts white except for dark bands on underwing and dark belly and undertail feathering. **HABITAT** Mostly far out to sea; occasionally close to land. **VOICE** Silent within its European range.

*adult*

**Adult** *flying; note the dark cap and white rump.*

# CORY'S SHEARWATER
## *CALONECTRIS DIOMEDEA*

**LENGTH** 45–55cm
**WINGSPAN** 100–125cm

Cory's Shearwater is common throughout its breeding range and, like other shearwaters, it favours isolated rocky islands for nesting. Strong onshore breezes improve the chances of them coming close to land.

**IDENTIFICATION** Large shearwater, similar to Great Shearwater but lacks that species' black cap and white nape band. Sexes similar. Bill large and yellow with black tip. Upperparts brownish except for darker wingtips and black tail; scaly effect caused by pale feather edges. At close range, faint pale base to tail sometimes visible. Underparts white except for leading and trailing edges to wings, which are dark, and brown face. **HABITAT** Breeds on islands; otherwise at sea. The species appears further north towards the end of the breeding season when sea temperatures rise. **VOICE** Wails and coughing screams on breeding ground; otherwise silent.

*CORY'S SHEARWATER*

# LEACH'S STORM-PETREL
## *OCEANODROMA LEUCORHOA*

**LENGTH** 19–22cm
**WINGSPAN** 45–48cm

Within its European range, Leach's Storm-petrel occurs from May to October, the winter being spent in the southern oceans. The best opportunities for seeing this species come with gales in autumn.

**IDENTIFICATION** Slightly larger than European Storm-petrel, with distinctly forked tail visible at close range. Wings relatively long and pointed. Plumage can appear all black. In good light, however, head, back and wing coverts look smoky grey; trailing edge of coverts shows pale feathering, producing a transverse wingbar. No pale bar on underwing. Rump conspicuously white; at close range, narrow grey bar revealed down centre. Varied flight pattern distinctive. Sometimes glides like shearwater then engages in darting, fluttering or hovering flight. Direct flight confident and powerful. **HABITAT** Breeds on remote islands; otherwise at sea.
**VOICE** Agitated churrs and hiccups at nest; otherwise silent.

*Erratic flight path recalls shearwater one minute and tern the next.*

LEFT: *Adult swimming.*

14–18cm **LENGTH**
36–39cm **WINGSPAN**

# EUROPEAN STORM-PETREL
### *HYDROBATES PELAGICUS*

European Storm-petrels (often referred to simply as Storm-petrels) nest on remote, rocky islands. They occasionally follow boats and congregate around fishing vessels to feed on offal.

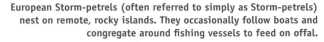

*When the bird is feeding its flight can look fluttering; it also uses its feet to patter on the water.*

**IDENTIFICATION**

A tiny seabird, superficially recalling House Martin. Plumage usually appears all black except for conspicuous white rump. At close range, brownish edges to wing covert feathers may be revealed as pale bands, and white band on underwing sometimes visible. Legs black and trailing and bill black and slender, bearing delicate tube-nostrils.

**HABITAT** Nests on sea cliffs and islands; otherwise at sea.

**VOICE** Churring and hiccuping from burrow; otherwise silent.

BELOW: *Adult swimming.*

ABOVE: *Adults feeding.*
BELOW: *Adult flying.*

# CORMORANT
### *PHALACROCORAX CARBO*

Seen in flight, the robust body and broad wings of the Cormorant give it a rather goose-like appearance. By contrast, on the water and at a distance Cormorants can resemble divers. They swim low in the water, with their heads tilted slightly upwards, and dive frequently.

**IDENTIFICATION** Adult looks dark at a distance; at close range, has scaly appearance due to oily greenish-brown feathers on upperparts having dark margins. Both *carbo* (see illustration) and *sinensis* races have white thigh patches in breeding season. Extensive white feather tips, especially in *sinensis*, make head and nape look white as breeding starts. Much of white feathering lost outside summer months. Juvenile brown and scaly; looks palest on underparts. **HABITAT** Breeds colonially, mainly around coasts in western Europe but on inland lakes elsewhere; overwinters mainly around sheltered coasts but also on inland waters. **VOICE** Guttural croaks at nest and roost; otherwise silent.

ABOVE: *Summer adult in flight.*
ABOVE RIGHT: *Winter adult swimming.*

LEFT: *The nest is an untidy mound of seaweed and flotsam, large enough to accommodate the incubating adult and two or three young*

RIGHT: *Adult in breeding plumage; the white thigh patch is flashed in courtship display. Bill large and dark with hooked tip. Race* carbo, *from northwest Europe, has yellow base to bill and white throat.*

65–80cm **LENGTH**
90–105cm **WINGSPAN**

# SHAG
### *PHALACROCORAX ARISTOTELIS*

Unlike its cousin, the Cormorant, the Shag is an entirely maritime bird, favouring deeper waters and rockier coasts than its relative. Shags are largely year-round residents, with adults faithful to the particular stretch of shore where they nest each year.

*The chicks take 53 days to fledge and are tended and fed by their parents for several weeks after this.*

*Breeding plumage quite distinct from Cormorant's, and shape of feather line round gape is also different.*

**IDENTIFICATION** Smaller than superficially similar Cormorant and seldom seen in similar habitats. Sexes similar. In poor light, adult looks all dark. At close range, breeding birds have oily-green plumage, bottle-green eyes, yellow gape and upturned crest. In winter, crest and sheen are lost or less obvious. Lores feathered on Shag, bare on Cormorant. Juvenile is pale brown with white chin; Atlantic birds have brown underparts but those from Mediterranean have white on belly. In flight, has proportionately shorter and more rounded wings than Cormorant and faster wingbeats.
**HABITAT** Rocky coasts.
**VOICE** Grunts and clicks.

*Non-breeding adult swimming.*

# PYGMY CORMORANT

*PHALACROCORAX PYGMEUS*

**LENGTH** 45–55cm
**WINGSPAN** 80–90cm

Pygmy Cormorants are colonial nesters and will often join colonies of other waterbirds. They prefer to nest among dense reeds for cover. Birdwatchers are more likely to see them swimming low in the water.

**IDENTIFICATION** Sexes similar. Compared with Cormorant, head and neck look proportionately short and tail looks proportionately long; these features are most noticeable in flight. Adult has mostly dark plumage except for chocolate-brown head. In breeding plumage, shows white flecks on head, breast and mantle. In winter, adult has whitish throat. Juvenile has brownish upperparts and paler underparts, belly and throat looking almost white. **HABITAT** Shallow, reed-fringed lowland lakes. **VOICE** Croaking calls at nest; otherwise silent.

*Summer adult, perched and drying wings.*

ABOVE: *Winter adult, perched and drying wings.*

LEFT: *Nesting **adult**.*

# GANNET
## *MORUS BASSANUS*

**The Gannet is Europe's largest breeding seabird and a common sight off many headlands along the coast of northwest Europe. If shoals of Mackerel or Herring are near the surface, Gannets plunge-dive from a considerable height.**

**IDENTIFICATION** Large size and black and white adult plumage distinctive. Adult looks all white except for yellow-buff head, black wingtips and dark legs. Feet webbed; at close range, pale blue visible along toes. Bill dagger-like and pale blue-grey. Juvenile is dark brown, speckled with pale spots; acquires white adult plumage over five years or so, the upperwing and back being the last to lose juvenile feathering. Flight pattern includes long glides on outstretched wings, deep, powerful wingbeats in direct flight and characteristic plunge-dive feeding method. **HABITAT** Breeds colonially on islands and inaccessible cliffs; otherwise at sea. **VOICE** 'Arr', 'urrah', heard at colonies and from breeding flocks; otherwise silent.

*In flight, body shape is distinctive, even from a distance.*

*juvenile*

*adult*

BELOW: *Adult Gannets at a breeding colony.*

# GREY HERON

*ARDEA CINEREA*

**LENGTH** 90–98m
**WINGSPAN** 175–195cm

The Grey Heron is the most widespread heron in Europe. It often stands motionless for hours on end, both when resting and when feeding. Grey Herons also stalk their prey on occasion, using a slow, deliberate pace followed by a lightning strike of the bill.

**IDENTIFICATION** Adult head, neck and underparts mostly whitish, except for black feathering on neck and on head; has black, trailing tuft of feathers on head. Bill large, dagger-like and yellow. Legs long and yellowish-green. In flight, Grey Herons look huge with long, broad and rounded wings. Wingbeats slow and leisurely, and head and neck held kinked and pulled in. Legs held outstretched with toes held together. **HABITAT** Wetland; sometimes on coasts. **VOICE** Call a loud and harsh 'frank'; young birds at nest give pig-like squeals.

*Large, dagger-like bill is perfectly adapted for fishing.*

*Adult, taking flight.*

**Juvenile** *similar to adult but underparts more grubby and streaked; black and white head markings less distinct.*

BELOW: *In* **adult***, back and upperwings grey except for flight feathers; black and white carpal feathers appear as 'black shoulder' on resting bird.*

78–90cm **LENGTH**
120–150cm **WINGSPAN**

# PURPLE HERON
*ARDEA PURPUREA*

Although seldom seen as well as or as often as the Grey Heron, the Purple Heron is nevertheless a locally common summer visitor to southern and central Europe wherever its habitat requirements are met. It also occurs as a vagrant north and west of its breeding range.

**IDENTIFICATION** Most attractively marked heron. Slightly smaller than Grey Heron, with more slender head and neck. Adult plumage appears mostly purplish-grey. Head and neck orange to buff, with black stripe along length down each side. Long breast feathers appear streaked and underparts look dark on standing bird. Upperparts purplish-grey. Juvenile appears more uniformly buffish-brown. In flight, adult upperwings look purplish-brown with black flight feathers; underwings look grey, except for dark maroon band forming leading edge. Best seen when commuting between roosting and feeding sites. **HABITAT** Extensive wetlands, especially in dense reedbeds. **VOICE** 'Kraank' call sometimes used, but mostly silent.

*In flight, head is held in snake-like kink. Note long, trailing legs and colourful upperwings.*

adult

**Adult** bird with eel.

adult

*Does not stand about in the open as much as Grey Heron, but is often flushed from the dense vegetation it favours.*

# NIGHT HERON
## NYCTICORAX NYCTICORAX

**LENGTH** 60–65cm
**WINGSPAN** 105–110cm

The Night Heron is a summer visitor to Europe, present from April to September; because of its colonial nesting habits, detailed maps show its precise distribution in tight groups. Although a few birds overwinter in the Mediterranean region, most migrate to tropical Africa.

**IDENTIFICATION** Sexes similar. Adult face, neck and underparts pale grey; whitish on forecrown and around base of bill. Back black and wings grey, the contrast most noticeable in flight. In breeding plumage sports long, white head plumes. Legs yellowish except at start of breeding season, when pinkish. Immature has black-tipped yellow bill and dark-brown plumage adorned with large, pale spots. Underparts streaked. **HABITAT** Wetlands. **VOICE** Raven-like 'kwaak' flight call.

*Adult has black bill, black crown and large, red eyes.*

*Relatively slow wingbeats make flight action seem almost mechanical.*

**juvenile**

*Adult perched.*

*As the name suggests, the Night Heron is most active after dark.*

45–47cm **LENGTH**
80–90cm **WINGSPAN**

# SQUACCO HERON
### *ARDEOLA RALLOIDES*

Present in the region from April to September, most European Squacco Herons then migrate to tropical Africa. Vagrants appear north of the breeding range in Europe, mostly in spring. At first glance, a flying Squacco Heron recalls a Cattle Egret.

**IDENTIFICATION** Sexes similar. In breeding plumage crown and nape streaked, feathers on lower nape being long and plume-like. Underparts white. Bill greenish with black tip and eyes yellow. Legs greenish-orange. In flight, shows pure white wings and back. In non-breeding plumage, adult has dull-brown upperparts and streaked head and neck. Still strikingly white in flight. Bill yellowish with black tip. Juvenile similar to non-breeding adult. **HABITAT** All sorts of wetlands. **VOICE** Harsh croaks heard in breeding season; otherwise silent.

ABOVE: *Adult in flight.* BELOW: *Adult standing.*

ABOVE: *Adult perched.*

# BITTERN
*BOTAURUS STELLARIS*

Bitterns are far more easily heard than seen: the male's loud, booming call can be heard up to 5km away on calm spring evenings in the vicinity of reedbeds. Most birdwatchers have to satisfy themselves with brief views of birds flying low over the reeds.

**IDENTIFICATION** Sexes similar. Large bird with mottled and marbled buffish-brown plumage. Darker streaks, barring and arrow-shaped markings afford excellent camouflage against reedbed. Neck long but often held in hunched posture. Cap and nape dark and shows dark moustachial stripe. Bill large, dagger-like and yellowish. Legs and feet yellowish-green with very long toes. When alarmed adopts motionless, upright posture with head and neck stretched skywards. In flight, often looks owl-like, with long and broad brown wings; trailing legs and forward-pointing head and bill clearly visible.
**HABITAT** Reedbeds; rarely in other wetland habitats – except during cold weather. **VOICE** During breeding season, male utters deep, resonant booming, 3–4 times in 5–6 seconds; otherwise silent.

ABOVE: *In flight, the brown plumage and rounded wings can make the Bittern resemble a giant Woodcock or owl.*

BELOW: *Alert **adult** with head and held outstretched – sky-pointing – as a sign of anxiety.*

*The Bittern's streaked and mottled plumage provides excellent cover among reedbeds.*

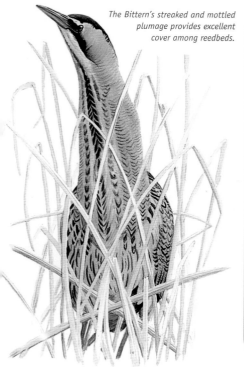

35–38cm **LENGTH**
53–56cm **WINGSPAN**

# LITTLE BITTERN
### *IXOBRYCHUS MINUTUS*

The Little Bittern is easier to see than its larger cousin. Vigilant scanning of a reedbed or wetland within the species' range will normally produce flight views, since Little Bitterns take to the wing regularly. Lucky observers may even see them clamber up reed stems.

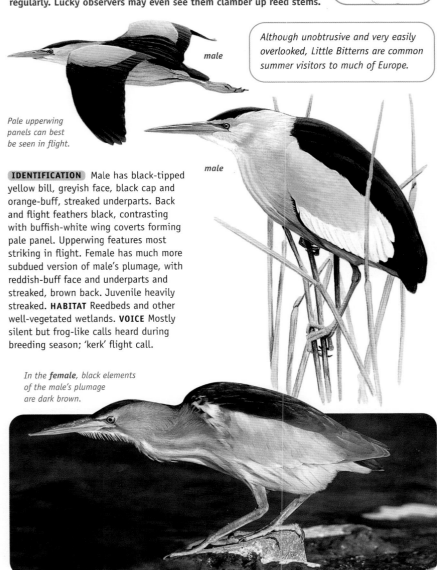

*male*

*Although unobtrusive and very easily overlooked, Little Bitterns are common summer visitors to much of Europe.*

*Pale upperwing panels can best be seen in flight.*

*male*

**IDENTIFICATION** Male has black-tipped yellow bill, greyish face, black cap and orange-buff, streaked underparts. Back and flight feathers black, contrasting with buffish-white wing coverts forming pale panel. Upperwing features most striking in flight. Female has much more subdued version of male's plumage, with reddish-buff face and underparts and streaked, brown back. Juvenile heavily streaked. **HABITAT** Reedbeds and other well-vegetated wetlands. **VOICE** Mostly silent but frog-like calls heard during breeding season; 'kerk' flight call.

*In the **female**, black elements of the male's plumage are dark brown.*

# SPOONBILL
## *PLATALEA LEUCORODIA*

**LENGTH** 80–90cm
**WINGSPAN** 115–130cm

The Spoonbill is a distinctly local species in Europe. In winter, birds from southeast Europe tend to move to coastal wetlands in eastern Mediterranean; Netherlands birds move down the Atlantic coast of northwest Europe.

**IDENTIFICATION** Sexes similar. Resting birds often have bill tucked in and so can be mistaken for Little Egrets. Feeding birds distinctive, and identified by bill shape and feeding method, when bill is swept from side to side. Adult plumage all white, although can look rather grubby; shows buffish-yellow on breast in breeding season and long plumes on nape. Legs long and black, and bill long and flattened with spoon-shaped tip. In flight, carries head and neck outstretched and legs trailing. Immature has black wingtips. **HABITAT** Shallow lakes, coastal lagoons. **VOICE** Mostly silent; occasional grunting sounds at nest.

*Outside the breeding season, Spoonbills are often seen flying in small flocks.*

*adult*

*In Europe, Spoonbills are under threat from marsh draining and pesticides; they are also sensitive to disturbance at breeding time.*

*The Spoonbill's flat-tipped bill is ideally suited for filtering out small water animals from soft sediment or the water column.*

55–65cm **LENGTH**

88–95cm **WINGSPAN**

# LITTLE EGRET

*EGRETTA GARZETTA*

**Wherever large, shallow lakes or coastal wetlands are found in southern Europe, you will find Little Egrets in summer. The species' range has expanded northwards in recent decades and it is now common in southern Britain (and Ireland) and breeds there.**

**IDENTIFICATION** The most common pure-white, heron-like bird in Europe. Sexes alike. Slender and elegant appearance, with long neck. Bill long, dark and dagger-like. Bare skin at base of bill yellowish in breeding season but otherwise darker. Also sports long head plumes in breeding season. Appearance remains similar throughout year. In flight, shows broad, rounded wings and trails its long legs behind it. Once prized and persecuted by the millinery trade for its long plumes, the species is now relatively common throughout its range. **HABITAT** Shallow lakes and wetlands; also coastal lagoons and saltpans. **VOICE** Harsh 'khaah' and other grating sounds heard at colony; otherwise mostly silent.

ABOVE: *Adult in flight.*

RIGHT: *Adult catching stickleback prey.*

BELOW: *Adult showing long, black legs and yellow feet.*

# CATTLE EGRET
## BUBULCUS IBIS

**LENGTH** 48–52cm
**WINGSPAN** 90–95m

In Europe the Cattle Egret's main breeding range is southern Iberia. But its range is expanding north and it bred in Britain for the first time in 2008. Cattle Egrets are active feeders, especially when they join herds of cattle or sheep.

**IDENTIFICATION** A stocky, white bird with a characteristic bulging throat. Sexes similar. Plumage pure white except during brief period of breeding season. Bill dagger-like and proportionately large; at height of breeding season pinkish-orange but otherwise yellow. Legs dull yellowish-green except, briefly, during breeding season, when pinkish-orange. In flight, wings broad and rounded, and legs trailing; neck held in typical hunched-up posture, giving large-headed appearance.
**HABITAT** Cultivated land and grassland, often alongside animals; also follows ploughs.
**VOICE** During breeding season, utters barking 'aak' and other calls; otherwise silent.

RIGHT: **Adults** following feeding cow.
BELOW: **adult**
BELOW RIGHT: **Adult**, at height of breeding season.

85–102cm **LENGTH**
140–170cm **WINGSPAN**

# GREAT WHITE EGRET
### *ARDEA ALBA*

Great White Egrets have a limited breeding range in the region but have recently spread to the Netherlands, north France, Spain and Latvia, and occur as vagrants as far north and west as Britain.

ABOVE: *Adult in flight shows long, broad wings and long, trailing legs; head and neck held in hunched posture.*

BELOW: *adult, non-breeding*

**IDENTIFICATION** Distinctly larger than Little Egret, with which it sometimes occurs, and with rather more statuesque proportions. Plumage pure white at all times; shows long, lacy plumes on lower back in breeding season. Bill black in breeding season but yellow at other times; patch of yellow skin at base of bill present at all times. Legs long; reddish on tibia in breeding season on adult but dark blackish at other times and in juvenile. **HABITAT** Extensive wetlands and large, reed-fringed lakes. **VOICE** Grating 'kraak' heard at colony and roost; otherwise silent.

*Adult, in breeding season.*

# DALMATIAN PELICAN

*PELECANUS CRISPUS*

Destruction by fishermen and wetland drainage have severely depleted the Dalmatian Pelican's numbers. They are often seen with White Pelicans, both on migration and at feeding or nesting sites.

**IDENTIFICATION** Similar in proportions and size to White Pelican but slightly larger. White plumage has blue-grey tinge; sports a back-curled mane in the form of curly feathers. Bill long and large and throat sac orange-yellow in breeding season but pink at other times. Legs grey in all plumages. In flight, adult seen from below has uniformly greyish-white wings, easily separating it from White Pelican. Seen from above, primary flight feathers are black, contrasting with otherwise pale plumage. Juvenile has more uniformly greyish-white underwing in flight than White Pelican. A consummate flier, able to soar and glide with ease.

**HABITAT** Shallow freshwater lakes.

**VOICE** Hissing and grunting calls heard at colony; otherwise silent.

*Adult, in breeding season.*

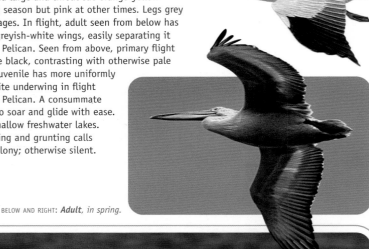

BELOW AND RIGHT: *Adult, in spring.*

140–170cm **LENGTH**
275–290cm **WINGSPAN**

# WHITE PELICAN
### *PELECANUS ONOCROTALUS*

**Northern Greece in spring offers the best opportunities for seeing this species in Europe. With its long, broad wings, the White Pelican is as proficient at soaring and thermalling as birds of prey. It is also well adapted to an aquatic life, the webbed feet enabling it to swim well.**

*Adult*, in breeding season.

The White Pelican is especially impressive in flight.

*Adult*, in breeding season.

BELOW: *Migrating flock.*

**IDENTIFICATION** Large, white waterbird. Often seen swimming in flocks when adult plumage looks all white, except for black wingtips. In good light, plumage can be seen to be tinged yellowish. Bill large and very long. Throat sac yellow to orange and shows bare patch of pink skin around eyes. Robust legs and webbed feet orange-yellow. From below, adult shows black flight feathers that contrast with otherwise white plumage. Juvenile has brownish plumage and yellow throat sac; shows brown flight feathers and brown leading edge to wing. **HABITAT** Shallow, lowland lakes and river deltas. **VOICE** Grunts, growls and mooing calls heard at nest; otherwise silent.

The capacious throat sac is used to engulf whole shoals of fish if feeding conditions are good.

# WHITE STORK
*CICONIA CICONIA*

**LENGTH** 100–115cm
**WINGSPAN** 155–165cm

Anyone who has visited bird migration hotspots at the Bosphorus in Turkey or the Straits of Gibraltar in southern Spain will have lasting memories of migrating storks. They are easy birds to see during the breeding season since they often nest on rooftops or churches.

**IDENTIFICATION** Unmistakable, given size and markings. Sexes similar. Standing, adult head, neck, back and underparts white; can look rather grubby. Wingtips black. Bill long, dagger-like and bright red. Legs long and red. In flight, soars impressively on long, outstretched wings, which look square-ended and have 'fingers' of primaries projecting. Body white except for black flight feathers when seen from above and below. Juvenile similar to adult but colour of bill and legs duller. **HABITAT** Feeds in wetlands and fields adjacent to towns and villages. **VOICE** Mostly silent; non-vocal bill-clapping at nest.

*Bill-clapping display of nesting **adults**.*

*Adult in flight.*

*adult*

95–100cm **LENGTH**
145–150cm **WINGSPAN**

# BLACK STORK
### *CICONIA NIGRA*

The Black Stork is a rare breeding bird in Europe. Most European birds migrate to tropical Africa. Especially when nesting, the Black Stork can be a shy and retiring bird that is difficult to see.

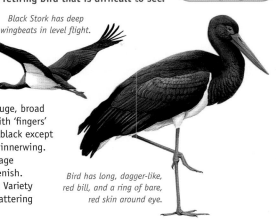

*Black Stork has deep wingbeats in level flight.*

**IDENTIFICATION**
Sexes similar. From behind, plumage of adult looks all black; in good light, oily sheen also visible. From other views, white underparts can be seen. Legs long and red. In flight, has huge, broad wings, which look square-ended with 'fingers' of primaries showing; plumage all black except for white underparts extending to innerwing. Juvenile similar to adult but plumage browner and legs and bill dull greenish. **HABITAT** Forested wetlands. **VOICE** Variety of soft calls; also non-vocal bill clattering at nest.

*Bird has long, dagger-like, red bill, and a ring of bare, red skin around eye.*

---

55–65cm **LENGTH**
80–95cm **WINGSPAN**

# GLOSSY IBIS
### *PLEGADIS FALCINELLUS*

The Glossy Ibis is found in its European breeding range mainly from May to August; birds then tend to disperse widely before embarking on autumn migration. From a distance, the Glossy Ibis looks like a cross between a Curlew and a heron.

**IDENTIFICATION** Waterbird with distinctive shape, even in silhouette. Pinkish bill large, long and curved downwards, and head rather large and bulbous in proportion to long neck. Non-breeding birds have pale streaks on head and neck. In flight, head and neck held outstretched and legs trail. **HABITAT** Wetlands. **VOICE** Crow-like 'kra-kra' sometimes heard near nest, but mostly silent.

*adult*

*Adult soaring.*

*Plumage mostly rich chestnut-maroon; in poor light can look all black, but in bright light shows green or purplish sheen to wings and back.*

# EGYPTIAN VULTURE

## NEOPHRON PERCNOPTERUS

**LENGTH** 60–70cm
**WINGSPAN** 155–180cm

**Present from April to September, Egyptian Vultures are found in warm climates such as central and southern Spain. They favour gorges or mountain slopes and from mid-morning soar to great heights.**

**IDENTIFICATION** In flight, silhouette recalls a miniature Lammergeier with its wedge-shaped tail; wings proportionately broader and shorter than that species'. Sexes similar. Seen from below, adult has black flight feathers that contrast with otherwise rather grubby white plumage; at close range, black-tipped yellow bill, bald yellow face and yellow or pink legs visible. Juvenile similar shape to adult but all dark; full adult plumage acquired gradually over four years or so. **HABITAT** Mountainous regions. **VOICE** Mostly silent.

ABOVE: *Adult in flight.*
LEFT: *adult*
BELOW: *juvenile*

100–115cm **LENGTH**
265–280cm **WINGSPAN**

# LAMMERGEIER
### *GYPAETUS BARBATUS*

The Lammergeier is Europe's scarcest and most local vulture species. It is found in the western Pyrenees, Turkey, the Caucasus, on Corsica and in northern Greece, with a total population of 50 to 100 pairs.

*juvenile*

*One of the most majestic of all birds in flight.*

*Adult soaring.*

*adult*

**IDENTIFICATION** A very distinctive bird of prey with very long and comparatively narrow wings and a long, wedge-shaped tail. Seen in good light, adults show orange-buff head and underparts; wings and tail black. At close range, black patch around orange eye can be seen along with black moustache-like feathers. Juvenile has similar flight silhouette to adult but is all dark. **HABITAT** Mountainous regions, often near gorges and ravines. **VOICE** Mostly silent.

85

# BLACK VULTURE
*AEGYPIUS MONACHUS*

**LENGTH** 100–110cm
**WINGSPAN** 250–290cm

The Eurasian Black Vulture is Europe's largest bird of prey and also one of its rarest. Although it was probably never numerous, persecution by farmers has reduced its numbers in the region to a few hundred pairs, the majority of these being found in central southern Spain.

ABOVE AND BELOW: *adult*

**IDENTIFICATION** Flight silhouette distinctive with long, broad and parallel-sided wings, which are square-ended but show splayed 'fingers' of primary feathers; soars with wings held flat. Head appears relatively small and tail is usually slightly fanned. Sexes similar. Plumage mostly dark brown but invariably appears all black because of distance at which most birds are seen. Seen at close range, has huge, black-tipped bill and bald head and neck with ruffled collar of feathers. Juvenile difficult to separate from adult in the field. **HABITAT** Seen at towering heights over all sorts of broken terrain, especially near mountains. **VOICE** Mostly silent.

95–105cm **LENGTH**
260–280cm **WINGSPAN**

# GRIFFON VULTURE

*GYPS FULVUS*

Although reduced in range and numbers, the Griffon is the commonest
vulture of the region and typically is a year-round resident. Given its
size and usual indifference to man, it is also the easiest to see,
especially when tens or even hundreds spiral on a single thermal.

**IDENTIFICATION** Large, broad-winged vulture. Sexes
similar. Adult has buffish-brown body plumage contrasting
with dark flight feathers; contrast visible from above and
below in flight and on perched birds. Head and neck bald
and whitish but sometimes stained; has collar of ruffled
feathers. In flight, looks small-headed and short-tailed.
Wings long and broad, narrowing towards tips and showing
pale barring against brown underwing coverts; soars with
wings held in shallow 'V'. Juvenile generally similar to
adult but underwing coverts rather pale with dark barring.
**HABITAT** Warm, mountainous regions. **VOICE** Utters
croaking calls near nest or roost; silent in flight.

*Being dependent on rising thermals, Griffon Vultures
are seldom seen in the air before ten in the morning.*

*Prior to taking to the air, often sits facing the sun
with wings slightly spread.*

ABOVE AND BELOW: *adult*

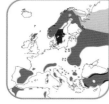

# GOLDEN EAGLE
*AQUILA CHRYSAETOS*

**LENGTH** 76–89cm
**WINGSPAN** 190–227cm

The Golden Eagle is a widespread, although never common, raptor of mountainous regions. It often flies very high, covering a wide range every day, but when hunting it will usually fly low, dropping suddenly on its prey with talons outstretched.

**IDENTIFICATION** A large eagle with a long tail and long, broad wings held in a shallow 'V' when soaring and gliding. Looks dark from below but shows buff, grey and dark-brown markings above with paler head. Strong wingbeats are followed by one- to two-second glides in normal flight, but prey may be surprised by a steep dive, or low-level glide. Immatures have white wing patches and white tail with dark terminal band. Adult plumage attained after five to seven years. **HABITAT** Mountainous regions, lowland forests and marshes; only where human habitation is absent. **VOICE** Mostly silent, but some yelping calls, rarely heard.

*juvenile, 1st winter*

*adult*

*immature, 3rd winter*

*The massive bill is impressive when seen close up; the crown and shaggy hind neck are washed golden-yellow.*

*adult*

Both Golden Eagles and Buzzards soar on raised wings, so caution is needed when bird is viewed from a distance; the eagle is much larger, although a distant bird's size is not always apparent.

70–90cm **LENGTH**
200–240cm **WINGSPAN**

# WHITE-TAILED EAGLE

*HALIAEETUS ALBICILLA*

A White-tailed Eagle in flight is an unforgettable sight and few people can fail to be impressed by its size. In winter, birds seldom rise to great heights, sometimes affording superb views in low-level flight.

**IDENTIFICATION** In flight, has immense wingspan with broad, parallel-sided wings, which are square-ended with primaries resembling splayed 'fingers'. Tail relatively short and broad; white in adult birds but dark in juveniles. When seen perched, yellow legs and bill can be seen in adult; juvenile bill dark but yellow at the base. Adult head looks paler than body. **HABITAT** Associated with sea coasts and extensive wetlands. **VOICE** Yelping call.

*adult*

*In many parts of their European range White-tailed Eagles are year-round residents, but birds from Russia migrate south and west in the autumn.*

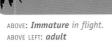

ABOVE: *Immature in flight.*
ABOVE LEFT: *adult*

# GREATER SPOTTED EAGLE
*AQUILA CLANGA*

**LENGTH** 62–75cm
**WINGSPAN** 160–180cm

Greater Spotted Eagles are still fairly common in parts of their eastern European range. Small copses and scattered woodland will sometimes serve as a breeding site, provided that wetland areas lie close by.

**IDENTIFICATION** Appreciably larger than Lesser Spotted Eagle, but this is not always easy to see in distant, solitary birds. Best feature for separation in flight seen from below is greyish flight feathers, which appear paler than rest of feathering on wings and body (converse true in Lesser Spotted Eagle). Seen from above, adult plumage looks all dark; that of juvenile shows heavy white spotting on wing coverts and inner flight feathers with white 'shafts' on all primaries. **HABITAT** Forest and scattered woodland close to wetland areas. **VOICE** Yapping call heard near nest.

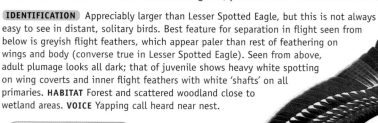

*The bird's leisurely flight on downward-bowed wings can give the impression of a much larger bird.*

*Juvenile is heavily spotted.*

LEFT: ***Adult** in flight.*
ABOVE: ***juvenile***

57–65cm **LENGTH**
135–160cm **WINGSPAN**

# LESSER SPOTTED EAGLE
*AQUILA POMARINA*

**Breeding sites for this species are limited because it requires undisturbed forest for nesting and marshes and wet meadows for feeding. Eastern Europe is the species' stronghold.**

**IDENTIFICATION**

Comparatively small eagle but with proportionately long, parallel-sided wings, which appear rather square-ended in soaring flight with 'fingers' of primaries clearly visible. Seen from below, can look all dark; in good light, flight feathers always darker than brown body feathers in both adults and juveniles, a good feature for separating from similar Greater Spotted Eagle. Seen from above, adult shows tail and flight feathers darker than body feathers, narrow white band on base of tail and white 'shafts' on inner primaries. Juvenile similar to adult but has numerous white spots on inner flight feathers.

**HABITAT** In European breeding range, favours forests adjacent to wetlands. **VOICE** High-pitched yapping call.

*adult*

*Juvenile shows white spotting on inner flight feathers.*

*adult*

# IMPERIAL EAGLE
*AQUILA HELIACA*

**LENGTH** 75–84cm
**WINGSPAN** 180–215cm

The Imperial Eagle is a rare bird in Europe. It hunts in open, lightly wooded lowland areas where there are scattered tall trees for nesting. Much time is spent sitting on a low perch, but feeding forays are made at high altitude, often at great speed.

**IDENTIFICATION** Adult is a very dark bird showing a creamy buff nape and greyish tail with a dark terminal band. Wings are long and narrow and held flat when soaring, but may be slightly raised with a flat tip when gliding. Tail appears long and narrow in adults, but juveniles show a more spread tail when soaring. Juvenile brownish-red, fading to paler buff-brown with streaked breast. Juveniles take four to five years to attain adult plumage. **HABITAT** Mediterranean steppe, mixed lowland habitats with some tall trees. **VOICE** Deep Raven-like 'gahk'.

*Immense, relatively long-winged raptor with white scapular patches.*

*adult*

*adult*

# SPANISH IMPERIAL EAGLE
*AQUILA ADALBERTI*

**LENGTH** 75–85cm
**WINGSPAN** 180–215cm

The Coto Doñana and environs in the south of Spain are one of the Spanish Imperial Eagle's strongholds; here the birds spend much of the day sitting in trees, where they are surprisingly easy to overlook.

**IDENTIFICATION** Seen in flight, wings look relatively long and parallel-sided; tail not normally fanned. Adult can look all dark but in good light shows dark brown plumage and white markings on scapulars and leading edge of innerwing; crown and nape are pale buff. Juvenile has pale-brown plumage except for dark flight feathers and tail; shows heavy white spotting on upper surface of flight feathers and, in good light, teardrop spots on wing coverts. **HABITAT** Open woodland and fields. **VOICE** Repeated, harsh barking call.

*immature*

*adult*

50–65cm **LENGTH**
130–150cm **WINGSPAN**

# LONG-LEGGED BUZZARD

*BUTEO RUFINUS*

In Europe, the Long-legged Buzzard is most easily seen in Greece and European Turkey between April and August. Compared to the Common Buzzard, it looks large, pale and relatively long-winged.

**IDENTIFICATION** Sexes similar. Adult plumage extremely variable but perched birds generally show noticeably pale head and breast; latter separated from pale vent and undertail by broad, rufous band across belly. Seen from below in flight, shows reddish-brown underwing coverts and dark carpal patches; flight feathers white but with conspicuous and contrasting black tips to primaries and black trailing edge to secondaries. From above, reddish-brown mantle and upperwing coverts contrast with dark flight feathers; tail and head look very pale. Juvenile similar to adult but with faint barring on tail and less uniform coloration overall. **HABITAT** Arid mountainous terrain and semi-desert. **VOICE** Mewing call, similar to that of Buzzard.

*adult*

*adult*

*Although dark forms of the species do occur, the **rufous form** (RIGHT) is most regularly encountered and certainly the easiest to identify with certainty in flight.*

50–60cm **LENGTH**
120–150cm **WINGSPAN**

# ROUGH-LEGGED BUZZARD

*BUTEO LAGOPUS*

The Rough-legged Buzzard's low-level flight, conspicuous white-based tail and habit of hovering make it easy to identify even at a distance. Its diet comprises mainly small mammals.

**IDENTIFICATION** Superficially similar to Buzzard in silhouette but slightly larger and with proportionately longer wings and tail. Like that species, the Rough-legged soars on raised wings, but also regularly hovers. Seen from below, typically shows dark and white pattern: has dark belly patch, dark carpal patches on wings and tail with faint barring towards tip and broad, dark terminal band. Seen from above, conspicuous pale base to tail appears as white rump. Seen perched, dark belly often noticeable and head can look pale, especially in young birds. **HABITAT** Nests on tundra; in winter, on marshes, moors and downs. **VOICE** Similar mew to Buzzard but louder and lower pitched.

*adult male*

*adult male*

93

# BUZZARD
### *BUTEO BUTEO*

**LENGTH** 50–55cm
**WINGSPAN** 115–130cm

Where it is common, the Buzzard often attracts attention to itself with its mewing, cat-like call. Furthermore, unlike many other large birds of prey, Buzzards spend quite long periods perched on posts and dead branches in the open, often yielding good views to observers.

**IDENTIFICATION** Medium-sized bird of prey. Sexes similar. Colour extremely variable but almost always some shade of brown. Soars on broad, rounded wings held in a 'V' angle with barred tail fanned out. Upperparts usually dark brown, although flight feathers contrastingly dark in paler birds. Seen from below, wings and tail barred, the trailing edge of wings and terminal edge of tail noticeably dark. Some birds show dark collar and dark carpal patches. At close range, black-tipped yellow bill and yellow legs visible. Almost pure-white birds are occasionally seen.
**HABITAT** Hilly country, open farmland with adjacent woodland.
**VOICE** Mewing 'peeioo'.

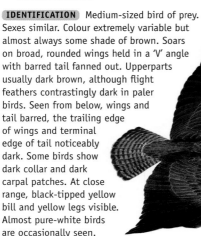

*adult*

RIGHT: *From below, Buzzards can be highly variable, with colouring ranging from largely dark to largely white; this is a typical* **adult***.*

**Adult** *tearing prey apart.*

55–69cm **LENGTH**
145–160cm **WINGSPAN**

# OSPREY
### *PANDION HALIAETUS*

An Osprey circling over a lake may resemble a large immature gull until it sights prey, when it will hover with deep, powerful wingbeats and dangling legs. It descends from its hunting flight in stages until ready to dive, which it does at high speed.

*The Osprey hits the water at high speed when fishing; if the fish is too large the Osprey will let it go, but birds have been known to drown as a result of claws catching in bones or scales.*

*adult*

BELOW: ***Adult** carrying a stick back to the nest, which is usually built at the top of a pine tree.*

*adult*

### IDENTIFICATION

The Osprey is a large, long-winged bird of prey, looking very pale below. Dark primaries and carpal patches give the underwing a distinctive pattern. Females and juveniles have a darker breast band on a buff background. The long tail has a broad, dark terminal band and three to four narrower dark bands. **HABITAT** Rivers, lakes, coastal areas. **VOICE** Shrill piping and yelping calls.

# HONEY BUZZARD
### PERNIS APIVORUS

**LENGTH** 50–60cm
**WINGSPAN** 135–160cm

Within their breeding range, Honey Buzzards are comparatively easy to see in flight, since they frequently soar over the forests and woods favoured as nesting sites with characteristically flat wings. When not in the air, however, they are secretive and seldom seen.

## IDENTIFICATION

Colour rather variable but usually dark brown above and pale underneath with dark barring. Seen from below in flight, wings are long and broad, tail is relatively long and head proportionately long and cuckoo-like. Shows pale throat but heavy barring from neck to base of tail; tail itself has several dark bars and conspicuous dark terminal band. On wings, flight feathers have dark tips and are barred, as are coverts. Dark patches on forewing are characteristic. At close range, pale head, yellow eyes (brown in juveniles) and yellow legs can be seen. **HABITAT** Breeds in mature woodland. **VOICE** Thin, mournful call, seldom heard.

TOP: *juvenile*
ABOVE: *adult female*

ABOVE: *adult male*

*adult male*

# SHORT-TOED EAGLE

62–67cm **LENGTH**
170–185cm **WINGSPAN**

*CIRCAETUS GALLICUS*

Short-toed Eagles favour open, warm habitats where there is an abundance of snakes. The usual method of hunting is to hover, or perhaps quarter low over the ground, dropping on to the prey with a rapid strike.

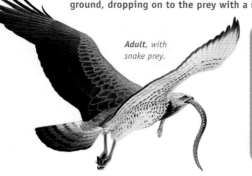

*Adult, with snake prey.*

adult

**IDENTIFICATION** A large, pale raptor, usually seen hovering or using updraughts, when underparts look very white. Wings broad and quite long in proportion to body size; tail narrow and square-ended. Darker head gives hooded appearance. Sexes have similar plumages but female is larger than male. May be confused with Osprey, but does not show dark carpal patches. **HABITAT** Dry, open habitats, with some maquis, garrigue or scattered trees. **VOICE** Fluting calls by male, harsher notes from female.

adult

Short-toed Eagles overwinter in Africa; they often migrate in mixed flocks of other raptors across well-known migration routes such as Gibraltar and the Bosphorus.

97

# BOOTED EAGLE
*HIERAAETUS PENNATUS*

**LENGTH** 45–50cm
**WINGSPAN** 100–130cm

**The Booted Eagle is still relatively common in Spain, but is rarer elsewhere in southern and central Europe. This is one of the most vocal of the eagles, with several wader-like calls uttered near the nest site and during courtship.**

**IDENTIFICATION** The smallest European eagle, occurring in both pale and dark forms. Dark form easily confused with Black Kite and juvenile Bonelli's Eagle; plumage varies from red-brown to blackish-brown, with buff tail darkening towards tip. For description of pale form *see* caption. Both dark and pale forms show a pale 'V' on upperparts formed by median upperwing coverts. Primary feathers in outstretched wings appear as typical eagle 'fingers'. **HABITAT** Wooded mountain slopes, open hilly country. **VOICE** Various whistling and cackling calls.

*dark form*

BELOW: *Pale form has pale underparts and wings except for dark flight feathers, dark-grey tail and greyish-buff head.*

LEFT: *pale form*

*The Booted Eagle can hang motionless at great height without hovering, and then dive straight down at breathtaking speed with legs extended forwards.*

65–70cm **LENGTH**
150–170cm **WINGSPAN**

# BONELLI'S EAGLE
*HIERAAETUS FASCIATUS*

Most Bonelli's Eagles remain near their breeding grounds all year, but outside the breeding season juveniles will migrate south towards the Mediterranean, where they will hunt over coastal marshes and plains. They are very widely scattered and nowhere common.

**IDENTIFICATION** Adults are distinctive with very pale belly, dark terminal band to long tail, and contrasting dark underwings; lesser underwing coverts are whitish and flight feathers greyish at base giving distinctive pattern, but general effect is of dark wings. A variable pale patch shows on the upper back. Sexes similar. Wingbeats are quick and shallow, with wings held level and slightly forwards when soaring. When gliding, wings are gently arched and show straight rear edge. Juveniles are pale pinkish-brown below and darker on back. **HABITAT** Mountainous and hilly country in Mediterranean region; sometimes marshes. **VOICE** Shrill, piping calls.

*adult*

RIGHT: *immature*
BELOW: *adult*

*Bonelli's Eagles often hunt in pairs along mountainsides and over rough ground, frequently using the same hunting areas every day; prey is usually captured on the ground and consists of medium-sized mammals such as Rabbits and birds such as partridges; birds are also sometimes caught in flight.*

# HEN HARRIER
*CIRCUS CYANEUS*

**LENGTH** 45–50cm
**WINGSPAN** 100–120cm

The typical flight pattern of the Hen Harrier comprises leisurely wingbeats and long glides. In windy conditions, the birds seldom have to flap their wings, holding them instead in a pronounced 'V' shape. They fly low over the ground.

**IDENTIFICATION** Male has mainly pale-grey plumage, feathers on breast and belly being palest of all. Wingtips contrastingly black and shows conspicuous white rump in flight. At close range and when perched reveals yellow iris, black-tipped yellow bill and yellow legs. Female has brown plumage with owl-like facial disc and streaked underparts; shows conspicuous white rump in flight and strongly barred tail and underwing. Juvenile similar to female. **HABITAT** Breeds on northern and upland moors and bogs; in winter, in lowland, open terrain, often coastal. **VOICE** Rapid, chattering 'ke-ke-ke' heard in nesting territory; otherwise silent.

*female*

*male*

BELOW: *Adult female and juvenile are very similar.*

BELOW: *male*

40–45cm **LENGTH**

105–120cm **WINGSPAN**

# MONTAGU'S HARRIER
## *CIRCUS PYGARGUS*

This harrier hunts by flying low over the ground, its skilled use of breezes enabling it to fly at strikingly slow speeds. A tell-tale rustle will cause it to swerve in mid-flight and plunge to the ground.

### IDENTIFICATION

Both sexes are superficially similar to Hen Harrier but wings look proportionately longer and more pointed. Male has mainly pale-grey plumage, palest on breast and belly. Seen from below, shows extensive black wingtips, two black wingbars and fainter, reddish wingbars on coverts; seen from above, has black wingtips, single black wingbar and white rump, less conspicuous than male Hen Harrier's. Female very similar to female Hen Harrier and best told by smaller white rump and wing shape. Juvenile similar to female but, seen from below, body and wing coverts reddish-orange. **HABITAT** Uses variety of habitats during breeding season including wetlands, arable fields, young plantations, heaths and moors. **VOICE** High-pitched 'yik-yik-yik' over breeding ground; otherwise silent.

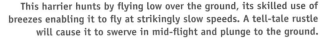

ABOVE: **Male** has greyish plumage with black wingtips and black bars on underwing. ABOVE RIGHT: *female*

*male*

RIGHT: **Female** has white rump like female Hen Harrier, but is smaller; wings also look more pointed.

# MARSH HARRIER
### *CIRCUS AERUGINOSUS*

**LENGTH** 50–55cm
**WINGSPAN** 115–130cm

With wings held in a pronounced 'V', Marsh Harriers quarter the reedbeds in a leisurely fashion, dropping down occasionally to catch a frog or small bird. When hunting, they seldom fly more than a few metres above the height of the reeds.

**IDENTIFICATION** Graceful bird of prey with relatively long wings and long tail. Occasionally seen perched but more usually observed in flight low over ground, often with legs dangling. Seen from above, male has dark-brown back and wing coverts, which contrast with blue-grey flight feathers and tail. Wingtips black, and head and leading edge of innerwing pale grey-buff. Seen from below, underwing blue-grey except for black wingtips, body dark brown and tail grey. Female has mostly chocolate-brown plumage except for pale-buff forehead and cap, throat and leading edge to innerwing. Juvenile resembles female but pale markings less distinct. **HABITAT** Reedbeds and wetlands; sometimes over nearby farmland. **VOICE** A plaintive, shrill 'kweeoo'.

RIGHT: *Adult male takes at least three years to acquire pale parts of plumage.*

*adult male*

*Adult female's plumage is mostly brown.*

When courting and nesting, male Marsh Harriers sometimes circle high.

# BLACK-SHOULDERED KITE

31–35cm **LENGTH**
145–165cm **WINGSPAN**

*ELANUS CAERULEUS*

**In Spain and Portugal Black-shouldered Kites are mainly year-round residents that start nesting comparatively early in the year, sometimes in February. They favour open terrain with scattered trees.**

**IDENTIFICATION** Sexes similar. Upperparts mostly pale grey and underparts white. Head looks superficially owl-like and has staring red eyes with black 'eyebrows'. Has black-tipped yellow bill and yellow legs. In flight, which is buoyant and graceful, black wingtips and black on leading edge of innerwing look conspicuous. Often hovers or glides with wings in 'V' shape. **HABITAT** Dry, open country with scattered trees. **VOICE** Mostly silent but utters thin scream in alarm.

*adult*

LEFT: *Seen perched, looks somewhat large-headed and short-tailed; black patch on innerwing shows as a black 'shoulder'.*

*juvenile*

*adult*

*Black-shouldered Kites often carry on feeding late in the evening, their pale plumage showing up well in the gloom.*

103

# BLACK KITE
*MILVUS MIGRANS*

**LENGTH** 55–60cm
**WINGSPAN** 145–165cm

The Black Kite is a migratory summer visitor to Europe, arriving in April or May and leaving in August and September to overwinter in sub-Saharan Africa. Black Kites may glide in a leisurely manner over lakes, but also visit rubbish dumps.

**IDENTIFICATION** In flight most easily confused with female Marsh Harrier. Sexes similar. Plumage mainly dark brown and can look all black in poor light. Head rather paler than body. Has black-tipped yellow bill and yellow legs. Tail forked, but not as deeply as Red Kite's. **HABITAT** Wooded lakes and open country. **VOICE** Gull-like whinnying call.

*adult*

*adult*

*adult*

Wings relatively long and broad and held flat when circling; tail is constantly twisted in flight to assist control.

60–65cm **LENGTH**
155–185cm **WINGSPAN**

# RED KITE
*MILVUS MILVUS*

Red Kites have a somewhat patchy distribution in Europe, being most common and widespread on the Iberian peninsula. Few birds of prey are more impressive in flight and the observer can only marvel at its mastery of the air.

*adult*

*Seen from above, tail is orange-red, and brown innerwings contrast with dark flight feathers.*

*adult*

*From below, rusty red body and underwing coverts contrast distinctively with pale head and white wing patches; wingtips are black.*

**IDENTIFICATION** Sexes similar. Plumage mainly reddish-brown with paler head and deeply forked tail. Has black-tipped yellow bill and yellow legs. In flight, soars effortlessly, often with wings slightly kinked forwards. Seen from below, body and leading edge of innerwing are reddish. Wings are long and show translucent whitish patch near tips; tail is pale rufous. **HABITAT** Typically associated with wooded valleys adjacent to areas of farmland or open country. **VOICE** Shrill, quavering 'weoo-weoo-weoo'.

*adult*

# GOSHAWK
## *ACCIPITER GENTILIS*

The best time of year to look for Goshawks is in the early spring, in the early morning, when pairs display above their territories. Birds can be seen circling and stooping, often with their white undertail feathers fluffed out like a powder puff.

**IDENTIFICATION** Large, dashing hawk, the female similar in size to Buzzard. Smaller male can be confused with female Sparrowhawk but note Goshawk's bulkier body, shorter tail relative to body size and longer wings, often held in an 'S' curve. Seen from below, both sexes look pale with grey barring on body, wings and tail; fluffy white feathers at base of tail often conspicuous. Both sexes have rather similar grey-brown upperparts. Juvenile has streaked underparts and less uniform upperparts. **HABITAT** Extensive forests, often of pine or beech.
**VOICE** Rapid, hoarse 'gek-gek-gek' heard at nest; otherwise silent.

*female*

*male*

*female*

Goshawks are resident across most of their range, but birds in the far north and east move south and west in the autumn.

30–40cm **LENGTH**
55–75cm **WINGSPAN**

# SPARROWHAWK
*ACCIPITER NISUS*

Sparrowhawks are often seen in low-level, dashing flight, but they will also occasionally soar, showing their short, rounded wings and long tail. The species has suffered greatly at the hands of man, both from the use of DDT and other agrochemicals and from sportsmen.

**IDENTIFICATION** Male has blue-grey upperparts and whitish underparts bearing strong reddish-orange barring on body and underwing coverts. Undertail feathers white and tail barred. Female has grey-brown upperparts and whitish underparts with grey-brown barring. At close range, both sexes show yellow legs and black-tipped yellow bill; iris of male orange, that of female yellow. Iris colour changes with age. Juvenile similar to female but browner and streaked below. **HABITAT** Mixed woodland, farmland with hedgerows; increasingly in urban areas. **VOICE** Harsh 'kek-kek-kek-kek'.

*Adult female chasing Chaffinches.*

*Sparrowhawks catch prey either by surprise attack from a concealed perch or flight close to a woodland edge.*

*juvenile*

*male*

# LEVANT SPARROWHAWK

*ACCIPITER BREVIPES*

The Levant Sparrowhawk has a limited breeding range in Europe, but on migration passes through the Bosphorus in spring and autumn. Its overwintering grounds are not known, but presumed to be in Africa.

*Levant Sparrowhawks favour warm lowland and coastal districts.*

*male*

**IDENTIFICATION** Dashing raptor, superficially similar to Sparrowhawk. Adult male seen in flight appears very pale underneath except for pinkish flush to breast, black wingtips and dark barring on tail. At rest, head and back appear uniformly blue-grey; shows white throat, white vent and faint pinkish barring on breast and belly. Adult female similar to adult male but barring on underparts more prominent. When seen in flight from below, black wingtips contrast with pale wings. Juvenile recalls adult female but has teardrop-shaped dark spots and streaks on breast and belly; underwings show dark barring. **HABITAT** Warm, dry woodland and farmland. **VOICE** Harsh screaming call uttered near nest.

LEFT: *male*
RIGHT: *female*

**LENGTH** 43–60cm
**WINGSPAN** 104–135cm

# SAKER FALCON
*FALCO CHERRUG*

The Saker Falcon may be seen circling high up with wings held straight and tail closed, or even hovering laboriously. In active flight, however, it has powerful wingbeats and may make its attack from a low-level flight path, dropping on to a small mammal at great speed.

**IDENTIFICATION** Sexes similar, although females are larger than males. Adult is greyish-brown above with pale-fringed feathers on the mantle. Head is noticeably pale with a lightly streaked crown. Underside is streaked, with the boldest markings on the flanks and 'trousers'. Most individuals show contrast on the underwing between pale flight feathers and darker coverts, although some very pale birds occur, where this is not obvious. Juvenile is generally darker than adult with bolder markings on the underside. **HABITAT** Open country, steppe. **VOICE** Harsh 'kek kek kek'.

*Plumage is overall much 'warmer' brown than similarly sized Lanner Falcon.*

43–52cm **LENGTH**
95–115cm **WINGSPAN**

# LANNER FALCON
*FALCO BIARMICUS*

This large falcon is rare in Europe. Lanners often hunt in pairs, covering vast areas and ones where few other birds of prey occur. They sometimes skim low over the ground to startle a ground-dwelling bird or small mammal, but they will also pursue birds through the air.

**IDENTIFICATION** Similar to Peregrine, but slightly slimmer with longer tail and uniformly broad wings with more rounded wingtips. Male has a rusty nape and dark blue-brown mantle with a pale, spotted underside. The larger female is similar but has a buff nape and more boldly spotted underside. In both sexes, the moustachial stripe is less pronounced than in the Peregrine. Juvenile is darker brown above than adult and more buff below with heavier brownish-black streaks. Flight feathers look pale on underwing. **HABITAT** Mediterranean region; dry open country, mountains. **VOICE** Similar to, but quieter version of, Peregrine's call.

*adult*

*Lanners lack the speed and agility of some falcons, but will still catch birds in flight.*

# HOBBY
*FALCO SUBBUTEO*

**LENGTH** 28–35cm
**WINGSPAN** 75–90cm

The Hobby is expert at catching large insects like dragonflies on the wing. The prey is seized by the talons in a downwards stoop and eaten in flight, unless it is a small bird, which will be taken to a perch and plucked. Hobbies often hunt late into the evening and take bats.

**IDENTIFICATION** In flight, the wings look long and pointed, and the tail appears short, giving the impression of a large Swift. Adult's white cheeks and moustachial stripes show well in sitting birds, as do the red 'trousers' and vent. The streaked underside looks dark in flight. Males and females are almost identical, apart from the smaller size of the male, but juveniles are browner with pale feather-edging and a pale crown, and they lack the red colour. **HABITAT** Open habitats, marshes, heathlands. **VOICE** Sharp, scolding 'kew kew kew kew kew'.

*Hobbies are widespread summer visitors to Europe, being most frequently seen in warm, open habitats such as heaths and extensive marshes.*

RIGHT: *Adults; the Hobby flies on swift wingbeats, interspersed with short glides when hunting.*

*adult*

25–30cm **LENGTH**
60–65cm **WINGSPAN**

# MERLIN
### *FALCO COLUMBARIUS*

The Merlin's small size is compensated for by its strong, dashing flight and ability to startle small birds by coming upon them suddenly from its low hunting flight. It will sometimes soar or hang in the wind high overhead, but will normally keep low down.

ABOVE: *juvenile*; RIGHT: *male*

**IDENTIFICATION** Europe's smallest bird of prey, with a neat, light outline. Wings appear short and relatively broad but tail looks long and square-ended. Resembles small Peregrine. Male is greyish-blue above with reddish-buff underside. Female is noticeably larger than male, dark brown above and strongly patterned below. Juvenile resembles female but is darker with white patches on nape. **HABITAT** Moorland, upland bogs; winter on lowland heaths, coastal marshes. **VOICE** Shrill 'kek kek kek'.

*female*

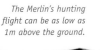

The Merlin's hunting flight can be as low as 1m above the ground.

When not hunting, the Merlin will sit on a low perch where there is a sweeping view of the moorland, adopting a very upright posture.

111

# KESTREL
*FALCO TINNUNCULUS*

The Kestrel is the commonest bird of prey over most of Europe. In direct flight, the wingbeats are fast and shallow with a few glides, but the most distinctive behaviour is the ability to hover in a fixed position on rapidly beating wings or on an updraught.

**IDENTIFICATION** Frequently seen hovering with a characteristic long-tailed silhouette and downward-looking head. Male is colourful with spotted brick-red back, black primaries and grey tail and head. Female is more uniform with heavily spotted chestnut plumage, a barred tail and brownish streaked head. At a distance the sexes can appear similar. Juvenile resembles female but is more streaked on the underside. **HABITAT** Cultivated country, heaths, moorland, roadsides and towns.
**VOICE** Piercing 'kee-kee-kee', especially at nest site.

LEFT AND RIGHT:
*Male is colourful and distinctive.*

BELOW: *Female has mainly chestnut plumage.*

Perched Kestrels have a noticeably upright posture.

*Its hovering flight distinguishes the Kestrel immediately from that other common and widespread raptor, the Sparrowhawk.*

29–32cm **LENGTH**
58–72cm **WINGSPAN**

# LESSER KESTREL
### *FALCO NAUMANNI*

Lesser Kestrels nest colonially in old buildings and on rock faces and are often seen hunting together when there is an abundance of flying insects, their favourite prey. They frequently nest near human habitation and show little fear unless directly persecuted.

**IDENTIFICATION**  Small falcon with narrow wings and a longish slender tail. Male is strongly coloured with unspotted chestnut back, blue-grey innerwing and hood and pale-grey tail with dark terminal band. Female is slightly larger than male and has barred tail. Juvenile resembles female. In all birds claws are pale, not dark as in Kestrel. **HABITAT** Mediterranean region; cultivated country, villages. **VOICE** Rasping two- or three-note calls and trilling notes at colonies.

*male* (LEFT) and *female* (RIGHT)

*Female* has chestnut colouring and shows dark spotting on upperparts; primaries are dark.

*Male* has blue-grey head and unspotted chestnut back.

# PEREGRINE FALCON

**LENGTH** 39–50cm
**WINGSPAN** 95–115cm

*FALCO PEREGRINUS*

Following a crash in its numbers, Europe's Peregrine population is now recovering. Prey, typically a medium-sized bird, may be spotted from a perch or from the air, and will be attacked by a high-speed stoop.

*juvenile*

*adult*

The flight of a Peregrine across an estuary will cause panic among gulls and waders, which will take to the air with the result that one at least will end up as prey.

*Small birds are often killed by the impact of the talons, but larger birds may be taken away to a perch to be killed and eaten.*

*Adult is steely grey above with a paler grey rump and pale underside with dark barring.*

**IDENTIFICATION** Large falcon with a compact body shape and broad-based, pointed wings. Shallow wingbeats with springy wingtips are characteristic, as is the dramatic high-speed stoop for prey from a great height. Adult is steely grey above with a paler grey rump. Has bold facial patterning with dark moustachial stripes. Juvenile is slightly slimmer and browner than adult, with pale feather edging on mantle and bold streaking below; facial markings less distinct than on adult and cere is grey-blue, not yellow. **HABITAT** Open, upland habitats; sea cliffs, coasts in winter. **VOICE** Shrill 'kek kek kek kek'.

55–60cm **LENGTH**
125–155cm **WINGSPAN**

# GYR FALCON
*FALCO RUSTICOLUS*

The powerful wingbeats of the Gyr Falcon enable it to fly quickly, low over the ground, and flush birds, which it then pursues and catches in flight. It will, however, also drop on to small mammals on the ground. It often sits on a low rock lookout between irregular feeding forays.

**IDENTIFICATION** Some birds, mostly from the high Arctic, are almost pure white, but dark lead-grey and brownish birds also occur in southern part of range. Southern birds have heavily barred plumage with pale patches and a pale forehead, darker eye patch and moustachial streak. The white underparts are heavily marked with spots and streaks, and the underwing shows almost translucent panels contrasting with darker coverts. Adult white high Arctic forms have almost no spots except on mantle, although dark tips to primaries can be seen; juveniles of this form are similar to adults but have black 'teardrop' marks on underparts. **HABITAT** Arctic tundra, high mountains; high Arctic seabird colonies. **VOICE** A hoarse 'kee-a kee-a kee-a'.

*White phase birds show hardly any spotting but do have dark wingtips.*

*Dark phase birds occur in the southern part of the range.*

*dark phase adult*

# RED-FOOTED FALCON

*FALCO VESPERTINUS*

**LENGTH** 28–31cm
**WINGSPAN** 65–75cm

Red-footed Falcons are frequently seen perching on a post or overhead wire, from which short forays are made to catch prey. Occasionally, acrobatic flights are made after high-flying insects.

**IDENTIFICATION** A small falcon resembling a short-tailed Kestrel at a distance. Male is distinctive with dark-grey plumage, pale, silvery primaries, deep rufous-red vent and thighs and red feet, eyering and cere; immature male similar to adult male but has paler underparts and pale face and throat. Adult female has orange or pale-yellow crown and underside, and barred, dark grey upperparts. Juveniles are streaked below and have darker, blotched upperparts and a barred tail, and like female have dark eye patches resembling a highwayman's mask. **HABITAT** Open heaths, cultivated land, steppe, marshland. **VOICE** Highly vocal; 'kew kew kew' flight calls.

*adult female*

*adult male*

**Adult female**
*has bright orangey
head and underside.*

*adult male*

116

36–42cm **LENGTH**
90–105cm **WINGSPAN**

# ELEONORA'S FALCON
### *FALCO ELEONORAE*

Eleonora's Falcons are at home on isolated, windy headlands in the Mediterranean, occurring from the Balearic Islands and Morocco eastwards to Cyprus. They arrive late in the season.

**IDENTIFICATION** Appears rather slender and dainty but is actually larger than the Hobby. Tail longer than on other small falcons. Wings long and slender, giving an angular outline in flight. Pale and dark morphs occur, pale morph being three times more numerous. Dark morph looks almost black in flight; pale morph shows pale cheek, dark moustachial stripe and dark, streaked underside. Underwing shows contrasting dark coverts and paler primaries in both morphs. Juvenile similar to light morph adult but with buffish underparts and heavy streaks. **HABITAT** Sea cliffs and headlands, arid deserts. **VOICE** Hoarse, kestrel-like chatter; not often heard.

*dark morph*

*pale morph*

*Eleonora's Falcons' flight is light and acrobatic, perfect for intercepting swallows and martins, and they often give long displays over their nesting sites.*

*Eleonora's Falcons delay nesting until late in the summer. Consequently their young are able to capitalise on the offspring of migrant songbirds returning south to Africa.*

ABOVE: **dark morph**
RIGHT: **pale morph**

117

# PHEASANT
*PHASIANUS COLCHICUS*

Originally introduced to Europe from Asia, pheasants are now widespread. Several strains are also regularly released for shooting, so a great variety of plumages is seen. Pheasants forage on the ground searching for plant food, but roost in trees at night.

**IDENTIFICATION** Male has brightly coloured, iridescent plumage, with red wattles and glossy green head, some showing well-developed 'ear tufts'. White collar is present in some individuals. Tail very long and barred. Purplish-chestnut plumage shows scalloped pattern due to bold markings on each feather. Female has paler brownish-buff plumage with strong pattern on upperparts and flanks. Barred tail is shorter. Juvenile resembles female, but with duller, less strongly marked plumage. **HABITAT** Woodland, copses, farmland, large gardens and orchards. **VOICE** Male has two-note crow, females have quieter contact notes.

ABOVE: *Male, landing.*

*female*

ABOVE: *female*; BELOW: *male*

# GOLDEN PHEASANT

(m) 85–115cm: (f) 65–85cm **LENGTH**
65–75cm **WINGSPAN**

*CHRYSOLOPHUS PICTUS*

Solitary Golden Pheasants seen in Europe are invariably escapes. In a few areas in Britain, however, birds have been released in sufficient numbers to form seemingly stable feral populations. These are thought to be the only viable non-captive populations outside China.

**IDENTIFICATION** Large, well-marked pheasant. Adult male has mainly orange-red body plumage except for yellow on crown and areas of blue and green on mantle and wings; shows conspicuous barring on nape. Tail broad and extremely long; brown with intricate pattern of fine, black lines. Adult female has roughly similar proportions to male. Body plumage mainly buffish-brown with dark barring. Juvenile similar to adult female but with shorter tail. **HABITAT** Mountain woodland and scrub in natural range; birds introduced into Europe favour conifer plantations. **VOICE** Male utters crowing call during breeding season; otherwise both sexes rather silent.

ABOVE: *male*; BELOW: *female*

# RED GROUSE
### *LAGOPUS LAGOPUS SCOTICUS*

**LENGTH** 37–42cm
**WINGSPAN** 55–66cm

Red Grouse are restricted to northern Britain and Ireland and are most often seen when flushed from dense heather. The low, gliding flight alternating with bursts of rapid wingbeats, and the frantic call, are all most visitors will observe.

**IDENTIFICATION** A plump gamebird that appears uniformly dark brown both on the ground and in flight; the wings are a dark grey-brown. Male is rich reddish-brown with red wattles and white-feathered legs. Female is pale buff-brown with pale feathered legs, but lacks the male's wattles over the eyes. Juvenile is buff-brown all over with pale feather margins. **HABITAT** Treeless heather moorland, mountain slopes. **VOICE** A hoarse, rattling 'ko-ah ko-ah ko-ah'.

*male*

*female*

*male*

37–42cm **LENGTH**
55–66cm **WINGSPAN**

# WILLOW GROUSE

### *LAGOPUS LAGOPUS LAGOPUS*

The Willow Grouse is the mainland Europe counterpart of Britain's Red Grouse. It is a widespread gamebird of open northern forests. Most birds are residents and do not migrate except in search of winter food and territories.

**IDENTIFICATION** A plump gamebird with liver-red to grey-brown plumage in summer and white plumage in winter. Male has red wattle over eye that is more prominent in spring, when white plumage is lost from the head first; by the end of summer male is more uniformly brown, but retains white primaries and black tail feathers, which are most obvious in flight. Female white in winter, but more tawny brown in summer than male and lacks his red wattle. **HABITAT** Mixed forests on mountain slopes, willow scrub. **VOICE** A hoarse, rattling 'ko-ah-ko-ah-ko-ah'.

*summer female*

*summer male*

*winter male*

35–57cm **LENGTH**
48–54cm **WINGSPAN**

# HAZEL GROUSE

### *BONASA BONASIA*

The Hazel Grouse is a bird of dense lowland forests, found particularly where there are damp gullies and mossy hollows rich in bilberry, birch and alder. These provide fruits, seeds and buds for food.

**IDENTIFICATION** A compact gamebird with a grey rump and grey tail ending in a black and white band. Male has a black chin patch, red wattle over the eye, and a short crest. Head and neck are finely barred and underside heavily blotched. Female has a warmer brown coloration overall and is generally less boldly marked. **HABITAT** Extensive mixed and coniferous forests. **VOICE** High-pitched whistle, recalling Goldcrest.

*male*

121

# PTARMIGAN

*LAGOPUS MUTA*

**LENGTH** 34–36cm
**WINGSPAN** 54–60cm

Harsh winter weather is not as much of a problem to Ptarmigan as poor conditions in early summer, when the chicks need a plentiful supply of insects. The variable plumage of the Ptarmigan helps it to blend in with the tundra as the snow recedes.

**IDENTIFICATION** Slightly smaller than Willow Grouse, which it resembles in winter, except that male has black lores in addition to red wattles. Both sexes appear all white in winter, except for black outertail feathers seen in flight. Plumage changes gradually through spring and summer, as snow melts, to more mottled grey-brown in male, and buff-brown in female. White primaries are retained in the wings, showing prominently in flight. Newly hatched young are downy and mottled buff-brown; juveniles similar to summer female but brown with darker feather edges. **HABITAT** Open, stony tundra, high treeless mountain slopes. **VOICE** Hoarse rattling 'karrrrrr k k k k k'.

*summer male*

*summer female*

*summer male*

*winter male*

*winter male*

*summer male*

ABOVE: *Nesting female.*

40–55cm **LENGTH**
65–80cm **WINGSPAN**

# BLACK GROUSE
### *TETRAO TETRIX*

The Black Grouse prefers marginal forest areas with easy access to open areas such as bogs and moors, where it is usually seen feeding on the ground. Through the spring males may be seen displaying out in the open at dawn.

**IDENTIFICATION** Almost all-black male, the size of a domestic hen, has white wingbars, white shoulder patches, white underwings and white undertail coverts. The black tail has a distinctive lyre shape and is used in the communal display. Female, often known as a greyhen, is warm brown above and grey-brown below with strong barring and speckling all over. The tail is shallowly forked. Juvenile similar to female but smaller and duller with pale central streaks on the feathers of the upperparts. **HABITAT** Woodland close to bogs and heather moors. **VOICE** Males make cooing calls and a sudden loud 'shoo-eesh'; females cackle.

*female*

*male*

*In flight, male's tail shape distinctive; female has slightly forked tail.*

LEFT: *female*
BELOW: *male*

123

# CAPERCAILLIE
*TETRAO UROGALLUS*

**LENGTH** 60–87cm
**WINGSPAN** 87–125cm

This large grouse family member is restricted to trees, and has an almost entirely vegetarian diet. It inhabits mature forests of pine, spruce, fir or larch. Pine needles are important in its diet.

ABOVE: *Displaying* **male**.
BELOW: *female*

*male*

*female*

**IDENTIFICATION** Both sexes are very bulky with broad wings and tails, and strong, heavy bills. Male appears dark blackish-grey at a distance, but has glossy green chest and dark-brown wing coverts and upper mantle. Large, white patches on shoulders and whitish speckles on flanks and tail break up overall dark effect. Female has rufous-brown upperparts with chestnut patch on chest and paler-brown underside. Most of plumage is heavily barred with black above and black and white below. Juvenile resembles female but is smaller and duller; young males develop distinctive plumage in their first winter, but do not reach full size until the next year. **HABITAT** Coniferous forest with some bogs and shrubby areas. **VOICE** Very loud popping sounds, followed by 'drum roll'; various grunts and gulps.

| 33–36cm **LENGTH** |
| 50–55cm **WINGSPAN** |

# BLACK FRANCOLIN
## *FRANCOLINUS FRANCOLINUS*

The Black Francolin is difficult to see, but its distinctive and far-carrying seven-note call, uttered from a low mound at dawn and dusk, advertises its presence. Normally it remains in thick, low cover and is difficult to flush.

**IDENTIFICATION** In flight this partridge-sized bird shows dark outertail feathers and rich-brown, dark-barred wings. Male has a mostly black head and underside with white ear coverts and white flecks on the flanks. Wings are dark brown with black feather-centres, and tail is finely barred with black and white. There is a broad, chestnut collar. Female has a pale head, chestnut patch on neck, and overall brown plumage with black arrow-marks on all feathers. Juvenile resembles female but has dull plumage and faint markings. **HABITAT** Low-lying shrubby areas near water; dried-up river beds. **VOICE** Harsh, shrill 'kek kek kek kek-ek-ek'.

*adult*

| 16–18cm **LENGTH** |
| 32–35cm **WINGSPAN** |

# COMMON QUAIL
## *COTURNIX COTURNIX*

*In flight, **Quail** shows relatively long, narrow wings.*

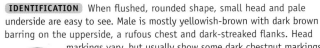

*Usually crouches but may stand higher to peer over vegetation.*

The Quail gives its presence away by the male's persistent call. This is heard for hours on end, particularly around dusk, coming from the ground in dense vegetation.

**IDENTIFICATION** When flushed, rounded shape, small head and pale underside are easy to see. Male is mostly yellowish-brown with dark brown barring on the upperside, a rufous chest and dark-streaked flanks. Head markings vary, but usually show some dark chestnut markings on the crown, through the eye, and on the cheeks and throat. Female resembles male but has less striking head markings; juvenile similar to female but has barred and spotted, not streaked, flanks. **HABITAT** Lowland grassland, agricultural land, pastures. **VOICE** Oboe-like 'wet-my-lips', repeated frequently. LEFT: *female;* BELOW: *male*

# RED-LEGGED PARTRIDGE

*ALECTORIS RUFA*

**LENGTH** 32–34cm
**WINGSPAN** 45–50cm

The Red-legged Partridge prefers dry habitats, often where there is some bare ground, and avoids woodland and very wet areas. It nests on the ground.

**IDENTIFICATION** A compact gamebird with overall greyish-brown colouring, but strongly marked flanks and head. Sexes are similar in appearance but males are larger. The head is grey and the rest of the upperparts and the chest are greyish-brown, but there is a more distinct grey band on the lower chest. The necklace meets over the bill and surrounds the white throat patch, and there is a bib of black streaks. The flanks are strongly barred with black and chestnut stripes on a white background. Juvenile lacks adult's head pattern and flank markings. **HABITAT** Open country, farmland, lowland heaths. **VOICE** Harsh repetitive 'kchoo kchoo-kchoo kchoo'.

*adult*

*adult*

# CHUKAR

*ALECTORIS CHUKAR*

**LENGTH** 32–34cm
**WINGSPAN** 47–52cm

Chukars rarely stray far from their home ranges, usually remaining in small groups; when flushed they fly strongly low over the ground.

**IDENTIFICATION** Compact, rounded gamebird. Sexes are very similar, showing grey heads and grey-brown upperparts, and a grey chest merging into a sandy underside. The white flanks are boldly barred with black and chestnut stripes and the black eyestripe extends down the neck to join on the chest, forming a dark necklace. Juvenile similar to adult but head and flank markings less distinct. **HABITAT** Dry, rocky mountain slopes, stony plains. **VOICE** Short 'chuck' sounds; louder rhythmic call when flushed.

*Adults have strongly patterned head and flanks, and red legs and bill.*

32–35cm **LENGTH**
46–53cm **WINGSPAN**

# ROCK PARTRIDGE
*ALECTORIS GRAECA*

**Rock Partridges fly only reluctantly, usually heading downhill and dropping to the ground quite quickly. They rarely stray far from their home ranges and usually live in small groups (coveys).**

**IDENTIFICATION** Very similar in appearance to the Chukar but chin and throat are pure white, not creamy buff, and the black necklace extends through the eyes and down to the base of the bill. Stripes on flanks are narrower and neater in appearance than on Chukar, and the chest and upperparts are greyer. The general impression at a distance is of very sharply defined set of markings. Juvenile similar to adult but, like on juvenile Chukar, head and flank markings are less distinct. **HABITAT** Dry treeless mountain slopes, often south-facing. **VOICE** A four-note call and various shorter contact notes uttered by members of coveys.

*Rock Partridges favour high mountain slopes.*

*adult*

---

32–34cm **LENGTH**
46–49cm **WINGSPAN**

# BARBARY PARTRIDGE
*ALECTORIS BARBARA*

**This partridge is likely to have been introduced into its few sites in Europe, as it is highly sedentary. It is secretive and remains concealed in low vegetation, running from danger to avoid breaking cover.**

**IDENTIFICATION** Very similar to Red-legged Partridge, but lacks that species' striking facial markings; the face and throat are grey and there is a collar of white spots on a dark-chestnut background, but no necklace. Most distinctive feature is the crown of dark chestnut with a light-grey supercilium. The upperparts are grey-brown with a pinkish tinge and the flanks are less boldly marked than in the Red-legged Partridge, with bars of black, buff and white. **HABITAT** Dry, open habitats with low bushes at low altitudes and mountains up to 3,000m. **VOICE** Repetitive 'kchek kchek' and other harsh calls; also Curlew-like call in flight.

*The Barbary Partridge will not fly unless approached very closely.*

*adult*

# GREY PARTRIDGE

*PERDIX PERDIX*

**LENGTH** 29–31cm
**WINGSPAN** 45–48cm

Grey Partridges avoid very wet and very arid areas as these do not provide the nutritious plant foods they require. They use cultivated fields, tracks for dust-bathing and ditches for drinking.

*Female (FAR RIGHT) has less pronounced horseshoe mark on belly than **male** (RIGHT).*

**IDENTIFICATION** This bird has a dumpy, rounded appearance, its head appearing particularly round with no neck. Underparts mostly grey. From a distance, upperparts look brown and plain, although on close inspection they are finely marked with darker brown and buff. Facial colouring is brick-red, contrasting with the grey underside. In flight, distinctive rusty outertail feathers are seen. Adult has dark chestnut horseshoe-shaped patch on underside, which is larger in male than female. Juvenile is browner than adult and lacks the horseshoe mark. **HABITAT** Lowland grassland, cultivated areas. **VOICE** Harsh 'keirr-ik keirr-ik' at night, 'pitt pitt pik pirr pik' calls when alarmed and fleeing.

male

*In many parts of its range, the Grey Partridge is in serious decline due to the adverse effect intensive farming has on its plant and insect food.*

27–30cm **LENGTH**
46–53cm **WINGSPAN**

# CORNCRAKE
*CREX CREX*

This very secretive bird is hard to see but is easily located by the male's far-carrying call. Although it keeps to dense cover in meadows and hayfields, the male will sometimes perch on a stone wall to call.

**IDENTIFICATION** Similar in size to Water Rail but with shorter, yellowish-brown bill and noticeably long rusty wings when seen in flight. Upperparts of adult are grey-brown with dark centres to the feathers that form broken lines running the length of the body. Neck and supercilium are greyish, but underside is mostly brownish-buff turning to reddish-brown with white barring on the flanks. Sexes are identical apart from the lack of grey on the neck and face of the female. Juvenile resembles female but is paler, with light spots on the wing coverts. Legs are flesh coloured, darker in juveniles than adults, and the eyes are pale brown. Flight is weak and the legs dangle. **HABITAT** Hay meadows, driest areas of marshes. **VOICE** Far-carrying, rasping 'crex crex' or 'crake crake'.

*adult*

*Flies low, quickly drops into cover and then runs to safety.*

*adult*

**Adult males** *utter their 'crex crex' call incessantly through the night and early morning.*

*adult*

129

# SPOTTED CRAKE

*PORZANA PORZANA*

**LENGTH** 22–24cm
**WINGSPAN** 37–42cm

**When seen in good light the Spotted Crake is not easily confused with any other small waterbird but its secretive habits make it difficult to locate. The 'whiplash' call, heard mostly at night, is the best guide to its presence.**

**IDENTIFICATION** A small, compact waterbird, which at a distance appears all dark grey-brown or greenish-brown, but in good light looks spotted. The undertail is pale buff, the short pointed bill is red at the base with a yellowish-orange tip, and the legs and feet are bright olive-green. Females resemble males but have less grey on the face and underparts, with slightly more spotting. Juveniles resemble females but lack any grey tones and have less spotting and duller, olive-coloured legs. **HABITAT** Sedges and rushes bordering lakes, ponds and rivers. **VOICE** Far-carrying 'dripping tap' call – 'hwitt hwitt'.

*adult*

*Migrant Spotted Crakes are sometimes easy to see and are more likely to feed out in the open than breeding birds.*

*Spotting on plumage only visible at very close range.*

*juvenile*

18–20cm **LENGTH**
34–39cm **WINGSPAN**

# LITTLE CRAKE
*PORZANA PARVA*

**Little Crakes prefer slightly deeper water to other small crakes; they are more inclined to swim and will also emerge into the open on the edges of reeds in the early mornings and at dusk.**

**IDENTIFICATION** Male is olive-brown above with the feathers showing dark centres and buff margins; at close range the scapulars and mantle show some pale streaks. The face and underside are slate-blue or grey with pale streaking on the rear flanks and undertail coverts, which are not as striking as in the Water Rail. Female is pale buff beneath, rather than grey, and has a whitish face with faint barring under the tail. Juvenile is similar to female but is paler below; shows white supercilium and pale mottling on the chest and flanks; barring on the underside is darker than in female. **HABITAT** Reedbeds and swamps with still water and floating vegetation. **VOICE** Low accelerating croaking sounds, ending in a trill.

ABOVE: *male*; BELOW: *female*

# BAILLON'S CRAKE

**LENGTH** 17–19cm
**WINGSPAN** 33–37cm

*PORZANA PUSILLA*

The Baillon's Crake's normal habit is to search for food among dense water plants and it rarely emerges into the open. It swims readily so is often found in areas of deep water in large swamps.

**IDENTIFICATION** A very small waterbird, the size of a House Sparrow, with colouring resembling a Water Rail. Adult upperparts are rufous brown with irregular whitish spots and streaks, and the feathers have dark centres. The face and chest are deep slate-blue and unmarked, but the rear flanks and underside as far as the tail are black with white barring. The legs are a dark flesh colour or dull olive, and the bill is green. The female is almost identical to the male but the throat and chest region are paler grey. Juveniles have the same upperpart colouring as adults, but are buff-coloured below and the bill is brownish. Has weak flight with dangling legs that is characteristic of smaller crakes. **HABITAT** Swampy areas with thick vegetation, streamsides, pond margins. **VOICE** Rasping sounds resembling a finger scratching a comb.

*Adult male has slate-blue face and chest.*

22–28cm **LENGTH**
38–45cm **WINGSPAN**

# WATER RAIL
## *RALLUS AQUATICUS*

The Water Rail is more often heard than seen, being usually well concealed within dense reedbeds. At night in spring, males utter a rhythmic crake-like 'kipp kipp' call.

*Plumage provides excellent camouflage in dense reedbeds.*

*adult*

**IDENTIFICATION** A secretive waterbird. Adult has mostly dark-brown colouring above and plain slate grey-blue below. The dark flanks are strongly barred and the tail is noticeably white beneath. The slender bill is red and slightly downcurved. The sexes are similar, but the female is a little smaller than the male with a slightly shorter bill. Juveniles are browner than adult on the underside and have a brown bill. In flight the long legs and toes trail conspicuously. **HABITAT** Reedbeds, marshes, well-vegetated river and lake shores. **VOICE** Harsh squealing and grunting sounds; nocturnal 'kipp kipp' call.

BELOW: *adult*

# MOORHEN
## *GALLINULA CHLOROPUS*

**LENGTH** 32–35cm
**WINGSPAN** 50–55cm

The Moorhen has adapted to a variety of wetland habitats and is as likely to be seen out in the open grassland as on a deep lake. Its fluttering take-off gives way to a strong flight, and it can also climb well.

*adult*

**IDENTIFICATION** At a distance adult appears all black with a red shield on the face and yellow tip to the bill. A horizontal white line along the flanks and the black and white pattern under the constantly flicked tail make confusion with any other waterbird unlikely. Seen more closely in good light the plumage is black only on the head, while the rest of the upperparts are very dark brown and the underside is deep slate-grey. Before the autumn moult the worn plumage looks dusty and the white lateral line may disappear. Juveniles are brownish overall with paler flanks and chest, white chin and throat, and a buff rather than white lateral line. The undertail pattern resembles that of the adult. **HABITAT** Wetlands, including urban park lakes, rivers, small ponds.
**VOICE** Varied, loud calls, including harsh 'krreck' and rhythmic 'kipp kipp kipp'.

BELOW: **Adults** *fighting*. RIGHT: *juvenile*

45–50cm **LENGTH**
90–100cm **WINGSPAN**

# PURPLE GALLINULE
### *PORPHYRIO PORPHYRIO*

The Purple Gallinule is a very scarce bird in Europe, found only in brackish marshes and areas of still water where there is ample plant material for it to feed on.

*White undertail is exposed frequently when bird is nervous.*

*adult*

*adult*

*adult*

**IDENTIFICATION** Adult has violet-blue plumage with brighter blue face, and red legs, eyes and bill. Undertail is white. Sexes similar but male is larger. After breeding, the bill is duller and has dark patches. The bluest birds are those from the western Mediterranean; the Egyptian race has green tinges on the scapulars and back, and the Middle Eastern race has a green head and is paler blue. Juveniles are grey, with dull-red bill and legs and white throat. **HABITAT** Marshes, reedbeds, tracts of bulrush, brackish swamps. **VOICE** Variable, deeper versions of Moorhen calls, low 'chock chock'.

*In Europe, Purple Gallinules are probably easiest to see at Albufera Marsh on Mallorca.*

# CRESTED COOT
## *FULICA CRISTATA*

**LENGTH** 38–42cm
**WINGSPAN** 75–85cm

The Crested Coot is a very rare bird in Europe. Where its restricted range overlaps with the Coot's, it can be difficult to pick out, even in the breeding season when its 'horns' are most prominent.

**IDENTIFICATION** Slightly larger than the Coot, but in other respects very similar. Sexes are identical. Adult has red knobs over the facial shield that can be seen at close range; at a distance they are not especially obvious and in winter they are smaller and duller than during the breeding season. In flight, wings lack the white edge to the secondaries seen in the Coot. Juvenile is drab brownish-black with a paler chin and throat, and a white centre to the belly. Adults and juveniles have slate-blue legs and feet. **HABITAT** Large water bodies with plenty of marginal vegetation. **VOICE** Two-note 'clukuk' and a metallic 'croo-oo-k'.

*Adult* very similar to Coot but has slate-blue legs and feet.

*adult*

36–38cm **LENGTH**
70–80cm **WINGSPAN**

# COOT
*FULICA ATRA*

An aggressive waterbird of larger bodies of water, the Coot defends a territory in spring against all comers. Coots prefer areas free of overhanging trees or steep banks and usually avoid fast rivers.

**IDENTIFICATION** A rounded, sooty-black waterbird, adult with gleaming white bill and facial shield and red eye. Sexes are identical, although the male is larger than the female. At close range, head and neck are seen to be the most intensely black, while flanks are greyer. In flight, wings have a pale rear margin. Juvenile is dull brown with pale face and throat, and a yellowish-grey bill. **HABITAT** Larger ponds and lakes, canals, urban park lakes. **VOICE** Loud repetitive 'kowk' and explosive shrill 'pitt'.

*The greenish feet have lobes on them to aid swimming; they are large and conspicuous on land but often hidden in flight.*

*Coots are widespread across Europe where suitable water bodies exist, and are resident in the south and west.*

*adults*

# CRANE
### *GRUS GRUS*

**LENGTH** 110–130cm
**WINGSPAN** 200–230cm

Cranes are solitary and nervous birds during the breeding season, but the rest of the year they congregate in large flocks. They nest in wetland areas.

*On migration and in their winter quarters Cranes form large flocks and are easier to observe than in the breeding season.*

**Adult** *Cranes are stately and imposing birds.*

*Cranes search for food by walking slowly and probing with the large bill; plant material is the commonest food in winter but in the breeding season frogs, ground-nesting birds and invertebrates will also be eaten.*

### IDENTIFICATION

A very large bird of upright posture, which moves in a steady and measured way on the ground. Sexes similar. Adult plumage is mostly grey but the head is much darker, appearing black at a distance, with a white band extending back from the red eye and a red crown. The chest and parts of the back have a pale-rufous tinge, and the tail and overhanging cloak of secondaries are darker. Juvenile is paler grey than adult with an unpatterned head and grey, rather than black, legs. In flight it shows long wings of even width with black flight feathers and a long extended neck and trailing legs. **HABITAT** Marshes, farmland, large boggy clearings in northern forests. **VOICE** Loud bugling calls, plus 'kroo-krii kroo-krii' calls by pairs.

*adult*

80–100cm **LENGTH**
170–180cm **WINGSPAN**

# DEMOISELLE CRANE
*ANTHROPOIDES VIRGO*

**The best chance of seeing wild Demoiselle Cranes in Europe is to visit Cyprus during migration time: small numbers pass in spring, and larger numbers in autumn.**

**IDENTIFICATION** Superficially similar to Common Crane but smaller. Sexes similar. Adult has mainly pale blue-grey plumage, but is black from throat and neck to breast and has broad, black supercilium bordering grey crown. White nape plumes arise from behind eye. Iris red. Black flight feathers mostly hidden at rest but conspicuous in flight. Legs dark and bill yellowish. Juvenile has grubby brownish-grey plumage and lacks adult's head and neck patterns.

**HABITAT** Steppe and upland grassland.
**VOICE** Grating, honking flock calls uttered on ground and in flight.

RIGHT AND BELOW: *adults*

# GREATER FLAMINGO

*PHOENICOPTERUS RUBER*

**LENGTH** 125–145cm
**WINGSPAN** 140–165cm

Flamingos are notoriously fickle in their breeding habits, attempting to nest only if feeding conditions are perfect and sometimes not even trying to breed in any given area for several years.

*adults*

*In flight, wings show black flight feathers and rosy-pink coverts; head and neck held outstretched and legs trailing.*

**IDENTIFICATION** Large and unmistakable bird, both standing and in flight. Adult plumage mainly pale pink but can look very washed out. Black-tipped pink bill is downcurved and banana-shaped. Neck very long and usually held in 'S' shape. Body compact and rounded. Juvenile is pale grey-brown with dark legs and black-tipped grey bill. **HABITAT** Shallow brackish lagoons and saline lakes. **VOICE** Flocks utter 'kaa-haa' calls.

*Legs of **adult** extremely long and pinkish-red; juvenile's are about two-thirds the length of the adult's.*

*The bill is used to filter out animals from the surface of the water: the head and neck are held downwards while the upside-down bill is swept from side to side.*

40–45cm **LENGTH**
105–115cm **WINGSPAN**

# LITTLE BUSTARD
### *TETRAX TETRAX*

Male Little Bustards display in the spring in the open; they give short rasping calls and make short jumps into the air. In flight they resemble gamebirds or possibly Mallards.

*female*

**Female** *lacks black and white neck pattern.*

*In spring, displaying male Little Bustards stand out in the open with their neck feathers splayed out.*

**IDENTIFICATION** A pheasant-sized bird with sturdy legs and a small head on a long thick neck. The overall body colour is speckled grey-brown with a white underside. Adult male has a strongly patterned black and white head and neck with a grey throat. Female lacks the male's black and white patterning, but has coarse speckling on the back. In flight, both sexes show white wings with black-tipped primaries and primary coverts, and a black and white tail rim. Juvenile is similar to female.
**HABITAT** Open grassy plains, large arable fields, grassy airfields. **VOICE** Snorting 'knerr' or 'pritt' calls, various grunts and whistles.

*male*

141

# GREAT BUSTARD

*OTIS TARDA*

**LENGTH** 75–105cm
**WINGSPAN** 190–260cm

The Great Bustard is a shy bird and is difficult to observe; it keeps to open plains where it can spot danger easily. The broad wings of the Great Bustard show a white panel in flight.

**IDENTIFICATION** Europe's heaviest bird. In the breeding season the displaying male has a bulging neck and a cocked-up tail that makes it appear even larger. Breeding males also have a strong chestnut chest band and white moustachial 'whiskers' extending back from base of bill. Outside the breeding season, male resembles female apart from his greater size. Female head and neck are grey with upperparts cinnamon-brown but strongly barred with black; the underside is white, giving the bird a three-coloured grey, brown and white appearance. Juvenile resembles adult female but has a buff neck. **HABITAT** Open grasslands, lowland areas, wide river valleys and plains. **VOICE** Mostly silent, but may give short, barking, alarm note.

*Female (ABOVE) is much smaller than male (RIGHT).*

*Male in full breeding plumage is very impressive; he performs an elaborate display in which he appears to turn inside out, exposing the white downy feathers.*

*male*

40–44cm **LENGTH**
77–85cm **WINGSPAN**

# STONE-CURLEW
### *BURHINUS OEDICNEMUS*

Stone-curlews are largely nocturnal, giving their
presence away by their eerie and far-carrying calls.
During the day they rest amongst low vegetation,
remaining motionless even when approached closely.

**IDENTIFICATION** A stocky wader with large, black and yellow eyes and stout, almost gull-like
bill, which is black at tip. Sexes similar. Adult plumage is mostly sandy brown with darker streaks;
underside is pale. At rest, wings show a white bar and dark lower edge; in flight, wings appear
black with paler panels. Tail appears relatively long. When standing, the tarsus joint is prominent.
Juvenile resembles adult but is less boldly marked. **HABITAT** Dry, open areas, semi-desert, arable
land, heaths. **VOICE** Curlew-like flight call, and various high-pitched whistling and shrill wader-like
calls at night.

*adult*

*adult* and *chick*

BELOW: *adult*

*Staring yellow and black eyes gives Stone-curlew a stern appearance.*

# OYSTERCATCHER
### HAEMATOPUS OSTRALEGUS

**LENGTH** 40–45cm
**WINGSPAN** 80–86cm

Oystercatchers are common where there are shorelines that provide molluscs to feed on, opening the shells with their powerful bills. They also take marine worms from mud.

*adult summer*

*Plumage is striking black and white with heavy orange bill; **adult winter** birds (above) acquire white collar.*

**IDENTIFICATION** Adults have striking black and white plumage, a red eye, an orange-pink bill and red-pink legs. In winter, adults acquire a white chin stripe on the otherwise black neck. Newly fledged juveniles are exceptionally well camouflaged to resemble lichen-covered rocks. First-winter birds are paler than adults with a larger, white throat patch. **HABITAT** Rocky shores, estuaries, large stony rivers, stony lake shores. **VOICE** Shrill piping calls, loud 'kubeek kubeek' alarm call.

*Adult calling.*

144

42–46cm **LENGTH**
77–80cm **WINGSPAN**

# AVOCET
### *RECURVIROSTRA AVOSETTA*

The Avocet uses its upcurved bill to sweep through liquid mud in search of tiny invertebrates; the side-to-side motion of the head is characteristic of this species.

*adult*

**IDENTIFICATION** A unique large, black and white wader with a strongly upcurved bill and long, blue-grey legs. The plumage is predominantly white with a black head and nape and black panels on the wings, which appear as oval panels in flight. From below, the Avocet looks all white in flight apart from black wingtips. Sexes identical and juveniles resemble adults except that the black element of the adult plumage is brownish instead. **HABITAT** Estuaries, coastal lagoons, saltpans, shallow lakes. **VOICE** Varied calls, including a ringing 'pleet pleet'.

*Avocets are attentive parents, accompanying their chicks when they feed and seeing off potential predators.*

*adult and chick*

*Adult feeding.*

145

# BLACK-WINGED STILT

*HIMANTOPUS HIMANTOPUS*

**LENGTH** 35–40cm
**WINGSPAN** 67–83cm

The Black-winged Stilt has the longest legs, proportional to its size, of any bird. Its long, slender bill is used to snatch insects on emergent vegetation, and to probe soft mud for aquatic larvae.

**IDENTIFICATION** A very long-legged wader with entirely black and white plumage. The wings and mantle are black and the underparts are white, but the degree of black on the head is variable. In flight the white rump and long white wedge on the back show clearly, as do the trailing pink legs. The head may be all white or show varying amounts of black. The sexes are very similar except that breeding female usually shows pure white head and neck. Juvenile is paler on the mantle than adult, with sepia tinges to the darker feathers. **HABITAT** Coastal lagoons, shallow lakes, saltpans. **VOICE** Varied short, nasal, bleating calls.

ABOVE AND BELOW: *adult male*

28–31cm **LENGTH**
75–85cm **WINGSPAN**

# LAPWING
### *VANELLUS VANELLUS*

The Lapwing is an agile bird in the air, performing displays over its territory at the start of the breeding season. The acrobatic swoops and dives are accompanied by the distinctive song. In winter, large flocks form near favoured feeding areas.

**IDENTIFICATION** Adult has glossy green upperparts and all-white underparts apart from rich orange undertail coverts, seen when bird dips its head during feeding. Male when breeding has solid black chin and throat. At a distance, Lapwing appears all black and white, and in flight shows long, broad, black and white wings with white tips to three outer primaries. In winter, feathers have pale margins which give a scalloped appearance to the mantle; cheeks are buff rather than white. Juvenile resembles winter adult but has shorter crest and browner chest. **HABITAT** Wet grasslands, marshes, open pastures. **VOICE** Shrill 'peeoo-wit' and other more scratchy sounds.

*Adults in flight.*

*Adults vigorously defend nests against predators such as Magpies.*

*adults and chicks*

*All adults have a long black crest but the male's is longer than the female's.*

*adult female*

# GOLDEN PLOVER

*PLUVIALIS APRICARIA*

**LENGTH** 26–29cm
**WINGSPAN** 67–76cm

The Golden Plover is a bird of open moorlands where the vegetation is short. It feeds on the ground, pursuing small soil invertebrates, and takes flight only if disturbed.

ABOVE: *Adult male breeding; White underwings are characteristic of the species and a good feature to look for in flying birds.*

LEFT: *juvenile*

**IDENTIFICATION** Plump wader with short bill and rounded head and spangled golden-brown upperparts. In summer, male has black face and black underside separated from upperparts by broad white border. In flight it shows white underwings contrasting with black belly. Female similar to male but has less black on underside, sometimes restricted to belly; face is greyer than male's and white border to the black areas is less distinct. Northern birds (Iceland and Scandinavia) have far more black than southern birds (Britain). In winter sexes are similar, with no black on the underside and more uniform plumage overall. Juvenile very like winter adult but may show some faint barring on the underparts.

**HABITAT** Breeds on moorlands, bogs; over-winters on lowland pastures.

**VOICE** A mournful, whistling 'pyuuh' or 'pyuu pu'.

*Belly white in winter and black in **summer adult** (RIGHT).*

27–30cm **LENGTH**
71–83cm **WINGSPAN**

# GREY PLOVER
*PLUVIALIS SQUATAROLA*

In the breeding season the Grey Plover is confined to the high Arctic, nesting on open ground. In autumn the whole population heads south and winters on estuaries and mudflats.

*winter adults*

*In flight, underwing pattern shows distinctive black axillaries against a white background at all times.*

*adult, breeding plumage*

Differs from Golden Plover in having much greyer speckled upperparts with no golden tinge.

**IDENTIFICATION** In summer, male is strikingly black below with pale head and white shoulders, and white-flecked upperparts. Female is duller than male and may show greyish cheeks and grey-brown upperparts. Winter adult (both sexes) lacks black belly and has more evenly marked dark grey, speckled upperparts. **HABITAT** Breeds on Arctic tundra; overwinters on muddy and sandy seashores. **VOICE** Whistling 'pleeoo-wee.

*Juvenile resembles winter adult (SEE ABOVE) but with pale-buff wash to plumage.*

149

# DOTTEREL

*CHARADRIUS MORINELLUS*

**LENGTH** 20–22cm
**WINGSPAN** 57–64cm

Remote mountain tops with sparse mosses and lichens are the preferred breeding habitat of the Dotterel. It is a very confiding bird on its breeding grounds.

**IDENTIFICATION** Distinctly patterned wader with no real affinity for water. In the breeding season, adult has broad, white supercilium and thin black and white chest band. Crown is very dark, framed by white eyestripes that meet on nape; face is whitish and rest of upperparts and neck are grey-brown. Belly is a rich chestnut with a darker centre and the undertail region is white. Female is generally brighter and more distinctive than male. In winter, colours fade to more uniform buff-brown with less markedly white supercilium. Juvenile resembles winter adult but has pale feather margins, which give a scalloped appearance. **HABITAT** Dry, open mountain plateaux; overwinters on arid grasslands. **VOICE** Soft 'pweet pweet' flight calls and trilling calls on ground.

*juvenile*

*female*

*Male incubating.*

15–17cm **LENGTH**
42–58cm **WINGSPAN**

# KENTISH PLOVER
### *CHARADRIUS ALEXANDRINUS*

**Most Kentish Plovers are summer visitors to Europe, spending the winter on the west coast of Africa, with small numbers on Mediterranean shores. It nests on the shore, and is subject to disturbance caused by human interference.**

**IDENTIFICATION** Small, pale plover. Adult shows less black on head than Ringed Plover and breast band is incomplete. Breeding male has chestnut crown and black patch on forehead; female has brown replacing black and a grey-brown crown. In winter, male resembles female, with both becoming duller in appearance. Bill and legs are black, and both sexes appear longer-legged than the Ringed Plover. Juvenile plainer than adult, with greyer upperparts. **HABITAT** Lagoons, estuaries, saltpans; mainly in Mediterranean. **VOICE** Short 'kip' or 'peep' sounds.

*male*

*In flight, shows broad, white wingbar; often looks relatively large-headed and short-tailed.*

*Male* only has chestnut crown during breeding season.

*adult male*

# RINGED PLOVER

*CHARADRIUS HIATICULA*

**LENGTH** 18–20cm
**WINGSPAN** 48–57cm

The Ringed Plover is a bird of northwestern sea coasts.
It is found on a variety of seashores, especially estuaries,
and broken, rocky shores, where there is an
abundance of invertebrate prey.

*Prominent white
wingbar seen in flight.*

**IDENTIFICATION** Small, stocky wader with mostly plain
colouring but striking facial markings. Upperparts of adult grey-
brown and underparts pure white; in summer, legs and bill base
are orange, but in winter bill may be all-dark. Head is strikingly
marked with black cheeks and black line over the brow; there is
a black chest ring. In winter, black fades and looks worn.
Sexes are almost identical, although some females
have less distinct black markings than males.
Juvenile resembles adult, but has
a scalloped appearance
on upperparts due to
pale feather edges,
and partial brownish
breast band. Striking white
wingbars show well in flight in both
adults and juveniles. **HABITAT** Seashores,
estuaries, large lake shores, tundra.
**VOICE** A rising 'tooip' whistle, and
a louder alarm 'te-lee-a te-lee-a'.

*adult and
chick*

*adult*

14–15cm **LENGTH**
42–48cm **WINGSPAN**

# LITTLE RINGED PLOVER

*CHARADRIUS DUBIUS*

**Little Ringed Plovers are summer visitors to Europe, arriving on their mostly inland breeding grounds in early spring. They have adapted well to human activities such as gravel extraction.**

**IDENTIFICATION** Small, slender wader. Sexes similar. Adult has dull-brown upperparts and pure white underparts with a strongly patterned head. Bright-yellow eyering stands out well against the black cheeks. Bill is all black and legs are dull pinkish-brown. When seen in flight, the lack of any wingbar at any time is diagnostic for this species. Juvenile looks like faded version of adult with indistinct head and chest markings. **HABITAT** Dry, open habitats, gravel beds, lake shores, and similar man-made sites. **VOICE** Falling 'kiu' flight call and plaintive 'krree-u krree-u'.

*adult and chick*

Little Ringed Plovers are absent from the far north and avoid densely vegetated areas and very wet habitats.

*adult*

153

# COLLARED PRATINCOLE

*GLAREOLA PRATINCOLA*

**LENGTH** 24–27cm
**WINGSPAN** 60–68cm

The Collared Pratincole rarely wades in water to feed, preferring drier, open habitats. Its normal method of feeding involves flying in a large flock in pursuit of airborne insects.

**IDENTIFICATION** No other European small wader (apart from Black-winged Pratincole) has combination of a very short bill, forked tail and long wings. At a distance, adult upperparts appear dark sandy or olive-brown with darker primaries and tail feathers. Underside is divided into pure white belly, light-olive chest and buff throat, clearly demarcated by thin black necklace stretching from eye to eye under chin. Gape of bill is bright red. Outside breeding season, adults have far less distinct necklace and more mottled throat and chest. Juvenile looks more speckled than adult because of pale margins to feathers; necklace is absent. **HABITAT** Dry, open habitats with shallow pools, large saltmarshes. **VOICE** Tern-like calls and short rhythmic nasal calls.

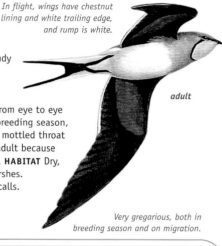

*In flight, wings have chestnut lining and white trailing edge, and rump is white.*

*adult*

*Very gregarious, both in breeding season and on migration.*

*adult*

25cm **LENGTH**
60–65cm **WINGSPAN**

# BLACK-WINGED PRATINCOLE
### *GLAREOLA NORDMANNI*

In west and northwest Europe, Black-winged Pratincoles occur only as vagrants. The species is rarely seen on passage; a trickle of birds is noted in early autumn, however, in the eastern Mediterranean.

**IDENTIFICATION** Superficially very similar to Collared Pratincole. Sexes similar. Summer adult at rest looks rather tern-like in silhouette. Plumage essentially dark sandy brown, palest on underparts. Has creamy-buff throat outlined and bordered by black and white lines. In flight, recalls tern or outsized hirundine. Shows forked tail and white rump. Upperwings uniformly dark sandy brown, lacking white trailing edge to innerwing and contrasting dark wingtip seen in Collared Pratincole. Underwing all-dark, lacking reddish-brown underwing coverts of Collared Pratincole. Winter adult (not seen in region) has pale feather margins on upperparts, giving scaly appearance, and less clearly defined throat markings. Juvenile recalls winter adult but looks even more scaly on back and on breast. **HABITAT** Steppe grassland, usually close to water. **VOICE** Churring calls at nest; squeaky call uttered in flight.

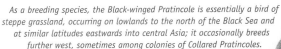
*summer adult*

*As a breeding species, the Black-winged Pratincole is essentially a bird of steppe grassland, occurring on lowlands to the north of the Black Sea and at similar latitudes eastwards into central Asia; it occasionally breeds further west, sometimes among colonies of Collared Pratincoles.*

*adult*

# LITTLE STINT
*CALIDRIS MINUTA*

**LENGTH** 12–14cm
**WINGSPAN** 28–35cm

This tiny wader uses its short bill to pick insects from the surface of mud or plants. It is an active bird when feeding, running and darting in search of prey.

*Looks small in flight; shows narrow white wingbar and dark line over white rump, and grey tail.*

**IDENTIFICATION** Smallest European sandpiper, all ages of which have black legs and short black bill. In summer upperparts are mostly rusty red with dark feather centres; the centre of the crown looks darker. In winter mostly grey-buff above and white below. Larger feathers have dark central shafts, visible at close range. Juvenile resembles summer adult but is paler with a white 'V' on the reddish-brown upperparts and white underparts.
**HABITAT** Breeds on tundra; overwinters on muddy wetlands.
**VOICE** A short 'tip' contact note and 'svee svee svee' display on breeding grounds.

*juvenile*

LEFT: *juvenile*
BELOW: *summer adult*

13–15cm **LENGTH**
30–35cm **WINGSPAN**

# TEMMINCK'S STINT

### *CALIDRIS TEMMINCKII*

Temminck's Stints prefer slightly richer habitats than Little Stints during the breeding season, nesting in grassy areas with willow scrub, usually near rivers or pools.

**IDENTIFICATION** Very small sandpiper with short legs and rather long tail. Breeding birds look greyish-buff above with some feathers showing dark centres and chestnut fringes. In winter adults have grey-brown plumage above and white underparts; grey colouring extends further down on chest and is more clearly demarcated than in winter plumage Little Stint. For description of juvenile, *see* caption. Paler clay-coloured legs also separate this species from Little Stint at all times. **HABITAT** Nests in tundra and mountainous Arctic regions; overwinters mostly on inland marshes. **VOICE** A ringing 'tirrr'.

*Adult displaying.*

*Juveniles are warm buff above with pale edges to the larger feathers, giving a scaly appearance.*

BELOW: *Adult in breeding plumage never as rusty red above as breeding plumage Little Stint; some adults show a few grey winter feathers on mantle.*

# DUNLIN
*CALIDRIS ALPINA*

**LENGTH** 16–22cm
**WINGSPAN** 35–40cm

**Huge flocks of Dunlin congregate on the shores of western Europe in autumn and winter. They are active feeders, seen in busy flocks.**

*Looks generally brown in flight, with distinct, narrow, white wingbar.*

*juvenile*

**IDENTIFICATION** Small wader. Sexes similar. In summer has black belly and mostly white underside. Upperparts are chestnut and black, neck and chest are streaked and undertail region is white. For description of winter adult, *see* caption. Juvenile recalls moulting adult, but black breast patch is replaced by darker streaks especially on flanks; upperparts have paler appearance than adult due to buff fringes to feathers. **HABITAT** Breeds on moorlands and tundra; overwinters on estuaries, sandy shores, lake shores. **VOICE** Harsh, rolling 'krreee' in flight; longer display over nest site.

LEFT: *Winter birds of all ages (**1st winter** seen here) lack the black belly and have evenly marked dark grey, speckled upperparts.* BELOW: *juvenile*

BELOW: *summer male adult*

18–20cm **LENGTH**
38–45cm **WINGSPAN**

# CURLEW SANDPIPER
### *CALIDRIS FERRUGINEA*

**For a brief period in summer the male Curlew Sandpiper has rich red coloration. Most birds seen in western Europe are juveniles in autumn.**

**IDENTIFICATION** In summer has rich red underside and dark upperparts. Fresh plumage looks 'mealy' at first owing to pale feather edges, but becomes darker with wear. Winter adults are very pale grey above with light streaking on upper chest; underparts pure white. For description of juvenile, *see* caption. In all plumages, long black legs, long, black, curved bill and white rump distinguish this species from other small sandpipers. **HABITAT** Breeds in high Arctic; overwinters on seashores, lakes. **VOICE** A clear, ringing 'krillee' in flight.

*Juveniles have buff-orange tint on upperparts and chest and pure white underside.*

*juvenile*

*summer adult*

# PURPLE SANDPIPER

*CALIDRIS MARITIMA*

**LENGTH** 20–22cm

**WINGSPAN** 40–44cm

The Purple Sandpiper overwinters further north than any other wader. It is usually found on rocky headlands and islands where there is some wave action.

*summer adult*

**IDENTIFICATION** The darkest of all small sandpipers, but with a thin white wingbar showing in flight. Adults in breeding plumage have strongly marked upperparts with brown, chestnut and whitish colours on larger feathers, and dull yellow legs and bill-base. For description of winter adult, *see* caption. Juvenile recalls winter adult but has more distinctly patterned appearance than adult. **HABITAT** Breeds on tundra and moors; overwinters on rocky shores. **VOICE** A short, variable, 'kewitt' call and an agitated call on nest site.

BELOW: *Winter plumage adult is dark grey above and paler grey below with dark streaks on breast.*

20–21cm **LENGTH**
36–42cm **WINGSPAN**

# SANDERLING
*CALIDRIS ALBA*

The Sanderling has a distinctive method of feeding on sandy shores, running in and out of the surf and snatching morsels of food from the sand as a large wave retreats.

*Winter adult in flight.*

**IDENTIFICATION** Small wader with relatively short, straight bill. In breeding plumage, has rusty-red upperparts with black markings on larger feathers giving a mottled appearance. Chest is rusty red, clearly demarcated from the pure white underside. For description of winter adult, *see* caption. Juvenile strongly marked above with black and white on upperparts, and with warm-buff tinge to mantle and neck areas. All ages and plumages have black legs and bill, with broad white wingbar seen in flight. **HABITAT** Breeds on high Arctic tundra; overwinters on sandy shores. **VOICE** A loud 'plitt' flight call; short frog-like trill in display.

ABOVE: *Winter adults* look all white at a distance, but at close range are seen to have pale grey upperparts with white fringes to feathers.

LEFT: *Summer bird has rusty-red upperparts and white underparts.*

161

# KNOT

*CALIDRIS CANUTUS*

When breeding on the tundra, the Knot population is spread out over a vast area, but in winter Knots gather in huge flocks. Estuaries in Britain are of global importance for the species.

*winter flock*

*summer plumage*

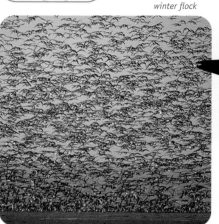

**IDENTIFICATION** In summer, adult has orange-red underside, white undertail coverts and mostly buff upperparts, strongly patterned with chestnut and yellow patches; the largest feathers have black and white markings on them. Winter adult has grey upperparts and white underparts. Juvenile very similar to winter adult, but has warmer brown or pinkish-buff wash with no grey tints. Black and white terminal bands on feathers of upperparts produce scalloped appearance. **HABITAT** Breeds on high Arctic tundra; overwinters on coasts.
**VOICE** Short, slightly nasal 'kwett' in winter; fluting calls on breeding grounds.

*juvenile*

30–35cm **LENGTH**
60–70cm **WINGSPAN**

# GREENSHANK
*TRINGA NEBULARIA*

The Greenshank is a scarce breeder in Scotland, but more widespread across Scandinavia. It is a common passage migrant in autumn.

ABOVE: *Pale wedge-shaped patch extending along the back is common to adults and juvenile.*
ABOVE RIGHT: **summer plumage adult**

**IDENTIFICATION** Mostly grey wader with long green legs and slightly upturned bill; sexes similar. In summer, grey upperparts have darker markings, forming bands along wings; arrow-shaped markings on breast and flanks give streaked effect. For description of winter adult, see caption. In flight, tail looks pale and white and wedge-shaped rump patch extends up the back in both adults and juveniles. **HABITAT** Breeds on bogs and marshes; overwinters on coasts, lake shores, riversides. **VOICE** Clear three-syllable 'chew chew chew' call.

*Juvenile* plumage browner than adult's, with neater streaks on neck and breast.

# REDSHANK
## *TRINGA TOTANUS*

**LENGTH** 27–29cm
**WINGSPAN** 55–65cm

The Redshank is both a familiar sight and sound on coastal marshes and wet meadows across much of Europe.

*The white trailing edge of the wing and white rump are evident in flight on juvenile and adult birds alike.*

*Breeding adult giving the alarm.*

**IDENTIFICATION** At all times adult has orange-red legs and reddish base to bill. Summer plumage grey-brown. Extent of dark markings on grey background varies considerably and birds from more northerly areas have darkest markings. In winter, darker markings fade and bird appears almost uniformly grey-brown above and very pale below. Juvenile has dull orange legs and base to bill. Shows dark streaks on underside and pale feather margins on mantle, giving slightly mealy appearance. End of tail is barred and outer edges of wings are dark. **HABITAT** Wet meadows, coastal marshes in summer; estuaries and shores in winter. **VOICE** A far-carrying and persistent 'klu-klu-klu' alarm call and a two-syllable 'tu-hu'.

*adult winter*

29–32cm **LENGTH**
55–65cm **WINGSPAN**

# SPOTTED REDSHANK

### *TRINGA ERYTHROPUS*

The Spotted Redshank breeds in the Arctic and winters on coasts. They feed by making distinctive stabbing movements with their long bill.

*winter adult*

**IDENTIFICATION** Elegant wader with long, red legs, which are darkest during the summer months. Sexes similar. In summer has sooty black plumage relieved by pale margins to feathers on the upperparts. Winter adult has essentially pale-grey upperparts and white underparts. Juvenile similar to winter adult but with grey barring on underparts. **HABITAT** Bogs and tundra in summer; coasts and estuaries in winter. **VOICE** A shrill 'chu-witt' call, plus a repetitive buzzing 'krruu-ee' uttered in display.

*The absence of a white wingbar in flight immediately distinguishes the Spotted Redshank from its cousin.*

RIGHT: *Both sexes of this distinctive long-legged, long-billed wader have very pale plumage in* **winter**.

BELOW: **partial breeding plumage**

165

# GREEN SANDPIPER
*TRINGA OCHROPUS*

The Green Sandpiper is a nervous bird, taking flight readily if disturbed, when it will give its clear, three-note call. Its usual habit, however, is to sit tight.

**IDENTIFICATION** From a distance, looks almost black and white both when feeding and when in flight; dark wings contrast with white rump and belly. Upperparts of adult dark olive-green, fading to grey-green on head. In winter, white spots seen in summer birds are absent and underparts look gleaming white. Juvenile has buff-brown spots on dark upperparts; neck and chest streaked. **HABITAT** Boggy areas with open woodland near by; streams, lake margins, watercress beds. **VOICE** A shrill, three-note 'tuEEt-wit-wit' given in flight.

*adult*

*Very black and white in flight; note the dark underwings.*

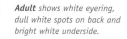

*Adult shows white eyering, dull white spots on back and bright white underside.*

*adult*

19–21cm **LENGTH**
50–55cm **WINGSPAN**

# WOOD SANDPIPER

### *TRINGA GLAREOLA*

The Wood Sandpiper is a common breeding wader of the far north of Europe and Scandinavia. From late summer onwards migrants turn up in western Europe; these are mainly juveniles.

*Barred tail and white rump are evident in flight and common to all ages.*

**IDENTIFICATION** Compared with other small sandpipers, such as Common and Green, has longer legs and is slimmer. Adults in worn plumage look brownish-grey; sexes similar. Juvenile is browner than adult and has streaked neck, chest and flanks. In flight all ages show pale underwings (wings of Green Sandpiper are dark below), barred tail and white rump. **HABITAT** Open forests with boggy areas, marshes, riversides. **VOICE** Flight call is a whistling 'jiff jiff'; rolling display call uttered on breeding sites.

BELOW: *breeding plumage*; BOTTOM: *adult in spring*

# MARSH SANDPIPER

*TRINGA STAGNATILIS*

**LENGTH** 22–25cm
**WINGSPAN** 50–55cm

The Marsh Sandpiper is instantly recognisable by its delicate proportions, especially its long, slender bill and legs. If seen in flight note its wedge-shaped white rump and trailing legs.

**IDENTIFICATION** Sexes similar. Adult in summer has grey to grey-brown upperparts and pale underparts with dark streaks. Adult winter plumage light grey above and almost white below. Dark shoulder patch contrasts with pale grey mantle; at close range dark feather quills and pale margins give slightly scaly appearance. Olive-green legs yellower in spring. Juvenile pure white below with browner upperparts than adult. **HABITAT** Lake margins and marshes in summer; lake shores and sheltered seashores in winter. **VOICE** A clear, whistling 'kiew', repeated frequently.

*Straight, thin bill characteristic of species.*

ABOVE: *adult breeding*
LEFT: *adult non-breeding*

The Marsh Sandpiper's proportionately long legs give it an elegant appearance.

19–21cm **LENGTH**
35–40cm **WINGSPAN**

# COMMON SANDPIPER
### *ACTITIS HYPOLEUCOS*

*Flies on strongly bowed, stiffly held wings.*

**The Common Sandpiper is a widespread breeding bird in Europe. In winter there is a migration southwards, although small numbers remain in northwest Europe.**

**IDENTIFICATION** Adult upperparts appear plain grey-buff at a distance, but darker feather centres and pale margins give delicately patterned appearance close up; this patterning is less obvious outside breeding season. Underside pure white with small white patch extending up in front of shoulder. Juvenile very similar to adult but with more scaly appearance owing to pale feather fringes. Legs always grey-green and bill dark brown with dull yellowish base. **HABITAT** Stony rivers and lake shores, sheltered seashores. **VOICE** A shrill and penetrating 'hee dee dee' call when flushed; song is a more rhythmic and longer version of alarm call.

*Short-legged wader with elongated body, accentuated by its crouching posture.*

*adult*

*adult*

*When perching on a boulder, the Common Sandpiper bobs its rear end constantly.*

# RUFF
*PHILOMACHUS PUGNAX*

**LENGTH** 26–32cm (m); 20–25cm (f)
**WINGSPAN** 54–56cm (m); 45–52cm (f)

In the breeding season male Ruffs gather in leks near their nesting sites and display their colourful plumage. They perform elaborate dances with much leaping and bowing. Females, non-breeding males and juveniles are much plainer looking.

**IDENTIFICATION** Unusual wader with distinctive appearance in breeding season and great variation between the sexes and individuals. For description of breeding male, *see* caption. Smaller female is also variable in appearance, having mostly buff upperparts with varying degrees of darker mottling and streaking. In winter adult male loses 'ruff' and resembles female, both sexes losing warm buff wash to plumage. **HABITAT** Sedge-covered swamps, wet meadows, lake margins, muddy pastures. **VOICE** Mostly silent, may make quiet drawn-out squeak.

*male*

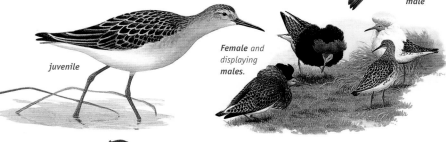

*juvenile*

**Female** and displaying **males**.

*male*

*Breeding male has elaborate neck and head feathers that may be any colour from black to white with numerous brown shades in between; the 'ruff' may be spotted, barred or plain.*

21–24cm **LENGTH**
49–55cm **WINGSPAN**

# TURNSTONE
### *ARENARIA INTERPRES*

The Turnstone is a familiar seashore bird in winter. Its name is appropriate as it does indeed find food by turning over stones with its short, strong bill.

*winter adult*

**IDENTIFICATION** For description of breeding-plumage male, *see* caption. Breeding-plumage female is duller than male, with darker streaked head and less chestnut on upperparts. In winter, upperparts of both sexes uniform grey-brown and head and neck mottled grey. Juvenile resembles winter adult but dark feathers have buff edges, giving scaly appearance. In flight, wings show bold black, white and chestnut patterning at all ages. **HABITAT** Breeds on coastal tundra; overwinters on seashores. **VOICE** Short, nasal alarm calls uttered by feeding birds, and longer urgent-sounding call given in flight.

RIGHT: *winter adult*
BELOW: *Breeding plumage male* has black and white facial markings, chestnut upperparts with darker bands, pure white underside and orange legs.

# WHIMBREL
*NUMENIUS PHAEOPUS*

LENGTH 40–46cm
WINGSPAN 75–85cm

There is some overlap in the breeding ranges of the
Curlew and Whimbrel, but the Whimbrel extends
further north. In winter it is found on the
coasts of all the southern continents.

**IDENTIFICATION** Smaller than Curlew but otherwise
superficially similar. Crown has two dark stripes and pale
supercilium. Sexes are similar and juvenile resembles adult apart from
pale buff spots on crown and wing coverts. **HABITAT** Tundra, moors and
bogs in summer; seashores in winter. **VOICE** A seven-note trill in flight;
a brief Curlew-like call in display.

*In flight, looks much smaller than
Curlew and has more rapid wingbeats.*

BELOW AND BOTTOM: *adult*

*More distinctive markings than Curlew,
with two dark stripes on the crown.*

50–60cm **LENGTH**
80–100cm **WINGSPAN**

# CURLEW
### *NUMENIUS ARQUATA*

The haunting melodious call of the Curlew is characteristic of upland moors in spring as males establish territories. Curlews normally live in large flocks in winter and are very vocal.

*adult*

**IDENTIFICATION** Large wader with long downcurved bill. Female larger than male and has longer bill, but both have similar plumage. In summer, fresh plumage has warmer yellowish tinge than in winter. Lower mandible is pink-flesh coloured in winter. Juvenile plumage very similar to adult; juvenile male has significantly shorter bill than juvenile female. **HABITAT** Upland moors and bogs in summer; coasts and marshes in winter. **VOICE** A mournful 'cour-lee'; also a tuneful bubbling trill when displaying.

*The long, curved bill of the Curlew is a perfect adaptation to feeding in damp ground.*

*The pale V-shaped area on the Curlew's back is clear when seen in flight.*

*adult*

# BLACK-TAILED GODWIT

*LIMOSA LIMOSA*

**LENGTH** 36–44cm
**WINGSPAN** 70–80cm

In the breeding season grazed freshwater marshes are favoured Black-tailed Godwit breeding sites. Their long legs enable them to wade in quite deep water and they feed by making deep probes into the mud.

**IDENTIFICATION** In breeding plumage head and neck are brick-red and upperparts and chest are mottled with black, chestnut and grey, the colours forming broken bars on upper chest. Underside is mostly grey-white. Amount of red coloration in breeding season is very variable, some adult females being almost grey in summer. Winter birds are pale grey above and grey-white below. Juvenile is warm buff below with brown and buff plumage above. **HABITAT** Breeds on damp meadows, boggy areas; overwinters on estuaries, marshes. **VOICE** Excited, nasal, 'kee-wee-wee-wee' calls uttered near nest.

*summer plumage*

ABOVE: *juvenile*; RIGHT: *winter adult*
BELOW: *Breeding plumage bird flexing its bill tips.*

33–42cm **LENGTH**
70–80cm **WINGSPAN**

# BAR-TAILED GODWIT
*LIMOSA LAPPONICA*

Bar-tailed Godwits breed on treeless tundra, and winter on coasts of western Europe and the Mediterranean. Feeding methods are more energetic than the Black-tailed Godwit's.

ABOVE AND BELOW: *winter adult*; RIGHT: *summer male*

**IDENTIFICATION** Superficially similar to Black-tailed Godwit, but shorter legged and stockier; if seen in flight, lacks that species' distinctive wingbars and tail markings. In summer-plumage male has a dark rusty-red underside and mottled chestnut and dark-brown upperparts; larger female has warm-buff underparts and slightly paler upperparts. In winter, both sexes are buff-grey above with white undersides; grey feathers have dark central shafts, giving lightly streaked effect above. Juvenile browner above than winter adult, with patterning similar to Curlew. **HABITAT** Breeds on tundra; overwinters on muddy shores. **VOICE** Nasal 'ke-vu' with variations for alarm or flight calls.

175

# GREY PHALAROPE
*PHALAROPUS FULICARIUS*

**LENGTH** 20–22cm
**WINGSPAN** 37–44cm

Grey Phalaropes breed in the high Arctic but regularly turn up in small numbers in northwest Europe on autumn migration, usually after storms. They feed in the characteristic phalarope way of swimming with rapid turns.

**IDENTIFICATION** Has broader, less pointed bill than Red-necked Phalarope. Breeding female has brick-red underparts, brown back and black and white facial markings. Breeding male similar to breeding female but colours less intense. Winter adults grey above and white below with black 'panda' mask through eye. Juvenile in autumn similar to winter adult but with irregular pattern of brown-fringed black feathers on otherwise grey upperparts. **HABITAT** Breeds on high Arctic tundra; overwinters at sea in tropical regions.
**VOICE** A sharp 'pik' alarm call; rolling 'prruut' uttered by female in summer.

ABOVE: *Grey Phalaropes stay out at sea for the whole winter.*

RIGHT: **winter adult**
BELOW: *Role reversal occurs in the breeding season, with the **female** having the brighter plumage.*

176

18–19cm **LENGTH**
34–40cm **WINGSPAN**

# RED-NECKED PHALAROPE
### *PHALAROPUS LOBATUS*

**The Red-necked Phalarope is instantly recognised by its habit of swimming in search of food, and often spinning round and round to stir up aquatic insect larvae, which it picks from the surface.**

**IDENTIFICATION** Bill very thin and pointed. For description of breeding female, *see* caption. Breeding male similar to female but colours subdued. Winter-plumage adults of both sexes, rarely seen in Europe, have ashy-grey upperparts and white underparts and look black and white at a distance. Juvenile recalls male with washed-out summer plumage showing paler flanks and undersides, and brown wash on neck. **HABITAT** Breeds on open tundra; overwinters at sea in tropical regions. **VOICE** Calls include short 'kitt' or 'kirrik' sounds.

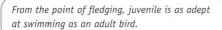

*From the point of fledging, juvenile is as adept at swimming as an adult bird.*

ABOVE LEFT: *juvenile*; ABOVE: *females*
BELOW: *Female has striking plumage in summer, with rusty-red neck and upper chest, slate-grey head and white throat.*

177

# WOODCOCK

*SCOLOPAX RUSTICOLA*

The so-called 'roding' flight of the male Woodcock is usually all that is seen of this very secretive bird. On spring and summer evenings the male flies with rather jerky wingbeats, usually at treetop height.

**IDENTIFICATION** Larger and more rotund bird than Snipe, with attractive red-brown plumage, particularly noticeable when seen from behind in flight. Upperparts rufous-brown and marbled with black and white; underside paler and barred with dark grey-brown stripes. Long bill is dark flesh colour, becoming darker at tip. Sexes similar and juvenile very similar. **HABITAT** Damp woodlands. **VOICE** A grunting 'oo-oorrt' call in flight, followed by a shrill squeak.

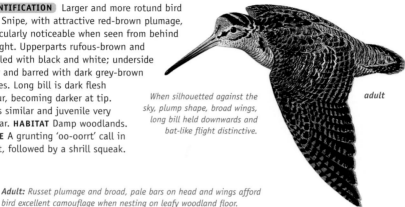

*When silhouetted against the sky, plump shape, broad wings, long bill held downwards and bat-like flight distinctive.*

*adult*

*Adult: Russet plumage and broad, pale bars on head and wings afford bird excellent camouflage when nesting on leafy woodland floor.*

25–27cm **LENGTH**
40–50cm **WINGSPAN**

# SNIPE
*GALLINAGO GALLINAGO*

In addition to its distinctive long bill, the Snipe also has a characteristic feeding action, unlike that of other waders. It probes into soft mud with a very jerky action.

*adult*

*Very long-billed wader with distinctively patterned head and back.*

*adult*

*Short tail is barred and has buff margin.*

*Legs dull green and bill pale reddish-brown with darker tip in both adults and juveniles.*

**IDENTIFICATION** Sexes similar. Upperparts are brown with pale stripes; larger feathers have dark centres and pale margins, giving scaly appearance. Flanks are barred and underside is greyish-white. Juveniles almost identical to adults. **HABITAT** Bogs, wet meadows, upper reaches of saltmarshes. **VOICE** A sneeze-like call when flushed; rhythmic, repetitive 'tick-a tick-a' on breeding grounds.

ABOVE: *Displaying* **adult**.

*adult*

# GREAT SNIPE
*GALLINAGO MEDIA*

**LENGTH** 27–29cm
**WINGSPAN** 45–50cm

**Boggy woodland clearings are usually chosen as nesting areas by Great Snipe. Males congregate in groups and display making chirping sounds and bill clattering.**

*adult*

**IDENTIFICATION** Larger and plumper than Snipe, with slightly shorter bill, longer legs, stronger barring on the belly and more strongly patterned wing coverts. In flight, white outertail feathers and white wingbars are diagnostic; bird also appears larger than Snipe, with more rounded body shape and wings. Flight pattern is more laboured than Snipe's and usually straight, not zigzagged; the bird settles rather abruptly by dropping into cover. In winter plumage becomes duller because of wear of buff and cinnamon feather margins. Sexes similar and juveniles essentially indistinguishable from adults in the field, although white markings are less clear. **HABITAT** Marshy areas in mountains and lowlands. **VOICE** Mostly silent, but gives short 'itch' call, and has a chirping display call on territory.

*Displaying **adult**.*

*Has darker belly than Snipe and distinctive white outertail feathers; plumage brightest during breeding season.*

*adult*

*Great Snipe have declined in many areas owing to habitat loss and excessive shooting.*

17–19cm **LENGTH**
36–40cm **WINGSPAN**

# JACK SNIPE
### *LYMNOCRYPTES MINIMUS*

*Relatively short bill is yellowish with a darker tip.*

The Jack Snipe is far less sociable than the Snipe and usually only seen when flushed. It prefers to feed in areas where there is some covering vegetation.

**IDENTIFICATION** Small, short-billed snipe with conspicuous pale-yellow stripes running along back. Overall impression is of greenish-brown patterned back and boldly marked head. Legs and feet are green. Sexes are similar and it is usually not possible to distinguish juveniles from adults. **HABITAT** Breeds on tundra bogs; overwinters on lowland marshes. **VOICE** A brief sneezing sound when flushed, otherwise silent except for muffled, whistling display call near nest.

*When keeping still among grasses and sedges, pale back stripes give Jack Snipe excellent camouflage. Very occasionally they venture across open marshy areas.*

16–18cm **LENGTH**
34–37cm **WINGSPAN**

# BROAD-BILLED SANDPIPER
### *LIMICOLA FALCINELLUS*

This wader is scarce with scattered breeding sites across northern Scandinavia and Siberia; in western Europe it is a scarce migrant. The bill tip and crown markings are the best features for identification.

**IDENTIFICATION** Slightly smaller than Dunlin, with longer body profile and more sharply downturned bill tip. In breeding and juvenile plumage, head shows pale stripes similar to Snipe, and pale supercilium. Upperparts pale in early summer owing to broad, pale feather fringes; these are lost with wear and plumage gradually becomes richer brown. In winter looks similar to winter-plumage Dunlin but the pale crown stripes can still be seen in good light and the legs appear muddy grey-green. Juvenile recalls breeding-plumage adult but with pale margins on upperparts. **HABITAT** Breeds on bogs in sub-Arctic. **VOICE** Rasping 'chrreeeit' and mechanical-sounding 'swirr swirr swirr'.

*The Broad-billed Sandpiper's snipe-like plumage and kink-tipped bill are good identification features.*

*breeding adult*

181

# GREAT SKUA
*STERCORARIUS SKUA*

**LENGTH** 53–66cm
**WINGSPAN** 125–140cm

The largest of all the skuas is an aggressive bird that allows no intruders, including humans, anywhere near its nest or young. Colonies are normally near colonies of other seabirds, where there are easy meals to be had.

**IDENTIFICATION** Bulky bird, adult reminiscent of juvenile gull but darker and far more heavily built. Juvenile similar to adult but usually darker; may show pale tips to larger feathers on upperparts. When standing on land, short legs and small feet obvious in all birds; when swimming, looks especially bulky and buoyant. **HABITAT** Seabird cliffs and islands in summer; overwinters at sea. **VOICE** Utters harsh 'tuk tuk' alarm calls and other fierce contact notes.

ABOVE: *juvenile*. BELOW: *Adults displaying. The white flashes on the dark wings are seen well in flight and during aggressive displays on land when the wings are raised over the head.*

*In flight, adult looks broad-winged and short-tailed, sometimes with two slightly projecting central feathers.*

46–67cm **LENGTH**
97–115cm **WINGSPAN**

# ARCTIC SKUA
### *STERCORARIUS PARASITICUS*

The Arctic Skua is the commonest of the skuas along the coasts of northwest Europe and the Arctic ocean. They often perform exciting aerial displays to startle a smaller bird into dropping a fish.

**IDENTIFICATION** Adult occurs in pale, intermediate and dark phases, pale being commonest in north and dark commonest in south of range. Dark phase birds have sooty brown plumage all over with darker cap and yellowish tone to sides of face. Pale phase birds are paler grey on mantle with grey-brown cap; flanks and ventral region light grey-brown and rest of underside, head and neck white. Pale phase birds show some straw yellow around the neck. Legs and bill are black in pale and dark phases, and both have all-dark wings with pale white flashes. Juvenile plumage very variable, pale phase birds having pale heads and light brown plumage with darker markings below, giving scaly appearance; dark birds are almost all dark with a slightly paler head. **HABITAT** Breeds on coasts near other seabirds; overwinters at sea. **VOICE** Utters a Kittiwake-like 'kee-aah', and short 'kukk' calls.

*Pale phase adult* chasing Kittiwake; has dashing, acrobatic flight when pursuing other birds.

Almost falcon-like appearance in flight, with long, slender wings and long tail.

LEFT: *dark phase*
BELOW: *intermediate phase adult*

183

# POMARINE SKUA
### *STERCORARIUS POMARINUS*

**LENGTH** 65–78cm
**WINGSPAN** 113–125cm

The Pomarine Skua's principal summer food is lemmings. It is very agile in the air, and also pursues seabirds, scaring them into dropping their food.

**IDENTIFICATION** Large, gull-like bird with heavy bill, large head and barrel-shaped body. Adult plumage very variable, with most birds occurring as pale phase and smaller number as dark phase. Pale phase birds are black-brown above and on upper chest and vent; belly white and nape pale yellow. Dark chest markings sometimes form complete band. Dark phase birds have sooty brown plumage all over; bronze wash to plumage seen only in good light. **HABITAT** Breeds on high Arctic tundra, overwinters at sea. **VOICE** Harsh, gull-like 'kowk' or 'geck' anger calls and higher mewing contact calls.

**pale phase adult**

**pale phase adult**

*Wings long and broad at base, and tail relatively long with twisted streamers in full adult plumage; both light and dark forms have white wing 'flashes' seen on both surfaces and showing very clearly in flight.*

**Juvenile** *pale brown with darker brown barring; white wing flashes are visible, but tail streamers are absent.*

**184**

35–38cm **LENGTH**
92–105cm **WINGSPAN**

# LONG-TAILED SKUA

*STERCORARIUS LONGICAUDUS*

The breeding success of the Long-tailed Skua is highly dependent on the populations of lemmings and other small rodents in the tundra; in bad rodent years it may fail to breed altogether.

**IDENTIFICATION** In breeding plumage adult has greyish-brown mantle and flanks, which contrast with darker wingtips and feathers. Cap is black and sides of face and neck are pale yellow; breast is pale, darkening towards ventral region. Bill short but thick. **HABITAT** Breeds on tundra; overwinters at sea. **VOICE** Short 'kreck kreck' calls, and more drawn-out cackling calls for display.

*adult*

*Smaller than other skuas, with narrow wings, long tail and slender body; like other skua species, however, powerful chest makes head appear relatively small.*

*Juvenile plumage variable, but most birds are very dark with paler feather margins, giving barred appearance; overall tone greyer than juvenile Arctic Skua.* BELOW: *adult*

*Of all the skuas, the Long-tailed Skua is the species most likely to be seen well inland on migration.*

# COMMON GULL
*LARUS CANUS*

**LENGTH** 38–44cm
**WINGSPAN** 110–125cm

The Common Gull is confined mainly to breeding colonies in northern Europe. In winter birds disperse to the seas and marshes close to their breeding sites.

*1st winter*

**IDENTIFICATION** Adult has black wingtips and grey mantle; head and body otherwise pure white and bill plain yellow during summer months. In winter head and neck show grey-brown flecks and bill duller than in summer adult, some individuals showing dark tip. Immature shows extensive brown in wings in first winter and broad, black terminal tail band. In second winter wings almost completely pale grey. Immatures have black bills at first, these becoming dull flesh colour before turning yellower in second winter. **HABITAT** Coasts, freshwater lakes, marshes. **VOICE** Shrill 'keeow' and mewing 'gleeoo' calls.

LEFT: *winter adult*. ABOVE: *Wings show black primaries with white flecks in flight.* BELOW: *summer adult*

**25–27cm** LENGTH
**70–77cm** WINGSPAN

# LITTLE GULL
*HYDROCOLOEUS MINUTUS*

From a distance, a Little Gull in flight appears to flicker as the dark underwing contrasts with the pale mantle. Its energetic and vigorous flight distinguishes it from other larger gulls.

LEFT: *juvenile*; ABOVE: *2nd autumn*; BELOW: *1st summer*

IDENTIFICATION Smallest gull of the region, with vigorous tern-like flight. Wings of adult are black on underside with trailing white edge. Mantle is pale blue-grey and rest of plumage is white but suffused with pale pink. In summer, head is all black; in winter, adult has paler head with dark-grey cap and black spot behind eye. In breeding season legs and bill are red; legs fade to flesh colour and bill becomes black in winter.

**HABITAT** Breeds on lake shores and marshes; overwinters at sea.

**VOICE** Harsh, short, tern-like calls; hoarse mewing calls uttered by juveniles.

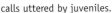

*summer adult*

*The bulk of the Little Gull population is found in northeastern Europe and Russia; in winter many move as far as southwest Europe and southern Britain.*

# BLACK-HEADED GULL

*LARUS RIDIBUNDUS*

**LENGTH** 38–44cm
**WINGSPAN** 94–105cm

*summer adult*

The Black-headed Gull is one of the commonest European gulls, breeding over a huge area of central Europe and Scandinavia.

**IDENTIFICATION** In flight all non-juvenile plumages show white leading edge to wing with black border to primaries on upperwing. Summer adult has dark chocolate brown head, colour extending to middle of head but not down back of neck. Bill red with dark tip and legs dark red. Juvenile is buffish white; subsequently, immature birds acquire grey mantle with brown and black wing coverts and black terminal tail band; legs and base of bill in immature birds are dark flesh coloured. **HABITAT** Sheltered seashores, lakes, marshes, urban parks, farmland. **VOICE** Utters harsh screaming calls; very vocal near nests and when in feeding flocks.

*White leading edge to upperwing diagnostic in all post-juvenile plumages.*

*Winter adult: head is white with two blackish smudges around eye and on neck; legs and bill paler than in summer.*

BELOW: *summer adult*

The Black-headed Gull is the most likely gull species to be seen following the plough.

188

36–38cm **LENGTH**
98–105cm **WINGSPAN**

# MEDITERRANEAN GULL

*LARUS MELANOCEPHALUS*

Mediterranean Gulls prefer flat areas such as saltmarshes for nesting, and are most widespread around the Mediterranean and Black Seas. Small numbers also breed in northwest Europe.

**IDENTIFICATION** In flight, wings of adult appear pure white at the tips. In winter, summer adult's black head is lost and bird appears white apart from dark smudges around and behind eye. First-winter bird has black terminal band on tail, black primaries, mostly grey secondaries and brownish-grey wing coverts. Second-winter bird has mainly pale grey mantle but still shows black near tips to primaries and partial black head. **HABITAT** Coasts and lagoons; lake shores mainly in Mediterranean area. **VOICE** Deep, nasal calls, mostly heard in spring; generally silent in winter.

ABOVE: *summer adult*

BELOW LEFT: *2nd winter*; BELOW: *winter adult*

BELOW: *In **summer plumage**, adult has black head with incomplete white eyering giving impression of eyelids.*

*From a distance, adult can look all white but close-up view reveals very pale grey mantle.*

189

# AUDOUIN'S GULL

*LARUS AUDOUINII*

**LENGTH** 48–52cm
**WINGSPAN** 127–138cm

Audouin's Gull is a rare breeding bird of the Mediterranean, nesting in colonies that are safe from human interference. It is a very graceful bird in flight.

*1st winter*

*Adult has very pale plumage.*

**IDENTIFICATION** Elegant gull with proportionately slender wings and relatively large bill. In flight, mantle looks pale silvery grey with trailing white edge and contrasting black tips to primaries; inner primaries have a few white flecks. Bill mostly red with black and yellow tip. Legs black. Juvenile has mostly grey-brown plumage, darker mantle and black bill. In second winter, juvenile shows dark primaries, mostly grey mantle, and black terminal band to white tail. At this stage bill is red, with black and yellow tip. **HABITAT** Remote Mediterranean headlands and islands. **VOICE** Donkey-like calls and 'mew' calls.

*adult*

*adult*

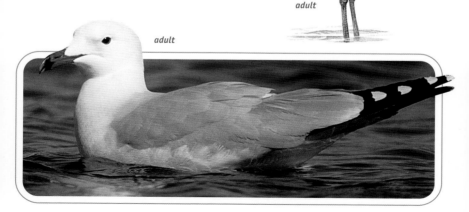

This is a rare gull, but the world population has increased since the 1970s to over 18,000.

42–44cm **LENGTH**
100–110cm **WINGSPAN**

# SLENDER-BILLED GULL
*LARUS GENEI*

The long, pointed bill, which is not especially slender, and the shallow forehead and long neck seperates the Slender-billed Gull from other gulls. It is good at catching fish and can make shallow dives.

**IDENTIFICATION** Adult similar to adult winter Black-headed Gull but completely lacking dark markings on head. Slightly larger than that species, however, with longer, broader wings and with slower wingbeats in normal flight. It often flies in 'V' formation like larger gulls. Adult has pale grey mantle with leading white edge to wings and black-tipped primaries; white

*summer adult*

underside is suffused with pink in summer. Long bill is orange with dark tip, and legs are paler orange than Black-headed Gull's. Juvenile has pale orange legs and bill, and wings have buff and dark brown coverts; shows tiny smudge of grey behind eye. If seen in mixed flocks with other gulls, appears to have proportionally long bill and small eye at all times. **HABITAT** Lagoons, deltas and large lakes around the Mediterranean, Caspian and Black Seas. **VOICE** Main call a deeper version of Black-headed Gull's call.

ABOVE: **non-breeding adult**

RIGHT: *In the **breeding** season the **adult** Slender-billed Gull shows a pink flush to its underparts.*

*Non-breeding birds sometimes gather in small numbers on saline lagoons and saltpans.*

191

# KITTIWAKE
*RISSA TRIDACTYLA*

**LENGTH** 38–40cm
**WINGSPAN** 95–120cm

Kittiwakes are found in huge noisy colonies around the sheer sea cliffs of Europe's northernmost coasts. At important mixed seabird colonies they are often the most numerous species.

Kittiwakes build their nests on tiny ledges on sheer cliffs.

ABOVE: *juvenile*. *Apart from conspicuous 'W' on wings, immature bird also shows blackish hind collar, black mark on face and dark tip to very slightly forked tail; bill black.* ABOVE RIGHT: *adult*

**IDENTIFICATION** Slightly larger than Black-headed Gull but has more compact body and proportionately long wings. Summer adult has bright white head, neck, underparts, rump and tail. At all times of year bill pale yellow, and legs and feet brownish-black. Juvenile has diagnostic blackish zigzag across grey and white upperwing. **HABITAT** Breeds on sheer, high sea cliffs; open sea in winter. **VOICE** Utters the musical cawing of its name, 'kit-ee-wak'.

*adult*

27–32cm **LENGTH**
90–100cm **WINGSPAN**

# SABINE'S GULL
*LARUS SABINI*

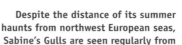

**Despite the distance of its summer haunts from northwest European seas, Sabine's Gulls are seen regularly from these coasts, in late autumn storms.**

*adult*

**IDENTIFICATION** Smaller than Kittiwake, with narrower wings, more deeply forked tail and buoyant tern-like flight action. Summer adult has dusky-grey head with thin black lower border around neck; lower neck and underparts pure white. Mantle is grey, and tail and rump are white; upperwing shows smart and diagnostic triangular pattern of grey coverts, white inner primaries and secondaries, and black outer primaries. In winter, the adult bird loses its dark hood but retains the dusky streaking on the nape of its neck. Bill black with yellow tip at all times; legs and feet blackish-grey. Juvenile has similar upperwing pattern to adult but with grey elements of plumage replaced by warm brown; shows dark tip to tail. **HABITAT** Arctic coastal lowlands; open seas in winter. **VOICE** Various grating cries and whistling calls.

ABOVE AND RIGHT: *juvenile*
BELOW: *summer adult*

# HERRING GULL
## *LARUS ARGENTATUS*

**LENGTH** 55–67cm
**WINGSPAN** 130–158cm

Herring Gulls are able to exploit a wide range of habitats and food sources. They can feed on the seashore and in the open sea, and can also scavenge in refuse tips.

*summer adult*

LEFT: *summer adult*

*1st winter*

*2nd winter*

Herring Gulls have very expressive calls and behaviour and can show aggression by defiant postures and loud calls.

**IDENTIFICATION** Adult plumage – silvery grey mantle with black wingtips flecked with white – is acquired in the fourth year. Large bill is yellow with orange spot near tip of lower mandible. Eye is yellow and legs are pink. Immatures are mottled brown in first winter with dark eye and bill, and dirty-pink legs. In second winter, have more grey in mantle, and iris becomes paler. Before attaining full adult plumage, black wingtips may look very pale, potentially causing confusion with Iceland or Glaucous Gulls. **HABITAT** All types of coastline, large lakes, rivers. **VOICE** Utters long 'aahhoo' calls and deep chuckling notes.

55–67cm **LENGTH**
130–158cm **WINGSPAN**

# YELLOW-LEGGED GULL

*LARUS MICHAHELLIS*

The Yellow-legged Gull is able to feed in a variety of ways and has adapted to modern fishing methods, following fishing vessels and scavenging on waste. It is the commonest gull in the Mediterranean.

*1st winter*

*adult*

**IDENTIFICATION** Very similar to, and formerly considered a race of, Herring Gull; adult differs in having yellow legs and darker grey mantle when compared to western European Herring Gulls. In winter, adult lacks dark mottling on head and neck, characteristic of Herring Gulls. At all times, bill is richer yellow and has larger red spot near tip than Herring Gull. Three separate races of Yellow-legged Gull are recognised by experts; these are very similar, and are not considered here. Immature birds are brown as juveniles and in first winter; legs dark. Acquire adult's white head and body plumage, grey mantle and yellow legs through successive moults over subsequent two years.

**HABITAT** Mediterranean region, Black Sea.

**VOICE** Utters raucous 'aahhoo' calls and deep chuckling notes.

*adult*

# LESSER BLACK-BACKED GULL

*LARUS FUSCUS*

**LENGTH** 52–67cm
**WINGSPAN** 130–148cm

This gull is a migrant over much of its range, spending its winters at sea but generally staying close to the coast in summer. In recent years some birds remain inland in winter, feeding on refuse tips.

**IDENTIFICATION** Occurs as three races in Europe, all of which have bright yellow legs. Adults of western race, *graellsii*, are slate-grey on mantle and can be confused with Yellow-legged Gull; wingtips show less white on black primaries than this species. Birds breeding around Baltic belong to race *fuscus*, and are black above, looking like slim Great Black-backed Gull but with only a single white spot on primaries. Scandinavian birds of race *intermedius* show characteristics of both of others. Juvenile has brown plumage, darker than juvenile Herring Gull, especially when seen in flight. Adult plumage acquired over subsequent two years. At successive moults, head and body become whiter, and brown on wings replaced by grey. **HABITAT** Coasts, marshes, agricultural land. **VOICE** Calls include variations on 'mew' calls; deeper and louder than Herring Gull.

*summer adult*

*1st-winter bird* (BELOW) *has all-dark flight feathers; in* **2nd winter** (LEFT), *acquires grey back and pale bill.*

*winter adult*

*Adult birds have more elongated proportions than Herring Gull; all races show distinctive yellow legs.*

64–78cm **LENGTH**
150–165cm **WINGSPAN**

# GREAT BLACK-BACKED GULL

*LARUS MARINUS*

The Great Black-backed Gull often breeds in the company of other seabirds, which become its source of food. It moves offshore in winter; over half the European population winters around Britain.

**IDENTIFICATION** Much larger and bulkier than Herring Gull, with large angular head, heavy bill and broad back. Sexes similar. Adult in summer has white head, neck, rump and tail. Back and upperwing slaty black with white tips to primaries forming row of white spots on closed wingtip. Underparts white. Bill yellow with red spot on lower mandible towards tip. Legs and feet pink. In winter, adult head and neck streaked with brownish-grey. Juvenile and immature plumages mottled dark brown and white, with whiter rump and blackish terminal band to tail; bill black. **HABITAT** Breeds on coastal islands, stacks, beaches and saltmarshes, occasionally inland at freshwater lakes; continental-shelf waters in winter. **VOICE** Utters deep barking 'owk uk-uk-uk'; also various other wailing and squeaking calls.

*1st winter*

BELOW: *Adult* in flight has more uniformly black upperwing than Lesser Black-backed Gull.

LEFT: *2nd winter*
BELOW: *adult*

197

# GLAUCOUS GULL
*LARUS HYPERBOREUS*

**LENGTH** 62–68cm
**WINGSPAN** 150–165cm

The Glaucous Gull prefers coastal breeding sites facing open seas, especially grassy cliffs. In winter they turn up on coasts of west Europe, numbers increasing in late winter as the weather deteriorates.

*1st winter*

**IDENTIFICATION**  Larger than Iceland Gull but usually smaller than Great Black-backed Gull. Looks pale and white-winged at all times. Summer adult has pale grey back and upperwing, otherwise plumage completely white, including wingtips. In winter, head and neck streaked brown. Pale eye, yellow bill with red spot, and pink legs and feet at all times. Immature plumages white with uniform pale mottled brown gradually lost by moulting until all-white by third year; bill pink with black tip. **HABITAT** Breeds on small islands on Arctic and sub-Arctic coasts; overwinters on bays and harbours. **VOICE** Short, high-pitched yapping and wailing calls.

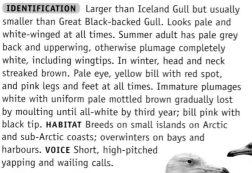

ABOVE: *2nd summer*
RIGHT: *adult*

*Winter adult has streaked head and neck.*

> In winter, the best places to look for Glaucous Gulls are harbours where fishing boats dock and process their catches.

52–60cm **LENGTH**
130–145cm **WINGSPAN**

# ICELAND GULL
*LARUS GLAUCOIDES*

The Iceland Gull breeds off the coast of Greenland and northeast Canada, but is seen in Iceland outside the breeding season. It also wanders as far as the coasts of Scandinavia and northern Britain.

*2nd winter*

**IDENTIFICATION** Smaller than Herring Gull, with more rounded head and smaller bill. Absence of black on wingtips at all times is good identification feature but may lead to confusion with Glaucous Gull; Iceland Gull is smaller and more graceful in flight. At rest, wingtips project further beyond end of tail. Juvenile and first-winter bird very similar to juvenile Glaucous Gull, with essentially white plumage mottled pale brown, but bill is brown-grey, not pale pink. Second-winter bird has pale, marbled grey upperparts and pale, streaked head and underparts. Pale grey bill has dark sub-terminal band. **HABITAT** Breeds on Arctic islands; overwinters at sea. **VOICE** Utters shrill version of Herring Gull's 'aahhoo' call.

TOP RIGHT: *2nd winter*
RIGHT AND BELOW: *winter adult*

# BLACK TERN
*CHLIDONIAS NIGER*

**LENGTH** 22–24cm
**WINGSPAN** 64–68cm

The Black Tern is a breeding bird of eastern Europe with many scattered colonies to the west. Birds return in May to breeding waters. It is the most widespread of the so-called 'Marsh Terns' (genus *Chlidonias*) in Europe.

**IDENTIFICATION** Smaller than all sea terns, with shorter, less forked tail. Summer adult dark slate-grey, with head almost black and upperwing ash-grey. Rump and uppertail grey. Underwing very pale grey, vent and undertail coverts white. In winter, grey upperparts and white underparts reminiscent of sea terns, but upperparts darker and with black smudge at shoulder. Moult between summer and winter plumages can give very blotchy appearance. Juvenile plumage has darker saddle. At all times bill black, long and fine, and legs and feet red-brown. **HABITAT** Continental, fresh or brackish waters, rich in floating and emergent vegetation. **VOICE** Squeaky harsh 'kik-keek' call; growling 'krrr' when on nest.

*adult, summer plumage*

*juvenile*

Flight light and erratic, with frequent dips to surface of water.

*adult, summer plumage*

*adult*

200

20–23cm **LENGTH**
63–67cm **WINGSPAN**

# WHITE-WINGED BLACK TERN
### *CHLIDONIAS LEUCOPTERUS*

The natural marshes and alkaline pools among the vast grasslands of Poland and Hungary are the White-winged Black Tern's favoured breeding areas. Birds arrive in mid-May.

**IDENTIFICATION** Breeding plumage bird has black head, neck and body, upperwings greyer and show bright silver-white wing coverts. Underwing shows black coverts and pale-grey flight feathers. Rump, vent and tail white. In winter, grey above and white below, with white collar and white rump contrasting with grey tail. Bill short and pointed, crimson when breeding, otherwise black. Legs and feet bright red in summer, darker in winter. Juvenile similar to winter adult but with darker, mottled brown back forming saddle.
**HABITAT** Natural flooded grasslands and swamps.
**VOICE** Call is a sharp churring 'keer'; shorter alarm notes.

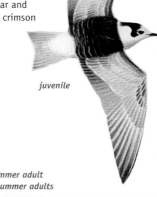

*juvenile*

LEFT: *summer adult*
BELOW: *summer adults*

# WHISKERED TERN
*CHLIDONIAS HYBRIDUS*

**LENGTH** 23–25cm
**WINGSPAN** 74–78cm

The Whiskered Tern occurs further south in Europe than the Black Tern, requiring a warmer climate than that species. The Camargue, in southern France, is a typical habitat.

**IDENTIFICATION** Relatively bulky size invites confusion with sea tern, but has shorter, less forked tail. Summer adult has jet-black crown and nape, contrasting with white lower face. Neck and rest of upperparts uniform grey, including rump and uppertail. Below white face underparts become dark slate grey, darkest on flanks. Vent and undertail coverts white. Upperwing grey, underwing coverts white. In winter much more like sea tern, with grey upperparts and white underparts. Bill dark crimson-red in summer adult but black in winter and juvenile. Legs and feet red at all times. Juvenile resembles winter adult, with dark brown back and pale grey upperwing, giving saddle effect. **HABITAT** Clear water, lakes and marshes with floating vegetation. **VOICE** Loud croaking and cawing 'krrerch'; sharper alarm call.

RIGHT: *juvenile*
LEFT AND BELOW: *breeding adult*

22–24cm **LENGTH**
48–55cm **WINGSPAN**

# LITTLE TERN
### *STERNA ALBIFRONS*

In Britain Little Terns are exclusively coastal, but elsewhere in Europe they are found along major rivers and around lakes as well. They arrive in Europe in April, and can be heard courting noisily.

**IDENTIFICATION** Smallest sea tern, with larger head, longer bill and more sharply forked tail than marsh tern of genus *Chlidonias*. Summer adult has black crown, nape and line through eye to bill; forehead white. Back pale grey fading to white uppertail. Underparts pure white. Upperwing grey like back, with blackish outer primaries forming dark leading edge, and whiter trailing edge. Bill long and slender, yellow with black tip. Legs and feet orange-yellow. Non-breeding adult has darker bill and larger white forehead than summer adult. Juvenile has browner-grey feathers on back and upperwing. **HABITAT** Coastal or riverine strips of bare shingle, sand with shallow lagoons, inlets. **VOICE** Rasping and churring 'kierr-ink' call; also shorter distinctive 'kik'.

TOP LEFT: *breeding adult*
LEFT: *courting pair*
BELOW: *breeding adult*

*Little Terns' size, narrow wings and bright, white appearance make identification easy.*

# SANDWICH TERN
*STERNA SANDVICENSIS*

**LENGTH** 36–41cm
**WINGSPAN** 95–105cm

Sandwich Tern colonies require access to shallow, sheltered waters, usually over sand for fishing. Nest sites are mostly on offshore islands, where ground predators are absent.

**IDENTIFICATION** Large and pale tern with long bill and head. Tail short but deeply forked. Wings long and narrow. In breeding season, Sandwich Tern has jet black cap with shaggy crest to rear. Back and upperwing very pale grey with silvery flight feathers. Rump and tail white. Underparts bright white. In winter, forehead becomes white and cap is mottled. At all times, adult has black bill with yellow tip, and black legs and feet. Juvenile resembles winter adult, but has shorter all-black bill and blackish flecking on upperwing and back. **HABITAT** Low-lying coasts with access to shallow, sandy-bottomed waters. **VOICE** Distinct disyllabic 'keerr-ink'; shorter, sharp alarm note.

*Deep, disyllabic call and bright white plumage allow easy identification.*

**breeding adult**

Most Sandwich Terns migrate to West African coasts for the winter; the Black Sea population only moves to the southern Mediterranean.

*Loses black forehead by late summer and acquires dusky wedge on outerwing through wear.*

LEFT: **non-breeding adult**
BELOW: *nesting **adults***

35–38cm **LENGTH**
100–115cm **WINGSPAN**

# GULL-BILLED TERN

*GELOCHELIDON NILOTICA*

The Gull-billed Tern is more catholic in its choice of colony sites than other terns and is less dependent on close proximity to water. It returns to European breeding sites in late April.

*breeding adult*

*breeding adult*

**IDENTIFICATION** Comparable in size to Sandwich Tern but has bulkier outline with heavier, more direct flight. In breeding season, has black crown reaching low down nape; white hindneck, face and underparts. Back, rump and tail ash-grey. Upperwing pearl-grey with duskier primaries towards tip. Underwing white except for dusky wedge near tip. Winter adult loses black cap but retains black mask. At all times in adult, bill black, thick and blunt, and legs and feet black. Juvenile darker than winter adult, with grey feathers of back and shoulders smudged brown; legs and feet red-brown. **HABITAT** Lowland coasts and deltas; inland to lakes, rivers and marshes. **VOICE** Loud, deep, trisyllabic grating call.

*breeding adult*

*breeding adult*

*Great care is needed to distinguish this species from Sandwich Tern; thick bill and harsh, grating call are best identification features.*

# CASPIAN TERN
*STERNA CASPIA*

**LENGTH** 47–54cm
**WINGSPAN** 130–145cm

The impressive-looking Caspian Tern is not common in Europe, being mainly restricted to the Baltic coasts. Breeding birds arrive in late April and forage for fish on large, sheltered waters, travelling some distance from the nest in order to do so.

ABOVE AND RIGHT: *breeding adults*

**IDENTIFICATION** Huge gull-sized tern with massive bill, round body, blunt wings and short tail. In breeding season, crown and shaggy nape black, and hindneck, face and underparts white. Back and upperwing silvery grey, darker towards wingtip. Underwing has large dusky patch at tip. Rump and tail whitish, sometimes with grey cast. In winter, cap more mottled with black speckling extending on to face; wings become darker with wear. Massive dagger bill is bright coral red in summer, more orange in winter with dark tip. Legs and feet black at all times. Juvenile has mottled black cap extending on to face, and irregular brown flecking on back. **HABITAT** Sheltered continental coasts with rocky islets, sand dunes, spits. **VOICE** Utters loud, deep, barking notes with short, sharp alarm call.

*breeding adult*

The Caspian Tern is shy at its breeding grounds and tends to choose more isolated locations in Europe to avoid disturbance.

33–38cm **LENGTH**
72–80cm **WINGSPAN**

# ROSEATE TERN
## *STERNA DOUGALLII*

Britain and Ireland are the most important breeding areas in Europe for Roseate Terns. There are a few pairs in northwest France and on the Azores but they are very rare throughout Europe as a whole.

**IDENTIFICATION** Similar to the Common Tern but has shorter wings and longer tail, giving slimmer appearance. In breeding season, adult has narrow, jet-black cap on crown and nape. Lower face, rump and tail white. Upperparts have blue-grey wash, paler than in Common Tern. Underparts washed with strong pink. Flight feathers pale silvery grey and translucent from below. Winter adult loses rosy wash and forehead becomes white. Long, narrow, black bill with red base seen at all times in adults. Legs and feet coral red in summer, dull red in winter. Juvenile has heavy brown spotting on upperparts, reminiscent of young Sandwich Tern. **HABITAT** Maritime coasts with low rocky islets, sand dunes. **VOICE** Calls include distinct rasping 'aakh' and whistled 'chewit'.

*Medium-sized, pale sea tern with long, flowing tail streamers; elegant in summer plumage.*

TOP, LEFT AND ABOVE: **breeding adult**

207

# COMMON TERN
## *STERNA HIRUNDO*

**LENGTH** 31–35cm
**WINGSPAN** 77–98cm

Common Terns are widespread throughout Europe in summer, returning to their nesting colonies in April. Most European birds overwinter in the tropical seas off West Africa.

*breeding adult*

**IDENTIFICATION** Often seen with Black-headed Gulls, but are fractionally shorter, with narrower, more pointed wings and long forked tail. Very similar to Arctic Tern, but with larger bill and head, stouter body and shorter tail; legs longer than Arctic Tern's. Summer adult has jet-black cap, pearl-grey upperparts with darker grey outer primaries and white rump and tail. Underparts white. In winter, adult has white forehead and mottled black cap. At all times adult has red, black-tipped bill, and red legs and feet. Juvenile is like winter adult but with ginger-brown mottling to back and forewing, and pale orange bill with black tip. **HABITAT** Along coasts and on inland fresh waters, sometimes on artificial platforms. **VOICE** Utters harsh rasping and emphatic 'key-yah' call; also short, sharp alarm.

RIGHT: *breeding adults*
BELOW: *breeding adult*

Common Terns select breeding locations on small, rocky islands or sandy shores; they will also nest on inland lakes or reservoirs, where they often choose artificial platforms.

33–35cm **LENGTH**
75–85cm **WINGSPAN**

# ARCTIC TERN
## *STERNA PARADISAEA*

*Shorter head and bill and longer tail give Arctic Tern subtly different flight shape from Common Tern.*

**Arctic Tern colonies are mainly confined to coasts, where grassy islands are favoured. They perform the longest migration of any bird, wintering in Antarctica.**

*breeding adult*

**IDENTIFICATION** Difficult to separate from the Common Tern, but has shorter bill and head, longer tail and much shorter legs. Summer adult pale blue-grey above, white below but with dusky grey wash on breast and belly. Rump and tail bright white. Jet-black cap, white cheeks and blood-red bill. White flight feathers, translucent from below, lack dark markings of Common Tern. Winter birds, not seen in region, have crown speckled white. Legs and feet coral-red in summer, darker in winter. Juvenile has white forehead, marked black cap and is pale grey above, lacking brown tints of other juvenile sea terns. **HABITAT** Inshore and offshore waters with grass-covered islets; sometimes inland along rivers. **VOICE** Utters shrill, nasal, grating notes and short, sharp alarm call; colonies very noisy.

LEFT AND BELOW:
*breeding adult*

# PUFFIN
### *FRATERCULA ARCTICA*

**LENGTH** 27cm
**WINGSPAN** 47–63cm

The Puffin is locally abundant, breeding in
large colonies on offshore islands and isolated
mainland cliffs. They prefer to excavate
nesting burrows on sloping peaty turf.

**IDENTIFICATION** Smaller than Guillemot and Razorbill, with obvious deep, colourful bill making
head appear large. Has black upperparts and white underparts in all plumages, smartest in breeding
adult, duller in juvenile. Summer adult has grey face and triangular bill, coloured bright red, blue-
grey and yellow. Brightness of bill much reduced in winter. Red eye has surround of blue-grey horny
appendages. Back, upperwing, rump and tail black. Underwing grey, rest of underparts white.
Legs and feet bright orange. Juvenile has flesh-coloured feet and small, blackish bill, thinner
than adult's. **HABITAT** Breeding colonies on sloping sea cliffs; open sea outside breeding
season. **VOICE** Least vocal of the auks; creaking, growling and grunting calls heard in
breeding season only.

*summer adult*

*summer adult*

The large, powerful bill is
slightly hooked to help the
bird hold slippery prey; the
bright colouring is lost in
the winter.

*summer adult*

*newly hatched chick*

*winter adult*

37–39cm **LENGTH**
63–68cm **WINGSPAN**

# RAZORBILL
*ALCA TORDA*

Razorbills nest on sea cliffs and among boulders on the coasts of northern Europe, sometimes in mixed colonies with their commoner relative, the Guillemot. Britain and Ireland hold half the world population.

**IDENTIFICATION** Size of Guillemot, with head, neck, back, upperwings and tail jet black in summer; underparts bright white. In winter throat and upper breast become dirty white and upperparts greyer. Breeding adult has deep, heavy black bill with neat white line across middle, and a white line connecting base of bill to eye; white on bill and eyeline duller in winter. Legs and feet black. Juvenile smaller than adult, browner and with bulbous bill. **HABITAT** Breeds on sea cliffs and boulders of undercliff; overwinters inshore or on open sea. **VOICE** Various growling calls.

ABOVE: *Lacking maneouvrability and ungainly in the air, Razorbills are in their true element underwater.*

summer
adult

juvenile

AUKS

# GUILLEMOT
## *URIA AALGE*

**LENGTH** 38–41cm
**WINGSPAN** 64–70cm

Guillemots are found around the coasts of northwestern Europe in densely packed cliff-ledge colonies. They catch fish by diving in pursuit of their quarry, and propel themselves using their wings, essentially 'flying' underwater.

BELOW: *Nesting **adult** with egg. The single egg is laid directly onto the cliff ledge and is sometimes incubated on the bird's feet; its distinctive shape may have evolved to stop it from rolling off.*

ABOVE: *The **bridled form** shows white spectacle round the eye.*

*Both Britain and Ireland are Guillemot strongholds; the more northerly birds tend to have darker summer plumage.*

**IDENTIFICATION** Longer-bodied and shorter-tailed than Razorbill. In summer, head, neck and upperparts dark brown, underparts mainly white. Flanks streaked with brown. White line across closed wing formed by white tips to secondaries. Dark furrow behind eye; this feature is white and extends around eye in so-called 'bridled' form, giving spectacled appearance. In winter, cheeks and neck white, upperparts greyer. At all times in adult birds, bill black, long and tapering, and legs and feet dark blue-grey. Juvenile has plumage like winter adult but smaller bill. **HABITAT** Breeds on rocky sea cliffs and stacks; overwinters in marine offshore and inshore waters. **VOICE** Growling and guttural rolling calls.

*Winter adult; note dark line running back from eye.*

39–43cm **LENGTH**
65–73cm **WINGSPAN**

# BRÜNNICH'S GUILLEMOT

*URIA LOMVIA*

Colonies of Brünnich's Guillemot are confined to high Arctic islands and coastal sea cliffs, such as on Svalbard. Winter ice formation forces them to disperse mainly to northern Arctic waters.

**IDENTIFICATION** Slightly larger and bulkier than Guillemot, with heavier bill and thicker head and neck. Plumage very similar to Guillemot. In summer adult has darker brown-black upperparts than Guillemot and white underparts; lacks brown flank streaks, and white breast meets brown-black throat in a sharp point. In winter upperparts retain blackish cast; white from throat extends onto face only below eye, not above as well, as seen in Guillemot. At all times adult has black, deep and strong bill, with white lower edge to upper mandible extending from base to mid-point. Legs and feet are brown to front, black to rear. Juvenile is smaller than winter adult, which it resembles in plumage except for mottled throat. **HABITAT** Breeds on Arctic sea cliffs and steep boulder slopes; open Arctic waters in winter. **VOICE** Utters growling and hoarse crowing calls.

RIGHT: *Summer adult has distinctive white gape streak.*

winter adult

summer adult

Winter ice formation forces Brünnich's Guillemots to be migratory, though dispersal is confined mainly to northern Arctic waters.

213

# BLACK GUILLEMOT
*CEPPHUS GRYLLE*

**LENGTH** 30–32cm
**WINGSPAN** 52–58cm

Black Guillemots nest in loose colonies in natural rock holes or crevices, often among boulders at the base of sea cliffs. Winter dispersal is undertaken only where necessary to avoid sea ice.

**IDENTIFICATION** Medium-sized auk with round body, smallish head and paddle-shaped wings. Strikingly different plumage patterns in summer and winter. Summer adult uniform dark chocolate brown except for large, white, oval patch on both upperwing and underwing coverts. In winter appears much whiter with back speckled grey and white; head, neck and underparts dirty white. Wing retains summer pattern. At all times, adult has sharply pointed black bill with vivid orange inside, and bright red legs and feet. Juvenile resembles winter adult but with upperparts and flanks more darkly mottled. **HABITAT** Breeds on sea cliffs and maritime boulder slopes; overwinters in shallow coastal seas. **VOICE** Utters a thin, shrill whistle.

ABOVE: *breeding adult*

*winter adult*

*Bright white wing patches clearly visible in flight; flies fast and low over water.*

*The bright gape is usually only seen during courtship displays.*

*breeding adult*

*breeding adult*

Nesting among boulders has made Black Guillemots vulnerable to predation by introduced North American Mink.

214

18cm **LENGTH**
40–48cm **WINGSPAN**

# LITTLE AUK
### *ALLE ALLE*

**Little Auks are the most northerly distributed of the auk family, breeding in colonies numbering millions on high Arctic islands. After breeding, Little Auks stay in cold northern waters unless forced south by late autumn storms.**

**IDENTIFICATION** Size of Starling, with smart black and white plumage showing narrow white lines on shoulder and white tips to secondaries, visible when wings closed. Bill very small and black. Body short and stubby with neckless appearance. Summer adult has black head, neck and breast. In winter, throat and breast white. Rest of upperparts black, underparts white. Juvenile similar to adult but browner. **HABITAT** Breeds on Arctic mountain and cliff scree slopes; cold open sea in winter. **VOICE** Twittering trills uttered at breeding colonies; whinnying alarm call in flight.

*Flies with very fast wingbeats; underwing paler than Puffin's.*

*breeding adult*

*winter adult*

*Storm-driven, exhausted Little Auks sometimes turn up on coastal lagoons in late autumn and early winter.*

*On the water the short, plump neck and almost bill-less profile are striking.*

*winter adult*

# ROCK DOVE
## *COLUMBA LIVIA*

**LENGTH** 31–34cm
**WINGSPAN** 63–70cm

The Rock Dove must be the best-known European bird due to the abundant populations of so-called Feral Pigeons that inhabit our towns and cities. Truly wild Rock Doves are shy, fast-flying birds, and are very wary.

**IDENTIFICATION** Much smaller than Woodpigeon. Adult is medium-sized, blue-grey pigeon with two obvious black bars across rear half of innerwing; plumage relieved on nape, neck and upper breast by green-purple gloss. Back, scapulars and innerwing paler ash-grey, tail with broad brownish-black terminal band. Bright white underwing coverts and lower back seen in flight. Bill lead-coloured, off-white at base. Legs and feet dull to bright red. Juvenile like adult but duller, except for sharing bright white on lower back. **HABITAT** Oceanic coasts and rocky areas; inland amongst open country; feral in towns. **VOICE** Various moaning, cooing calls.

*Black wingbars obvious in flight.*

*adults*

*The continuing encroachment of the feral form (ABOVE) is the greatest threat to the Rock Dove's (LEFT) survival.*

40–42cm **LENGTH**
75–80cm **WINGSPAN**

# WOODPIGEON
### *COLUMBA PALUMBUS*

The Woodpigeon is a powerful flier able to employ fast jinks and swerves to avoid predators; its undulating, wing-clapping display is well known. In western Europe the population is mainly resident.

*White crescent on wing and **adult**'s neck patches diagnostic.*

**IDENTIFICATION** Largest pigeon in Europe. Adult easily identified by blue-grey plumage with white neck patch, white wing crescents and black terminal band to longish, full tail. Sides and back of neck glossy green with purple sheen. Breast warm mauve-pink. In flight, adult's white wing crescents very obvious; also shows blackish primaries with white outer webs sometimes showing as pale panel. Bill is reddish with yellow tip and off-white patch at base. Pale yellowish eye. Legs mauve-pink. Juvenile much duller than adult; lacks white neck patch. **HABITAT** Woodland and scrub; agricultural fields next to woods in winter. **VOICE** Multisyllabic cooing, with emphasis on second note.

*From a distance, overall impression is of a grey bird, but at closer range browner back and pink breast discernible.*

*adult*

# STOCK DOVE
### COLUMBA OENAS

**LENGTH** 32–34cm
**WINGSPAN** 63–69cm

Stock Doves are found mostly in the lowlands, although they will venture into the uplands where suitable habitats occur. Their nests are usually sited in tree-holes.

*Flight action faster than Woodpigeon's.*

**IDENTIFICATION** Adult plumage mainly grey. Head and underbody bluer and sides of neck have glossy green sheen. Upper breast has warm pink wash. Grey tail has broad black terminal band. Bill grey-buff, off-white at base. In flight, upperwing shows paler grey central panel and twin black bars on tertials. Eye brown with grey orbital ring. Legs bright pinkish-red. Juvenile browner and duller than adult, lacking any green sheen. **HABITAT** Border of woodland and open country. **VOICE** Disyllabic, warm, cooing 'oo-look'; also growling calls at nest.

*Medium-sized, blue-grey pigeon, slightly smaller than Rock Dove, which it resembles except that it never has any white in its plumage at any age.*

*adult*

*adult*

31–33cm **LENGTH**
48–56cm **WINGSPAN**

# COLLARED DOVE
*STREPTOPELIA DECAOCTO*

Collared Doves expanded north and west into Europe very quickly from 1930 onwards, reaching Britain in the 1950s and Norway in the 1960s. This spread is continuing.

*Flight action is fast, with clipped wingbeats.*

**IDENTIFICATION** Larger than Turtle Dove, with longer tail and uniform pale, sandy grey plumage. Adult has pale-grey crown. Face, neck and breast pinkish-buff, fading to cream on belly and undertail coverts. Narrow, white-edged black half-collar. Back, scapulars and smaller wing coverts sandy grey-brown. Greater coverts and secondaries show grey panel next to darker, dusky primaries. Underwing coverts white. Uppertail brown with whitish tips to outer feathers. Broad, white terminal band to undertail. Bill black. Eye dark red with pale orbital ring. Legs and feet mauve-red. Juvenile duller than adult, lacking black half-collar. **HABITAT** Mixed habitats of gardens, farms, orchards and town avenues. **VOICE** Repeated, penetrating, unmusical cooing.

*adults*

*In western Europe Collared Doves favour mixed habitats such as gardens, orchards and parks, where they readily use buildings and wires for perching.*

# TURTLE DOVE
*STREPTOPELIA TURTUR*

**LENGTH** 26–28cm
**WINGSPAN** 47–53cm

The Turtle Dove, with its deep, purring, cooing song, is a quintessential summer bird of Europe. They are migratory and spend the winter in Africa.

*adult*

**IDENTIFICATION** Smaller and slighter than Collared Dove. Adult has blue-grey crown with face, neck and breast warm pink. Patch of narrow black and white lines on neck. Back and rump brown with indistinct dark flecking. Closed wing has dappled pattern with black-centred, rich brown feathers. In flight, shows blue-grey greater coverts and dusky flight feathers. Complicated tail pattern of white-tipped black feathers, except for central pair, which are wholly brown. Undertail black, rimmed white, contrasting with cream underparts. Dark bill with pale tip. Yellow eye with crimson orbital ring. Legs reddish. Juvenile duller, lacking neck patch. **HABITAT** Warm woodlands, open scrub, orchards and parks. **VOICE** Deep, purring 'coo', which may sound 'frog-like' at a distance.

*Small, slim dove with thin neck, protruding round head and deep chest; has comparatively long, wedge-tipped tail and swept-back wings.*

*adult*

*adult*

32–34cm **LENGTH**
55–60cm **WINGSPAN**

# CUCKOO
### *CUCULUS CANORUS*

The Cuckoo's silhouette in flight can resemble a small falcon or hawk; however, a prolonged view will reveal that the Cuckoo has a distinctive rowing flight action. It is migratory, with European adults flying to Africa in July; juveniles follow several weeks later.

*Adults in flight.*

*adult*

ABOVE: *Unlike falcon or hawk, Cuckoo has weak flight action with rapid wingbeats not raised above the horizontal; wings are pointed.*

**IDENTIFICATION** Similar in size to Collared Dove but with longer tail. Adult male has slate-grey head, breast and upperparts. Underparts, from lower breast to undertail coverts, white with close, narrow blackish barring forming pattern of transverse lines across underbody. Upperwing darker grey-black, underwing paler. Darker tail feathers tipped and spotted white. Female similar to male but browner with buff breast band; occasional form has grey replaced with rufous, barred black. Decurved bill has yellow base with darker tip. Legs and feet yellow. Juvenile similar to rufous female but differs in having barred throat, white nape and white edges and tips to dark feathers. **HABITAT** Woodland, scrub, parkland and open uplands. **VOICE** Familiar male call 'cu-coo'; female makes repeated bubbling notes.

BELOW: *Juvenile rufous with pale nape patch. Has a squeaking hunger call; it is fed by its 'parent' even when it is already quite well grown.*

# GREAT SPOTTED CUCKOO

**LENGTH** 38–40cm
**WINGSPAN** 58–61cm

*CLAMATOR GLANDARIUS*

The Great Spotted Cuckoo feeds mainly on caterpillars, which it searches for by hopping along the ground. The prey is taken to a perch, where irritant hairs are removed by wiping.

*Juvenile* unmistakable in flight, with black cap, chestnut primaries and disproportionately long tail.

This impressive bird is strikingly patterned, has a long tail and perches prominently.

*adult*

*adult*

**IDENTIFICATION** Much larger than Cuckoo, with crest, broader wings and tail. Adult has blue-grey crested crown; upper face and neck blackish-brown. Rest of upperparts dusky brown with prominent white tips to scapulars, underwing coverts and long graduated tail. Chin, throat, foreneck and breast have warm orange-buff wash; rest of underparts off-white. Underwing coverts cream. Longish, stout, grey-black bill. Red eyering. Brown-grey legs and feet. Juvenile recalls bright adult but lacks crest; whole of crown dark brown. Light tips to feathers are cream not white, and bright chestnut primaries conspicuous in flight. **HABITAT** Warm Mediterranean scrub; open woodland. **VOICE** Loud harsh rasping calls and double 'kioc-kioc'.

33–35cm **LENGTH**
70–73cm **WINGSPAN**

# BLACK-BELLIED SANDGROUSE

*PTEROCLES ORIENTALIS*

The Black-bellied Sandgrouse is the larger of the two European species of sandgrouse and is found mainly in Spain and Turkey. Nesting birds are well camouflaged and usually nervous of people.

*Adults in flight.*

*adult*

**IDENTIFICATION** Heavy-bodied, pigeon-like bird with short, pointed tail and broad, pointed wings. Male head, neck and breast grey with chestnut and black half-collar on foreneck. Grey breast separated from black belly by narrow black and white bands. Back and upperwing ochre-yellow with blackish flecking. Flight feathers grey-black. Underwing shows black flight feathers and white coverts. Pointed tail barred yellow and black. Female and juvenile are duller than male; breast is spotted. **HABITAT** Flat plains on sandy soils, steppes. **VOICE** Musical cluckings and low bubbling notes, heard mostly in flight.

31–39cm **LENGTH**
54–65cm **WINGSPAN**

# PIN-TAILED SANDGROUSE

*PTEROCLES ALCHATA*

In Europe, the Pin-tailed Sandgrouse is confined to the warm, arid steppes of Spain, Portugal and Turkey, with a northerly outlying population on the stony Crau plain, in southern France.

**IDENTIFICATION** Both sexes have brown bill, white feathered legs and grey feet. Male has chestnut face, black throat, black margins to chestnut breast band; underbody and underwings white. Back and upperwing have greenish marbling, white-edged maroon wing coverts and black-barred yellow rump. Dark tail streamers. Female similar to male but with crown and nape streaked black, more yellow, less chestnut and more fine black barring on upperparts. Juvenile resembles dull female. **HABITAT** Warm arid Mediterranean steppes, dried-out marshes. **VOICE** Noisy and distinctive repeated 'chata-chata' flight call.

*adult*

*adult*

# BARN OWL
*TYTO ALBA*

**LENGTH** 33–35cm
**WINGSPAN** 85–93cm

A hunting Barn Owl is a beautiful sight, with its slow, buoyant flight, hovering and swift plunges into the undergrowth for prey. Not strictly nocturnal, it can be seen in the half-light of winter afternoons.

**IDENTIFICATION** Smaller than Tawny Owl but with longer, narrower wings. Adult from south and west European race has warm, vermiculated yellowish-brown upperparts contrasting with clear silver-white underparts. Crown, nape, back and rump warm yellowish-brown with soft grey mottling and rows of tiny blackish spots. Coverts on closed wing similar; in flight shows warm-buff flight and tail feathers with dark-brown barring. Face has complete heart-shaped white facial disc with dark rusty eye pits and black eyes. Underparts, including feathered legs, silky white. Feet grey-brown. Bill pinkish. Adult from central European race has buff body underparts and underwing coverts. Similar in other respects to white-breasted race. Juvenile resembles adult as soon as down is lost. **HABITAT** Open lowlands with small woods, hedges and fields; upland grasslands and heaths. **VOICE** Screeching, whistling and snoring notes in breeding season.

*adult*

*adult*

*adult*

*dark-breasted adult*

*adult*

37–39cm **LENGTH**
95–100cm **WINGSPAN**

# TAWNY OWL
*STRIX ALUCO*

*adult*

**In northwest Europe the Tawny Owl is the most likely owl to be encountered by the casual observer, as the adaptability of the species makes it tolerant of humans. It is a nocturnal species.**

**IDENTIFICATION** Medium-sized, broad-winged owl with large, rounded head and no ear tufts. Mottled, barred and streaked plumage varies from rufous-brown to grey-brown. Greyish facial disc bordered blackish with white eyebrows, lores and sides to chin. Eyes large and black. Crown, neck and back brown, boldy streaked with black. Prominent line of white-spotted scapulars. Flight feathers softly barred dark brown. Underwing buff-brown. Underparts greyer and usually paler with uniform blackish streaks. Bill yellowish-grey. Legs and feet buff, feathered; claws grey. Juvenile similar to adult, once down has been lost. **HABITAT** Deciduous or mixed woodlands, forest and parks in towns. **VOICE** Classic melodious hoot 'huit-houuu'; common call 'ke-wick'.

*Looks bulky in flight, with big head, short tail and broad wings.*

*juvenile*

*adult*

*The Tawny Owl may be mobbed by smaller birds, giving away its presence.*

*In daylight the Tawny Owl's neat, rounded appearance and pale spots on the closed wing make identification straightforward.*

225

OWLS

# GREAT GREY OWL

*STRIX NEBULOSA*

**LENGTH** 65–70cm
**WINGSPAN** 135–160cm

The Great Grey Owl often hunts by day, using forest glades, bogs and adjacent open moorlands. Although usually a sedentary species, it can become nomadic in response to fluctuating populations of its mammalian prey.

*Great Grey Owl is a huge owl and could be mistaken for an Eagle Owl or Ural Owl; it is proportionately longer-winged than either species, slimmer-bodied than Eagle Owl and shows less barring on wings than Ural Owl.*

**IDENTIFICATION** Large, round head, long wings and tail. Adult plumage dark brown-black and white, appearing grey at distance. Head, back, rump and tail are pale grey, profusely streaked and barred dark brown. Dark blotching on back. Indistinct rows of pale spots on scapulars and coverts. Closed wing is brown, heavily streaked and barred blackish. Facial disc striking, with concentric fine black and grey barring, bright white eyebrows, lores, moustache and chin. Bright-yellow eye and bill. Underbody pale grey, heavily streaked dark brown. **HABITAT** Dense, mature boreal pine, fir forests and adjacent moorland. **VOICE** Deep, muffled, pumping hoots with squealing and growling alarm notes.

*adult*

*adult*

*adult*

60–62cm **LENGTH**
125–135cm **WINGSPAN**

# URAL OWL
*STRIX URALENSIS*

In summer, the Ural Owl hunts along forest fringes and in glades. In winter it moves towards villages or farms, where more open habitats and cultivation can provide an easier source of food.

**IDENTIFICATION** Larger than Tawny Owl, with longer tail. Adult plumage pale grey. Head, neck, back and underbody pale grey with uniform pattern of dark brown streaks. Circular, pale brownish-grey facial disc neatly outlined in dark brown. Eyes blackish-brown. Edges of scapulars white, forming distinct rows of pale spots down back. Wings grey with warmer brown tones to broadly barred flight feathers. Underwing contrastingly marked with whitish, black-tipped coverts and dark-brown barred flight feathers. Tail grey with broad, dark-brown bands. Bill yellow. Legs and feet feathered, buff-grey. Juvenile similar to adult once fully fledged. **HABITAT** Temperate forests of Europe with glades; also overwinters in parks and around villages. **VOICE** Deep hoot of three di- or trisyllabic notes; also harsh croaks.

*adult*

*adult*

*adult*

The survival of this sedentary species is dependent on the availability of a year-round feeding territory and, in central Europe, undisturbed woodland habitat.

# LONG-EARED OWL
*ASIO OTUS*

**LENGTH** 35–37cm
**WINGSPAN** 90–100cm

The Long-eared Owl is distributed widely throughout Europe wherever there are trees. It is often found in agricultural areas with small woodland copses in the breeding season.

*adult*

**IDENTIFICATION** Smaller than Tawny Owl, though appears tall and thin when alarmed. Adult plumage ground colour is rufous-brown on upperparts, only slightly paler on underparts. Most feathers fringed pale buff. Crown, neck and back streaked and barred with black. Closed wing shows white shoulder and white covert spots. Flight feathers are rich orange, barred blackish. Facial disc warm orange-buff divided by point of grey crown and white eyebrows. Prominent, blackish, pale-fringed ear tufts. Eyes bright orange. Bill grey. Underparts buff-brown with heavy, blackish arrowhead streaks. Belly and undertail unstreaked. Legs and feet feathered, buff; claws grey. Juvenile similar to adult but with closer and less regular barring. **HABITAT** Woodland copses and scrub with open habitats for hunting. **VOICE** Quiet, but far-carrying, repeated 'oo' notes; young like squeaking gate.

*adult*

*The ear tufts are erected when the owl is alarmed.*

*adult*

37–39cm **LENGTH**
95–110cm **WINGSPAN**

# SHORT-EARED OWL

*ASIO FLAMMEUS*

The Short-eared Owl can be identified by its long, narrow wings, buoyant flight and often horizontal posture when perched. It will feed both by day and at night.

*adult*

**IDENTIFICATION** Long-winged owl with fairly small head, often confused with Long-eared Owl. Adult plumage yellowish-buff, heavily streaked with black. Head and neck buff with bold, dark streaks. Back so heavily streaked it appears mostly blackish. Rump paler with fewer streaks. Tail yellowish-buff, broadly barred dark brown. Striking facial disc surrounded by heavy black spotting. Pale-buff cheeks and reversed white brackets between yellow eyes sunk in blackish pits. Underbody clearer, warm buff with lighter streaks. In flight, wing shows dark carpal patch and dark tip. Bill grey. Legs and feet feathered, buff. Juvenile similar to adult but with broader, pale tail-tip. **HABITAT** Open country, moorlands, rough grazing, sand dunes, marshes. **VOICE** Low-pitched hollow 'hoo-hoo-hoo' series of notes; hissing and rasping calls at nest.

ABOVE AND RIGHT: *adult*

*Ear tufts are very small and seldom seen.*

229

# EAGLE OWL
### *BUBO BUBO*

The Eagle Owl's direct and purposeful flight action is similar to that of a Buzzard, so care is needed to identify it; it is the only large owl with ear tufts.

**IDENTIFICATION** Largest European owl; barrel-shaped with prominent ear tufts. Adult plumage usually warm brown, heavily marked on upperparts with thick, black streaks and spots. Flight feathers barred black. Paler brown underparts have black droplets on breast; narrower streaks and fine dark bars on belly and flanks. Head has laterally flattened blackish ear tufts and well-marked pale-grey facial disc with bright orange eyes. Chin and throat show furry, whitish ruff. In flight the dark leading edge to wing contrasts with yellowish flight feathers, barred blackish. Feathered legs and feet. Bill black. Juvenile paler and fluffier than adult, lacking ear tufts, and has more completely barred underparts. **HABITAT** Wilderness with rocky crags and mosaic of woods and open country. **VOICE** Deep, booming, far-carrying disyllabic hoot with sharp, croaking alarm call.

*adult*

*adult*

The Eagle Owl is a truly impressive bird when seen standing on a cliff ledge or when flying down prey in a fast glide.

*adult*

53–66cm **LENGTH**
142–166cm **WINGSPAN**

# SNOWY OWL
## *BUBO SCANDIACA*

The Snowy Owl requires huge expanses of tundra when breeding. In flight it is an active hunter and is surprisingly swift in its chase and falcon-like capture of prey. It sometimes moves south in winter if prey is in short supply.

*adult female*

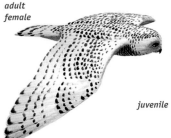

*juvenile*

**IDENTIFICATION** Mainly white owl with relatively small, round head and long, rounded wings. Golden-yellow eyes sunk in dusky pits. Bill black. Legs and feet densely feathered, white with black claws. Adult male almost entirely creamy white. Occasional small, dark-brown spots on underwing coverts hardly noticeable. Adult female ground colour is white but heavily spotted and chevronned dark brown over whole of upperparts and most of underbody. Pure white face and centre of breast stand out. Juvenile has dark-grey head and body; rest of plumage like adult female, but more strongly barred. **HABITAT** Arctic tundra, from sea level into uplands. **VOICE** Loud, booming double hoot and barking alarm; silent outside breeding season.

*Very large, essentially white owl, exceeded in size among European owls only by Eagle Owl.*

*adult male*

# LITTLE OWL
## *ATHENE NOCTUA*

**LENGTH** 21–23cm
**WINGSPAN** 54–58cm

The Little Owl is widely distributed across Europe, and is a bird of open country. It likes an abundance of perches from which it can hunt prey and watch for danger.

*adult*

*An upright posture is adopted when the bird is alarmed.*

*adult*

*adult*

*adult*

**IDENTIFICATION** Small, dark owl with longish legs. Adult upperparts dark brown-grey, spotted and flecked with white. Crown and nape closely spotted white. Back more uniform dark brown with whitish fringes to lower neck feathers, scapulars and coverts, creating pale lines. Tail has four pale-brown bars. Facial disc buff-grey, more rectangular than round, with prominent pale eyebrows and yellow eyes. Underparts paler buff-grey with gorget of heavy streaks on upper breast, finely streaked on belly and flanks. Bill grey-brown. Legs feathered buff-white; feet brown. Juvenile similar to adult but paler; plumage is more uniform with less streaking and spotting. **HABITAT** Lowland agricultural habitats in west; more arid rocky gorges and plains in east. **VOICE** Hollow, rising whistle, sometimes repeated in crescendo; chattering warning call.

19–20cm **LENGTH**
53–63cm **WINGSPAN**

# SCOPS OWL
## *OTUS SCOPS*

The Scops Owl is a nocturnal, arboreal species, which requires secluded perches for daytime roosting and plenty of open varied habitats in which to find prey.

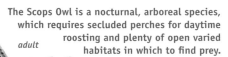

*adult*

*With its excellent camouflage and habit of roosting during the day in mature trees and bushes, the Scops Owl is very hard to see.*

**IDENTIFICATION** Small, large-headed owl with slender body and fairly long wings. Adult seen with either brown-grey or rufous upperparts; both have blackish streaks, bars and delicate pattern of vermiculations. Scapulars show as prominent line of black-tipped white feathers. Facial disc with incomplete blackish-brown border, mainly on sides. Shape accentuated by prominent streaked ear tufts, which are often flattened sideways. Paler brown to buffish-white underparts with dark-brown streaks and vermiculations. Outer flight feathers broadly barred buff. Underwing paler buff. Bill blue-black. Eye yellow. Legs feathered, buff; feet grey. Juvenile inseparable from adult. **HABITAT** Warm, dry lowlands in open mixed woodland; parks with old hollow trees. **VOICE** Repeated, short, human-like whistle, reminiscent of slow time signal pips.

*adult*

*adult*

233

# PYGMY OWL
*GLAUCIDIUM PASSERINUM*

**LENGTH** 16–17cm
**WINGSPAN** 34–35cm

The Pygmy Owl's fast, undulating, almost urgent flight is reminiscent of a small woodpecker. When perching, it often waves its tail up and down or sits with it cocked like a flycatcher.

**IDENTIFICATION** Tiny, small-headed owl, roughly size of Hawfinch. No real facial disc but curved rows of brown and buff spotting and white eyebrows and white sides to chin neatly frame face. Adult has dark-brown upperparts, spotted and barred with whitish-buff. Shows two whitish curves back to back on nape, and buff-spotted brown crown. Throat and sides of breast brown, barred black. Rest of underparts white, streaked blackish, extending up centre of breast. Relatively long narrow tail, brown with white barring. White bars on brown flight feathers. Eyes yellow. Legs and toes feathered, white. Juvenile similar to adult but duskier, with less pale spotting and barring. **HABITAT** Taiga and montane coniferous forest. **VOICE** Monotonous, fluty, repeated whistle; various hissing notes.

*adult*

The combination of stern expression, white barred tail and absence of pale, spotted scapulars allows separation from Tengmalm's Owl.

*Adult with Blue Tit prey.*

24–26cm **LENGTH**
55–62cm **WINGSPAN**

# TENGMALM'S OWL
## *AEGOLIUS FUNEREUS*

In the north, Tengmalm's Owl prefers spruce and birch forests where these border open moorlands, but in central Europe montane mixed forests are preferred; here it uses old Black Woodpecker nesting holes.

**IDENTIFICATION** Smallish, dark owl with large, square head and longish tail. Adult upperparts dark brown with copious white spotting on crown, and fewer, larger spots on nape and back. Broad white edges to scapulars show as pale braces. Wing coverts and flight feathers dark brown, finely spotted with white. Tail dark brown with rows of tiny white spots. Squarish grey facial disc outlined in black. Yellow eyes set in dark pits. Underparts pale greyish-white, spotted with light brown. Bill yellowish-grey. Legs and feet feathered, white. Part-fledged juvenile dark chocolate brown with white eyebrows and moustache; white spotting on wings. Similar to adult in other respects. **HABITAT** Taiga lowlands; montane coniferous forests with rides and clearings. **VOICE** Soft, far-carrying, repeated short whistles; short, smacking yelp.

*Range of Tengmalm's Owl overlaps with smaller Pygmy Owl, with which it can be confused.*

*adult*

*adult*

# HAWK OWL
*SURNIA ULULA*

**LENGTH** 36–39cm
**WINGSPAN** 75–80cm

Russia contains huge areas of suitable habitat for Hawk Owls, but they also breed in Scandinavia, where they move into more southerly habitats in periodic population irruptions. The Hawk Owl could easily be mistaken for a Sparrowhawk in flight.

*adult*

**IDENTIFICATION** Adult has strongly patterned blackish and pale-grey plumage. Crown, nape and back blackish-brown, spotted white. Large whitish shoulder patch. Closed wing dark brown with few white spots. Flight feathers dark with whitish bars. Rump pale, barred blackish. Long, dark-brown tail narrowly barred pale grey. Face whitish with broad, blackish, curved borders to facial disc. Breast and belly very pale grey, narrowly barred blackish. Wings short and pointed. Eyes striking pale yellow. Bill yellow-horn. Legs and feet feathered white. Juvenile paler and fluffier than adult, with more barring; other characteristics similar to adult. **HABITAT** Arboreal; pine and birch forest in tundra with clearings. **VOICE** Trilling, hooting notes and screeching alarm call.

*adult*

*The Hawk Owl has a fierce expression that reflects its voracity as a predator of small mammals and birds; it is also an aggressive defender of its nest, repeatedly attacking intruders.*

# RED-NECKED NIGHTJAR
*CAPRIMULGUS RUFICOLLIS*

**LENGTH** 30–32cm
**WINGSPAN** 65–68cm

The Red-necked Nightjar prefers open habitats with bare patches of dry, sandy soil and scattered trees to use as song-posts. The Stone Pine woods of the Coto Doñana in Spain are a typical habitat.

**IDENTIFICATION** Adult has mostly rufous-brown plumage with complex variegated markings. Greyish crown, brown back, rump and tail variously streaked black. Pale-buff tips to scapulars and coverts create pale lines across closed wing. Warm rufous-pink collar and throat relieved by narrow, white moustache and broad, white spots to side of chin. Underparts pale rufous-brown with narrow, black bars and greyish band across breast. In flight, both male and female show white wing spots and long white patches on outertail feathers. Juvenile resembles dull adult with more buff plumage. **HABITAT** Stone Pine woods; plantations with open, sandy ground. **VOICE** Repetitive, low-pitched, double knocking 'cut-oc, cut-oc'.

*Adult female with chick.*

*Larger than Nightjar, with longer wings and tail and large head.*

*male*

26–28cm **LENGTH**
57–64cm **WINGSPAN**

# NIGHTJAR
*CAPRIMULGUS EUROPAEUS*

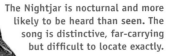

The Nightjar is nocturnal and more likely to be heard than seen. The song is distinctive, far-carrying but difficult to locate exactly.

*adult male*

*The Nightjar is a summer visitor to Europe; it is thought the entire population overwinters in sub-Saharan Africa.*

**IDENTIFICATION** Shape similar to small falcon or Cuckoo. Adult plumage dark grey and rufous-brown with heavy black barring and delicate pattern of vermiculations. Head, nape, back and rump grey, lightly streaked with black. Long, grey tail, barred black outer feathers tipped white in male, buff in female. Scapulars and coverts edged silvery white, showing as pale lines. In flight, rufous-brown flight feathers heavily barred black, showing white patch near wingtip in male, buff patch in female. Underparts brown, finely barred black, becoming rufous towards undertail. White moustache. Bill very short; black with wide gape. Juvenile resembles pale adult female, but lacks wing and tail spots. **HABITAT** Dry, open conifer woods, scrub, sandy heaths and semi-deserts. **VOICE** Monotonous whirring 'churr'; disyllabic 'kwa-eek' note.

*male*

*female*

237

# SWIFT
*APUS APUS*

**LENGTH** 16–17cm
**WINGSPAN** 42–48cm

The Swift is entirely aerial except for nesting. Abundant insect food is available only in the short summer months, so Swifts migrate to Africa for winter; they arrive in Europe in early May and are gone by late August.

**IDENTIFICATION** Medium-sized, all-brown swift, with small white throat patch. Very similar in size and shape to Pallid Swift, but wings slightly narrower and tail more noticeably forked. Greyish forehead visible at extremely close range. In bright sunlight pale upper surface to flight feathers. Powerful rapid flight with winnowing wings. Juvenile bird essentially indistinguishable from adult, showing long, crescent-shaped wings, short, forked tail and all-dark plumage. **HABITAT** Aerial; usually in and around towns and villages. **VOICE** Shrill screaming whistle in breeding season.

**Adults:** *The Swift's familiar crescent shape is ideal for rapid sustained flight.*

adult

*Parties make screaming calls as they fly together.*

juvenile

16–17cm **LENGTH**
42–46cm **WINGSPAN**

# PALLID SWIFT
### *APUS PALLIDUS*

*Note blunter, broader wings than Swift, which do not seem to beat as quickly.*

The warm, sunny, coastal Mediterranean towns are where Pallid Swifts look most at home. Bright sunlight and a dark background aid identification, allowing the pale sandy colour to be seen well.

*adult*

**IDENTIFICATION** Similar in size to Swift but subtle differences in shape and colouring are important for identification. A slightly bulkier bird than the Swift overall, particularly noticeable in broader wings and shorter, more rounded tail forks. Adult and juvenile essentially indistinguishable. Plumage brown with pale margins to feathers creating sandy effect in good light. Forehead greyish-white. Slightly darker brown saddle on back contrasts with paler rump and upper surface to wings. Prominent white throat patch. Underbody pale sandy brown caused by pale margins to most feathers. **HABITAT** Mediterranean zone, around towns, villages and coasts. **VOICE** Screaming whistle in breeding season, deeper than swift.

*adult*

20–22cm **LENGTH**
34–60cm **WINGSPAN**

# ALPINE SWIFT
### *APUS MELBA*

*adult*

The Alpine Swift is common and well distributed across all of southern Europe. It is an impressive bird to watch, with its powerful, fast flight, easy glides and chattering call.

**IDENTIFICATION**

*adult*

Much larger than its European relatives, with bulky body and long, broad, crescent-shaped wings. Upperparts warm sandy brown, appearing paler when pale margins to fresh feathers are evident. Black patch in front of eye noticeable at close range. Chin and throat white. Broad, sandy-brown breast band. Lower breast, belly and flanks are white. Underwing brown with darker brown flight feathers showing above and below wing. White chin hard to see but large white belly patch obvious. Juvenile shows more prominent white tips to brown feathers than adult. **HABITAT** Aerial over southern European mountains, coasts and open country. **VOICE** Loud, shrill, chattering call during breeding season.

# WHITE-RUMPED SWIFT
*APUS CAFFER*

**LENGTH** 14cm
**WINGSPAN** 34–36cm

The White-rumped Swift has only recently been found in Europe, where it is found in the southern tip of Spain. This population is remarkable; it lays its eggs in the nests of the Red-rumped Swallow.

**IDENTIFICATION** Smallish, slim-bodied swift with long, deeply forked tail and dark plumage. Adult has mainly blue-black colour to body and wings, with noticeable narrow, bright white band across upper rump. Greyish crown and line over eye, small whitish chin and silvery sheen to underwing flight feathers, visible at close range. Long, narrow wings give distinctive silhouette. Juvenile shows more whitish tips to body feathers than adult and less blue-black sheen to dull, dark plumage. **HABITAT** Rocky habitats; in vicinity of coastal towns in southern Spain. **VOICE** Whistle beginning as chatter, merging into trill.

*adult*

*Very fluttery flight, lacking power of larger relatives.*

The forked tail helps distinguish this species from Little Swift. The largely black underparts help separate it from House Martin.

# LITTLE SWIFT
*APUS AFFINIS*

**LENGTH** 12cm
**WINGSPAN** 34–35cm

The Little Swift is sometimes suspected of breeding in southern Spain and is observed on a scarce but regular basis feeding over coastal marshes in the southern Iberian peninsula. Elsewhere in Europe, it is a rare vagrant.

**IDENTIFICATION** Small compact swift. Recalls House Martin in plumage details but easily recognised as a swift species by silhouette. Sexes similar. Adult has dark sooty-brown plumage except for square, white rump and white throat; forehead greyish. Tail relatively short and square-ended. Juvenile similar to adult but plumage not as dark. **HABITAT** Nests in buildings and on cliffs; otherwise entirely aerial. **VOICE** High-pitched screaming call uttered in flight.

*adult*

*adult*

16–17cm **LENGTH**
24–26cm **WINGSPAN**

# KINGFISHER
### *ALCEDO ATTHIS*

Kingfishers need small, sheltered bodies of
clear water for fishing, where the birds can
see fish from a suitable perch before
plunge-diving for capture.

**IDENTIFICATION** Small kingfisher with long
bill and relatively large head. Adult has crown,
nape, moustache and all upperparts bright blue,
tone varying with light and viewing angle. Pale
sheen on back. Crown and wing coverts have
pale blue spotting. Scapulars, flight feathers
and tip of tail darker blackish-blue. Face,
underbody and underwing coverts rich
orange-chestnut, paler on throat and
centre of belly. White spots in front
of eye, on side of neck and under chin.
Long dagger-shaped bill, all black in male,
with reddish base in female. Legs and feet
coral red. Juvenile lacks brilliance of adult,
and has greener upperparts and bluish-grey
breast. Legs dull orange. **HABITAT** Streams,
rivers and lakes with surrounding vegetation.
**VOICE** Song comprises Starling-like bubbling
whistles; also plaintive chattering whistle calls.

*adult female*

The **male** presents the
**female** with a fish during
the courtship display.

If there is no suitable perch, the
Kingfisher will hover for several
seconds with rapid wingbeats
before plunging after prey.

# WHITE-BREASTED KINGFISHER

*HALCYON SMYRNENSIS*

White-breasted Kingfishers favour perches that are 1–3m above water. Long periods are spent simply watching for fishing opportunities, but the birds will also take terrestrial insects.

**IDENTIFICATION** A beautifully marked, distinctive kingfisher. Sexes similar. Adult has striking white throat and chest, and chestnut head, neck, breast and underparts. Back, tail and wings iridescent blue except for black tips to primaries and black and chestnut wing coverts. Bill proportionately massive and bright red; legs and feet bright red. Juvenile similar to adult but duller. **HABITAT** Wetlands of all types; also occasionally hunts over dry land. **VOICE** Utters loud rattling calls and shrill whistles.

*adult*

BELOW: *Adult's bright colouring is distinctive.*

25–26cm **LENGTH**
45–46cm **WINGSPAN**

# PIED KINGFISHER
### *CERYLE RUDIS*

The Pied Kingfisher is a widespread tropical species; in Europe, it is restricted to the southern coasts of Turkey. It is essentially resident throughout its range, but it is a rare, regular winter visitor to Cyprus.

**IDENTIFICATION** Distinctive and well-marked kingfisher. Adult male has striking black and white marbled upperparts. Underparts essentially white except for two black breast bands. Adult female similar to adult male but has one, not two, black breast bands. Juvenile similar to adult female but has chest band grey not black. All birds have black bill and feet. **HABITAT** Always found close to water; generally fresh water but sometimes also coastal. **VOICE** Loud, high-pitched screaming call.

*adult male*

*adult female*

# HOOPOE
## *UPUPA EPOPS*

**LENGTH** 26–28cm
**WINGSPAN** 42–46cm

The Hoopoe spends a lot of time on the ground catching insects, walking with a rather short, pigeon-like gait.

*adult*

*Disproportionately large, rounded wings show well in flight; Hoopoe has erratic, bounding flight action, reminiscent of a giant butterfly.*

*adult*

*When disturbed, Hoopoe freezes and will not rise until approached very closely.*

*In flight, looks strikingly black and white; on the ground, however, it can be surprisingly difficult to spot, especially on broken terrain.*

*adult*

**IDENTIFICATION** Adult has head, neck, back and underbody pale brownish-pink, with warmer pinkish shade on breast. Long erectile crest of pink feathers, tipped with white and black. White crescent on rump. At rest, transverse black and creamy-white barring crosses wings and shoulders, the foremost bar being pale orange. Tail black with wavy white band near base. Undertail coverts whitish. In flight, primaries are black with single white crescent near tips. Long, slender, decurved bill, black with pinkish base. Legs and feet black. Juvenile duller than adult, with dingy cream barring and shorter bill. **HABITAT** Warm, dry, open, varied landscapes with some trees and bare ground. **VOICE** Song low, far-carrying mellow 'oo-oo-oo'; cawing contact calls.

30–32cm **LENGTH**
66–73cm **WINGSPAN**

# ROLLER
### *CORACIAS GARRULUS*

The Roller is a spectacular bird of warm, dry southern and central European lowland habitats. It uses the old nest holes of other species to nest in, and perches in trees to locate and drop down onto prey.

**IDENTIFICATION**

*adult*

Large crow-like bird, with very brightly coloured plumage. In flight, upperwing shows two-tone blue coverts and blackish flight feathers. Underwing shows pale blue coverts and blue black-tipped flight feathers. Adult has head, neck and underbody pale green-blue. Forehead and chin whitish, with narrow black eye-mask. Back chestnut, rump purple-blue. Shoulder iridescent cobalt blue with pale green-blue coverts and blue-black flight feathers. Tail blue-black with pale greenish outer webs and dark tips to feathers. Strong, decurved and slightly hook-tipped black bill. Legs and feet black. Juvenile has similar pattern to adult, but all colours duller.
**HABITAT** Warm continental lowlands, old open forest, heaths and grasslands. **VOICE** Rasping, accelerating rattle; harsh, short contact call.

*adult*

The Roller selects mainly large insects such as mole crickets, characteristic of dry, warm lowlands, but will also steal nestling birds and catch small reptiles.

*adult*

In the breeding season the male performs an acrobatic mating dance, where he dives rapidly towards the ground with half-rolls, like a Lapwing.

# BLUE-CHEEKED BEE-EATER

*MEROPS SUPERCILIOSUS*

| LENGTH | 28-30cm |
| WINGSPAN | 46-48cm |

This species breeds in northwest Africa and locally from the Middle East to northwest India with small numbers in Turkey. It is a very rare vagrant to Europe, mainly in late spring.

**IDENTIFICATION** Attractive bee-eater. Sexes similar. Adult mainly green with bluish rump and lower back, and rusty-red underwing. Head markings distinctive. Has black eyestripe and white forehead grading to sky blue supercilium. Cheeks sky blue and throat yellow, grading to orange-red. Tail streamers extremely long, at least twice length of those of European Bee-eater. Juvenile similar to adult but plumage duller and tail streamers much shorter.
**HABITAT** Open, arid terrain, usually close to water.
**VOICE** Bubbling, ringing disyllabic 'prr-ipp'.

*adult*

*adult*

*adult*

*adult*

*adult*

27–29cm **LENGTH**
44–49cm **WINGSPAN**

# BEE-EATER
*MEROPS APIASTER*

The Bee-eater breeds in warm, sunny open landscapes in the drier parts of Europe. Sandy or clay banks are required for colonial nesting tunnels.

*adult*

**IDENTIFICATION** Slim, long-winged bird with distinctive flight silhouette and multicoloured plumage. Adult has chestnut crown, nape and back shading to yellowish-brown on scapulars and rump. Uppertail dark shiny green, duller below with central two feathers darker and elongated. Wing coverts chestnut, surrounded with bluish-green. Flight feathers shiny blue, dark-tipped. Whitish forehead and narrow pale blue supercilium. Black eye-mask and black border to bright yellow throat. Underparts pale turquoise-blue. Underwing orange with darker tipped flight feathers. Long, slim, black decurved bill. Eyes reddish. Legs and feet brownish-black. Juvenile resembles dull adult but greener on back and wings. **HABITAT** Warm open habitats with mixed agriculture; clumps of trees, often near rivers. **VOICE** Liquid bubbling 'pruupp'.

*The Bee-eater prefers to be in close proximity to water, which ensures an abundant supply of large insects such as dragonflies; it goes after them with a typical slow glide.*

*adult*

*Hot, sheltered valleys with clumps of trees are the Bee-eater's favoured habitat, but it will inhabit treeless grassy plains if there are places to use as perches.*

*adult*

# RING-NECKED PARAKEET

*PSITTACULA KRAMERI*

**LENGTH** 27–43cm
**WINGSPAN** 42–48cm

The Ring-necked Parakeet is an established alien species (its natural range is Asia and Africa). The suburban western fringes of London are a stronghold.

ABOVE: *male*

BELOW: *female*

*With its neck stretched, the pink elements of this **male's** neck 'ring' are obvious; the species is sometimes called Rose-ringed Parakeet.*

**IDENTIFICATION** Colourful and distinctive bird with a long-tailed outline in flight. Sexes similar. Adult male has mainly green plumage but dark flight feathers are noticeable on the wing. Has red bill and eyering, and pinkish neck ring, dark-bordered towards lower margin. Adult female is similar but lacks markings on neck or throat. **HABITAT** Open woodland, suburbs and parks. **VOICE** Announces its presence (including in flight) with loud, squawking calls.

*Several other populations of this and other species of parrot and parakeet have become established in the wild across Europe.*

16–17cm **LENGTH**
25–27cm **WINGSPAN**

# WRYNECK
### *JYNX TORQUILLA*

The Wryneck needs open, warm, sunny habitats, often with bare sandy ground where it can easily find ants. It nests in trees using the old site of another species.

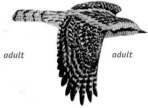

*adult*          *adult*

*The nest hole is usually situated in a tree branch rather than on the main trunk.*

**IDENTIFICATION** At a distance, adult appears mottled grey and brown; at close range very finely marked. Grey crown, sides to mantle and back bordered by black scapular stripe, which connects on side of neck with elongated black eyestripe. Wings brown with heavy dark barring and vermiculation. Long, grey full tail has transverse black bars. Throat and upper breast yellowish with short black bars. Lower breast and belly creamy white with dark spots. Bill, legs and feet pale brown. Juvenile slightly paler than adult, with less barring. **HABITAT** Lowland woodland fringes, orchards, parks and large gardens. **VOICE** High-pitched, ringing 'pee-pee-pee', like small falcon.

*adult*

*Similar in size to Nightingale but longer and slimmer, with plumage recalling Nightjar.*

# GREEN WOODPECKER

*PICUS VIRIDIS*

**LENGTH** 31–33cm
**WINGSPAN** 40–42cm

Although it is traditionally a forest species, the Green Woodpecker has adapted to habitat loss and is now also found in more open terrain with trees. Its preferred food is ants and it often feeds on the ground.

**IDENTIFICATION** A large, bulky woodpecker. Adult male has red crown extending on to nape; he has black face patch with red moustachial stripe set in black. Upperparts bright green with bright yellow rump and brown-black primaries, barred cream. Tail dark greenish-grey with faint cream spotting. Rear of face, sides of neck and underparts pale, clear yellow except for darker barring on flanks. Bill grey with yellowish lower mandible. Legs and feet grey. Adult female similar to male but has smaller black face patch and lacks red moustache. Juvenile plumage pattern similar to adult but colours dulled by white spotting and barring on upperparts; dark bars on underparts.

**HABITAT** Open, broad-leaved, lowland forest with clearings; parks, gardens and heaths.

**VOICE** Ringing laugh known as a yaffle; alarm call is a short 'kyack'.

*juvenile*

*adult female*

*adult male*

*adult male*

Signs of Green Woodpecker attacks can often be seen on forest anthills.

Red centre of the male's moustachial streak hard to see in poor light.

25–26cm **LENGTH**
38–40cm **WINGSPAN**

# GREY-HEADED WOODPECKER
### *PICUS CANUS*

The Grey-headed Woodpecker is found across the middle latitudes of Europe wherever woodland is plentiful. It reaches higher altitudes in the mountains than its close relative, the Green Woodpecker.

**IDENTIFICATION** Adult male has grey head marked only with red forecrown and narrow black moustache above whitish throat. Back, scapulars and wing coverts pale but intense green. Rump yellow. Breast and underbody pale grey. Tail greenish. Folded flight feathers brownish-black, barred with white. In flight, upperwing shows an even green colour, except for dark brown-grey primaries conspicuously barred white. Underwing dark grey, barred white. Bill dark grey, yellowish towards base. Female has no red on crown and is similar to but duller than male. Legs and feet of both sexes grey. Juvenile browner and scruffier than adult. **HABITAT** Open deciduous woods and riverine carr; montane larch woods in central Europe. **VOICE** Short drumming; repeated fluty whistles slowing and descending in pitch.

*Smaller than Green Woodpecker, with less robust bill.*

*adult male*

*adult female*

*adult male*

251

# BLACK WOODPECKER
### *DRYOCOPUS MARTIUS*

**LENGTH** 45–47cm
**WINGSPAN** 64–68cm

The Black Woodpecker's noisy and showy behaviour makes it easy to track down. When foraging on trees it climbs with very pronounced bounds, using its massive bill to chisel rapidly into wood.

**IDENTIFICATION** Largest European woodpecker, half the size again of the Green Woodpecker. Adult male glossy black with scarlet forehead and long crown. Adult female browner and lacking plumage gloss, with red on crown restricted to small patch above nape. Massive, grey-brown, chisel-like bill with darkish tip. Legs and feet dark grey. Juvenile resembles adult, but with grey chin and red on crown less extensive or sometimes absent. **HABITAT** Mature northern taiga; southern montane deciduous forests with mature tall trees. **VOICE** Loud, far-carrying drumming; loud, melodious, repeated notes – often in flight.

*adult male*

*adult male*

*adult female*

*adult male*

*Large trees are required for nest sites, and the Black Woodpecker's ability to excavate living wood creates many opportunities for other hole-nesting species.*

22–23cm **LENGTH**
34–39cm **WINGSPAN**

# GREAT SPOTTED WOODPECKER

*DENDROCOPOS MAJOR*

The Great Spotted Woodpecker gleans food from cracks and holes in timber and excavates rotten wood to search for beetles. It is largely resident in Europe and is Europe's commonest woodpecker.

**IDENTIFICATION** Blackbird-sized, strong-billed pied woodpecker. Upperparts almost wholly black, relieved by large white scapular patches, lines of white spots across flight feathers and white barring on outertail feathers. Adult male has crimson nape patch, absent in female. Face, including eyering, mainly white with black moustache connecting with black nape and with black extension bar on to sides of breast. Enclosed white patch on sides of neck. Underparts creamy white with pinkish-red vent area and 'trousers'. Bill, legs and feet dark grey. Juvenile has black-bordered red crown, dirty-white underparts and less distinct white barring on wings than adult. **HABITAT** Adaptable to various habitats with trees; prefers open, mature, deciduous woods. **VOICE** Loud drumming; call is a sharp 'tchicc' and short rattle of similar notes.

*adult male*

*female*

*adult male*

*juvenile*

The loud drumming made by the repetitive striking of the Great Spotted Woodpecker's bill on hollow trees can be heard in European woods from early January.

253

# SYRIAN WOODPECKER
## DENDROCOPOS SYRIACUS

**LENGTH** 22–23cm
**WINGSPAN** 34–39cm

The Syrian Woodpecker spread northwestwards into central Europe during the 20th century; it replaces the Great Spotted Woodpecker in the warmer, drier, open lowland habitats of the Balkans.

**IDENTIFICATION** Similar to Great Spotted Woodpecker. Adult has generally black upperparts and white underparts. On face, black moustachial line turns up and back, but stops before joining with back of neck, giving more open-looking white face than Great Spotted Woodpecker's. Male has red nape. Bolder white barring on wings but tail almost completely black – lacking white bars as on outer feathers of Great Spotted Woodpecker; vent paler pink than that species. Bill, legs and feet dark grey. Juvenile similar to adult but has red crown and flank streaks. **HABITAT** Warm, open landscapes with scattered trees. **VOICE** Long, loud drumming; call soft, short 'chjuck'.

*adult female*

*adult male*

*adult male*

The close similarity of this species to the Great Spotted Woodpecker hinders identification in newly colonised areas.

20–22cm **LENGTH**
33–34cm **WINGSPAN**

# MIDDLE SPOTTED WOODPECKER
### *DENDROCOPOS MEDIUS*

**The stronghold of the Middle Spotted Woodpecker is the Hornbeam-oak forests of mainland central Europe. It prefers old stands of forest, with a mosaic of coppiced undershrubs and large standard trees.**

**IDENTIFICATION** Smaller, less cleanly marked version of Great Spotted Woodpecker. Adult male has red crown, which is shorter and duller in female. Remainder of upperparts black with white scapular patches (smaller than on Great Spotted Woodpecker), white barring across flight feathers and white outertail feathers, barred black. Face white with black moustachial border not connecting with black on nape. Downward extension of moustache onto sides of throat gives way to black streaking, extending down flanks. White chin and throat shading to dirty yellowish breast. Belly and vent pinkish. Bill, legs and feet grey. Juvenile similar to adult but duller, with less contrast and fewer flank streaks. **HABITAT** Mixed deciduous woods of Hornbeam and oaks, parkland elms and riverine alder. **VOICE** Drumming rare; far-carrying Jay-like 'quahh'; contact call soft and short.

*adult*

*adult*

*adult*

*The Middle Spotted Woodpecker prefers broad-leaved forests, but where these are not available will occupy old orchards or riverine alder.*

255

# LESSER SPOTTED WOODPECKER

*DENDROCOPOS MINOR*

The Lesser Spotted Woodpecker does not need large trees, as foraging and nesting usually take place in smaller side branches. The bird's behaviour, small size and unobtrusiveness make it difficult to spot.

**IDENTIFICATION** Smallest pied woodpecker, about size of Nuthatch. Adult upperparts predominantly black with heavy white barring across back and wings; black tail with outer feathers barred white. Male has short red crown; white in female. Rear of crown black. Buff-white face above black moustache curving upwards around ear coverts, with downward-extending bar. Underparts buffish-white, streaked black on flanks, with black spots on undertail coverts. No red around vent. Bill, legs and feet grey. Juvenile similar to adult, but with browner and more streaked and spotted underparts. **HABITAT** Open, broad-leaved woodland; riverine alders, parks, orchards and tree-lined avenues. **VOICE** Quiet, high-pitched drumming; soft whistling 'pee-pee-pee', repeated up to 20 times.

*adult male*

*Distinguished from Great Spotted Woodpecker by small size and absence of white patches on wings.*

*adult male*

*adult male*

*This tiny woodpecker avoids dense stands of mature forest, particularly conifers.*

24–26cm **LENGTH**
38–40cm **WINGSPAN**

# WHITE-BACKED WOODPECKER

*DENDROCOPOS LEUCOTOS*

The White-backed Woodpecker is the largest pied woodpecker in Europe. It requires large tracts of relatively undisturbed old-growth forest with a high proportion of dead and decaying timber.

*adult males*

**IDENTIFICATION** Large pied woodpecker. Adult upperparts predominantly black with heavy white barring across wings, and white lower back and rump. Black tail has barred white outer feathers. Male crown red, extending slightly on to nape; female crown black. White face with black moustachial stripe turning up, but not connecting with black nape, and extending down to break into heavy black streaks covering sides of breast and flanks. Chin and throat white. Breast pale-buff, lower belly and vent bright pink-red. Bill, legs and feet grey. Juvenile similar to adult but has black streaks intermixed with red crown, greyish flanks and less red around vent. **HABITAT** Extensive deciduous or mixed forests. **VOICE** Long, loud accelerating drumming. Low, quiet 'kjuck' and other hoarse squeaks.

21–22cm **LENGTH**
32–35cm **WINGSPAN**

# THREE-TOED WOODPECKER

*PICOIDES TRIDACTYLUS*

Although insect larvae are important in its diet, Three-toed Woodpeckers regularly ring spruce trees with holes to extract sap. This species is mainly a sedentary European resident.

*adult males*

**IDENTIFICATION** Adult of northern race has black nape, face and moustache with white rear supercilium and white stripe under ear coverts. Back and rump white with ragged black border. Wings and tail black with narrow, white barring on flight feathers and outertail feathers. Underparts buff-white with grey barring on sides of breast and flanks and black-spotted undertail coverts. Male has yellow crown; this black with white flecks in female. Alpine race darker, with less white on back and heavier markings on underparts. Bill, legs and feet grey. Juveniles of both races greyer on underparts than respective adults. **HABITAT** Northern, dense, moist, coniferous forests; central montane steep-slope spruce forests. **VOICE** Long, rattling drumming; contact call soft, longish 'gjug'.

# SHORE LARK
## *EREMOPHILA ALPESTRIS*

**LENGTH** 14–17cm
**WINGSPAN** 30–35cm

In Sweden and Finland the Shore Lark breeds in the driest stony areas of tundra, where the dominant sparse vegetation is lichen. In the southern mountains it chooses similar habitats on the bare upland plateaux.

**IDENTIFICATION** Adult male has pale yellow face and throat with black forecrown and black mask curving down below eye. Black gorget across upper-breast. Reddish-brown rear crown and nape with tufted black feathers on sides of crown forming 'horns'. Facial markings made more striking by abrasion through winter into spring. Rest of upperparts warm brown, heavily mottled with black. Tail black with brown centre and white outer feathers. Lower breast and belly white with pinkish-brown wash and faint black streaking on flanks. Adult female is duller and more heavily streaked than male. In both sexes bill grey, and legs and feet black. Juvenile recalls adult but is speckled and lacks face pattern. **HABITAT** Sub-Arctic or Arctic lowland tundra or montane plains; on coasts in winter. **VOICE** Subdued twittering song of thin musical notes.

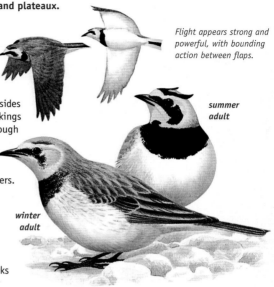

*Flight appears strong and powerful, with bounding action between flaps.*

*summer adult*

*winter adult*

*Smaller and slimmer than Skylark, with crouched appearance when seen on ground.*

*summer adult*

18–19cm **LENGTH**
30–36cm **WINGSPAN**

# SKYLARK
### *ALAUDA ARVENSIS*

Traditionally a species of steppe grassland, the Skylark has adapted to a variety of habitats; it does not require trees as it feeds and nests exclusively on the ground. The familiar song is often delivered in flight.

*adult*

*Short-distance flight is fluttery; over longer distances flight action is strong and undulating.*

**IDENTIFICATION** Smaller than Song Thrush, with a stout bill that distinguishes it from pipits. Sexes similar. Adult upperparts buff, streaked blackish-brown. Crown well streaked, with short crest prominent only when erect. Pale buff supercilium and surround to dull buff cheeks. Closed wing shows blackish buff-edged coverts forming wingbars. Tail blackish-brown with white edges. In flight, wings show clear white trailing edge. Underparts buff-white with heavy streaking across breast and flanks. Bill grey-brown. Legs and feet pale brown. Juvenile recalls adult but has heavily speckled white on upperparts with black drop-shaped markings on breast. **HABITAT** Grasslands in lowlands and uplands; cultivated fields. **VOICE** Loud melodious warbling flight-song; call is a liquid rippling 'chirropp'.

*adult*

*adult*

*One of Europe's commonest larks, the Skylark does not require such warm and dry conditions as many of its relatives.*

# WOODLARK
*LULLULA ARBOREA*

**LENGTH** 15cm
**WINGSPAN** 27–30cm

The Woodlark prefers habitats often found where heathland meets woodland edge. Here the ground is usually well drained, with low vegetation cover for nesting and trees for perching.

**IDENTIFICATION** Smaller and slighter than Skylark, though plumage superficially similar with buff upperparts, heavily streaked blackish. Adult has face well marked with bold white supercilia meeting on nape, and dark brown surround to warm buff cheeks. Hindneck and rump pale whitish-buff. Head has small crest at rear of crown. Closed wing shows black and white bar at wing bend. Tail short and dark, with white spots at tip. Underparts buff-white with necklace of prominent black streaks. Fine bill, dark grey-brown with paler base. Legs and feet pink. Juvenile similar to adult but has less well-marked face and white spotting on upperparts. **HABITAT** Warm, dry, sandy lowlands with heathland vegetation and scattered trees. **VOICE** Flight-song is a beautiful descending series of rich, mellow, fluty whistles.

*adult*

# CRESTED LARK
*GALERIDA CRISTATA*

**LENGTH** 17cm
**WINGSPAN** 29–38cm

The Crested Lark prefers warm, open plains with low vegetation and is most at home in grassland or cultivated areas with some bare ground. It is able to take advantage of human-modified habitats and can be found on urban sites.

**IDENTIFICATION** Bulky, Skylark-sized bird with long bill, spiky crest, deep chest and upright stance. In flight it looks compact with broad wings and short tail. Adult plumage ground-coloured, sandy-buff on upperparts and underparts. Blackish streaking most obvious on crown, including crest and back, and on chest and flanks. Face strikingly marked with cream supercilium and eyering forming spectacle; also neat black moustachial and malar stripes. Dark tail with buff outer feathers. Underwing coverts bright orange-buff. Longish dark grey-brown bill. Legs and feet flesh coloured. Juvenile has shorter crest than adult, darker upperparts with white speckling and whiter underparts. **HABITAT** Open, dry plains with low vegetation; artificial habitats such as waste ground. **VOICE** Song from ground or in flight is loud with fluty whistles and mimicry.

*adult*

17cm **LENGTH**
28–32cm **WINGSPAN**

# THEKLA LARK
### *GALERIDA THEKLAE*

In Europe, Thekla Larks are associated with Mediterranean habitats and there is considerable overlap in Spain with Crested Larks. Thekla Lark prefers complex habitats with open soil, trees and bushes, walls, and cereal fields.

**IDENTIFICATION** Same size as Crested Lark but slighter build, shorter bill and fuller fan-shaped crest are all useful identification features. Adult upperparts greyish-brown; underparts show greyer chest and whiter belly. Distinct blackish streaks on crown, whole of neck and back. Rump rufous. Finely streaked throat. Heavy black spotting on greyish-brown chest extends on to flanks. In flight, underwing appears dull grey-brown. Bill grey-brown with paler base. Legs and feet flesh-coloured. Juvenile similar to adult but has shorter crest and upperparts speckled with white; almost inseparable from juvenile Crested Lark. **HABITAT** Mediterranean mixed habitats of forest edge, scrub and cultivated plains. **VOICE** Loud, fluty song with whistled notes and mimicry, alarm-call is a repeated fluting whistle.

*adult*

---

18–19cm **LENGTH**
34–42cm **WINGSPAN**

# CALANDRA LARK
### *MELANOCORYPHA CALANDRA*

The Calandra Lark's heavy bill, long legs and bulky body are all helpful in identification. The wings are broad and give the bird a powerful and direct flight action; they are very dark underneath, another useful pointer for identification.

**IDENTIFICATION** Larger than Skylark with broader wings, short tail and heavy bill. Adult has crown, nape, back and wings buff-brown with blackish feather centres forming streaks. Warm brown face with creamy supercilium and narrow eyering. Dark brown tail with white outer feathers. Underparts creamy white with blackish patches on sides of breast and warm yellowish wash, spotted black extending down on to flanks. In flight, shows white trailing edge to wings and black underwing. Bill grey-brown with dark tip. Legs and feet pale brown. Juvenile similar to adult but more speckled on upperparts and throat and lacking clear blackish patches on breast. **HABITAT** Grassland steppes of lowland plains and upland plateaux; in cultivated fields. **VOICE** Loud, rich fluty song interspersed with grating notes; shrill buzzing contact call.

*adult*

# SHORT-TOED LARK
## *CALANDRELLA BRACHYDACTYLA*

**LENGTH** 13–14cm
**WINGSPAN** 25–30cm

The Short-toed Lark feeds unobtrusively on the ground, often making use of ruts and vegetation to obscure its presence. Compared to Lesser Short-toed note the long tertials that cover the wing point at rest and a cleaner-looking breast.

**IDENTIFICATION** Smaller and paler than Skylark, with compact body, neat finch-like bill and no crest. Adult upperparts sandy-buff, lightly streaked dull brown. Crown warm rufous-brown. Off-white supercilium contrasts with brown cheeks. Closed wing shows line of blackish-centred coverts with pale buff margins. Pale buff rump contrasts with blackish tail with white edges. Underparts clear white with faint sandy wash across breast and darker brown patches on breast sides. Bill grey-brown with yellow base. Legs and feet brown. Juvenile similar to adult but more obviously speckled on

upperparts and has gorget of dark streaks across upper breast. **HABITAT** Dry, open steppes on plains and undulating landscapes; often in fields in winter. **VOICE** Song from ground or in flight is shrill, jingling and melodious with swallow-like twittering.

*adult*

*adult*

13–14cm **LENGTH**
24–32cm **WINGSPAN**

# LESSER SHORT-TOED LARK
### *CALANDRELLA RUFESCENS*

The Lesser Short-toed Lark favours more open, sandy ground than the Short-toed Lark. Compared to that species note Lesser Short-toed's prominent wing point, streaked breast and pale forehead.

**IDENTIFICATION** More heavily streaked upperparts and chest than Short-toed, with long wing point and tiny bill. Adult upperparts rufous-brown with blackish feather centres, particularly on crown and mantle. Pale cream supercilia frame brown face and meet across pale forehead. Underparts buffish with brown wash on chest, and gorget of black streaks extending to flanks. Wings brown with pale feather edgings; three primaries project at rest. Bill pale grey-brown with darker tip. Legs and feet yellowish. Juvenile similar to adult but more speckled. **HABITAT** Continental steppes and semi-deserts, especially sandy ground with low shrubs. **VOICE** Long, continuous and melodious song in flight; quite loud, rippling alarm call.

*adult*

18cm **LENGTH**
26–31cm **WINGSPAN**

# DUPONT'S LARK
### *CHERSOPHILUS DUPONTI*

Dupont's Lark is remarkably reluctant to fly, preferring instead to run. Clumps of vegetation are used for nesting and concealment and it is hard to see. Its beautiful, mournful flight song is usually heard just before dawn.

**IDENTIFICATION** Smaller than Skylark with long bill and no crest. Adult upperparts brown, heavily streaked with blackish-brown. Face well marked with long buff-white supercilium and eye ring forming spectacle; pale grey half-collar surrounds brown cheeks. Mantle, scapular and wing feathers are edged buff, giving scaly effect. Underparts white with heavy black spotting across chest and streaking down flanks. Long, decurved grey-brown bill. Long, brownish-white legs. Juvenile similar to adult but upperparts less streaked; pale feather edges create scaly look. **HABITAT** Dry, open, Mediterranean steppes with sparse vegetation; cereal fields in winter. **VOICE** Song is beautiful mixture of fluty notes and finch-like twittering.

*adult*

263

# SWALLOW
## *HIRUNDO RUSTICA*

**LENGTH** 17–19cm
**WINGSPAN** 32–35cm

The Swallow is found throughout nearly the whole of Europe, and is absent only from the Arctic, deserts and the highest mountains. It hawks for insects over pastures, along hedges, woodland edge and over water.

ABOVE AND RIGHT: *adult male*

*Long tail streamers and steady, gliding flight make this species easy to identify.*

**IDENTIFICATION** Classic swallow shape with small bill and long, forked tail streamers. Adult upperparts and breast band shiny blue-black. Forehead, chin and most of throat above breast band rich rufous-red. Underparts, including underwing coverts and long undertail coverts, buff-white, with black undersurfaces of flight feathers and black underside to tail. When spread, tail shows white spots towards the tips of all but outermost feathers, which are elongated into streamers. Female has shorter streamers than male. Bill and feet black. Juvenile similar to adult but has less shiny plumage, paler head, mottled breast band and shorter forked tail. **HABITAT** Aerial above pasture, open water, villages and farms. **VOICE** Song is a pleasant warble with some rattling notes; alarm call is a loud, short 'chit'.

*male*

16–17cm **LENGTH**
32–34cm **WINGSPAN**

# RED-RUMPED
# SWALLOW

*HIRUNDO DAURICA*

The Red-rumped Swallow is a very attractive member of the swallow family, but care is required to identify it when seen from a distance. It favours rocky upland habitats where it can hawk for insects.

**IDENTIFICATION** Sexes similar. Adult has crown, mantle, scapulars and upperwing coverts blue-black, not as shiny as Swallow. Wings and tail brown-black, including undertail coverts, which gives effect of whole tail having been dipped in black paint. Broad, pale chestnut band across nape, and chestnut lower back shading to buff rump. Forehead and cheeks speckled rufous-buff. Underparts buff, faintly streaked black. Underwing coverts buff, contrasting with blackish flight feathers. Bill black. Legs and feet brown-black. Juvenile duller than adult, with much shorter tail streamers. **HABITAT** Aerial over meadows and pasture, open water and villages; in warm latitudes. **VOICE** Quiet, twittering, chattering song; short, descending, whistling alarm note.

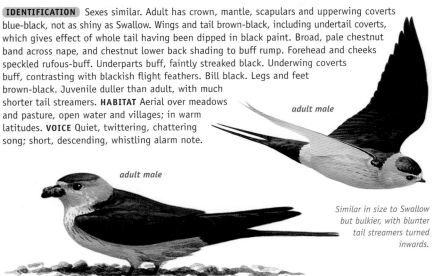

*adult male*

*adult male*

Similar in size to Swallow but bulkier, with blunter tail streamers turned inwards.

Note rich buff band on nape and mostly rufous face with neat blue-black cap.

*adult male*

265

# CRAG MARTIN
*PTYONOPROGNE RUPESTRIS*

**LENGTH** 14cm
**WINGSPAN** 32–34cm

The Crag Martin prefers sheltered valleys, warmed by the southern summer sun. It has a graceful, slow flight, repeatedly quartering along the same sheltered crag or cliff.

*adult*

**IDENTIFICATION** Heavier and more bulky than Sand Martin, with broad wings, almost unforked tail and uniform dusky plumage. Adult upperparts dusky brown-grey. Underparts dark buff with smoky tone. Underwing coverts blackish. At close range buff throat is speckled with dark brown. Lateral tail coverts show pale chevrons. In flight white spots are visible towards tips of tail feathers. Bill black. Legs and feet dark brown. Juvenile similar to adult but has warmer plumage tones, with paler throat. **HABITAT** Mountainous regions and river valleys and gorges with exposed rock. **VOICE** Quiet, but persistent, guttural twittering song. Short, single-note contact call.

*adult*

# SAND MARTIN
*RIPARIA RIPARIA*

**LENGTH** 12cm
**WINGSPAN** 27–29cm

The Sand Martin is a common bird around bodies of water, particularly if there are nearby sandy banks for its colonial nest tunnels. Sand Martins are wholly migratory, the European population wintering in Africa south of the Sahara.

**IDENTIFICATION** Smallest hirundine in Europe, with short, slightly forked tail. Adult has whole of upperparts, including flight and tail feathers, dark greyish-brown, often with sandy tone. Brown extends down onto cheeks and broad band across breast, with light brown smudges on flanks. Rest of underparts white. Underwing dusky brown. Throat often speckled or shaded with brown. Black bill, legs and feet. Juvenile similar to adult but upperparts less uniform with pale fringes to feathers. **HABITAT** Aerial, in vicinity of sandy banks and near to water. **VOICE** Harsh, twittering, quiet song; harsh, grating, single-syllable contact call.

LEFT: *adult*; BELOW: *adult*

12.5cm **LENGTH**
26–29cm **WINGSPAN**

# HOUSE MARTIN
### *DELICHON URBICUM*

The House Martin's association with human habitats has made its range extensive throughout Europe. It nests in loose colonies and, once a building is chosen, many nests are built on the eaves and walls sheltered by the roof.

*adult*

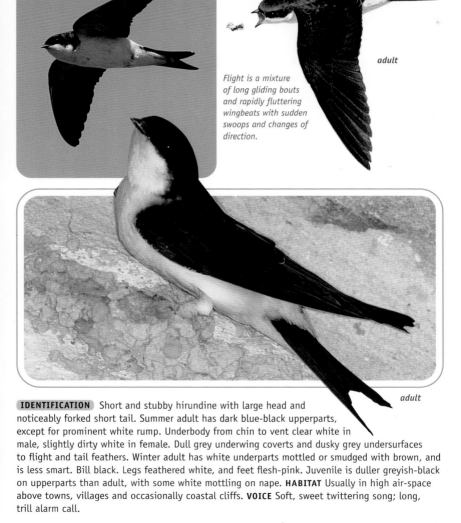

*adult*

*Flight is a mixture of long gliding bouts and rapidly fluttering wingbeats with sudden swoops and changes of direction.*

*adult*

*adult*

**IDENTIFICATION** Short and stubby hirundine with large head and noticeably forked short tail. Summer adult has dark blue-black upperparts, except for prominent white rump. Underbody from chin to vent clear white in male, slightly dirty white in female. Dull grey underwing coverts and dusky grey undersurfaces to flight and tail feathers. Winter adult has white underparts mottled or smudged with brown, and is less smart. Bill black. Legs feathered white, and feet flesh-pink. Juvenile is duller greyish-black on upperparts than adult, with some white mottling on nape. **HABITAT** Usually in high air-space above towns, villages and occasionally coastal cliffs. **VOICE** Soft, sweet twittering song; long, trill alarm call.

# TREE PIPIT
*ANTHUS TRIVIALIS*

**LENGTH** 15cm
**WINGSPAN** 25–27cm

The Tree Pipit feeds and nests on the ground but requires trees for look-outs and song-posts. It also likes parkland and heathland in the early stages of woodland colonisation and will use young conifer plantations.

*Displaying **adult**.*

**IDENTIFICATION** Smart pipit with clear markings. Adult head, nape, back and wings warm buff-brown with black streaks on back. Face well marked with yellowish supercilium and eyering, and brown eyestripe. Cream margins and tips to blackish-brown wing feathers give closed wing a striking pattern. Rump unstreaked. Tail dark brown with white edges. Chin and throat buffish-white, warmer yellowish on breast and flanks with bold brown-black spotting. Belly and undertail coverts buff-white. Bill dark grey-brown with pale flesh-coloured base. Legs and feet flesh-pink. The hind claw (*see* photo above right) is distinctly shorter than Meadow and other ground-dwelling pipits. Juvenile very similar to adult, with buffer ground colour and more streaking. **HABITAT** Mosaic of open grassland or heath and woodland edge or forestry plantations. **VOICE** Loud, rich song starting with rattle, ending in descending piping notes; loud 'tseeep' call.

TOP AND ABOVE: ***adult***

14.5cm **LENGTH**
22–25cm **WINGSPAN**

# MEADOW PIPIT
### *ANTHUS PRATENSIS*

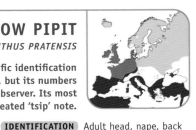

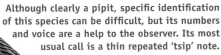

Although clearly a pipit, specific identification of this species can be difficult, but its numbers and voice are a help to the observer. Its most usual call is a thin repeated 'tsip' note.

*adult*

**IDENTIFICATION** Adult head, nape, back and wings have variable ground colour of greenish-olive to dark buff-brown, with blackish streaks prominent on crown and back. Mantle sometimes shows pair of indistinct buffish braces. Face shows thin, off-white supercilium. Rump brighter, usually olive-brown, faintly streaked. Underparts greyish-white to olive with chest band of narrow blackish spots and streaks extending on to flanks. Bill grey-brown. Legs pinkish-buff. Juvenile has heavier streaking on upperparts than adult, and cleaner, brighter, pale margins to wing feathers; underparts warmer yellowish-olive. **HABITAT** Open, completely vegetated landscapes, particularly grasslands, bogs and tundra. **VOICE** Flight-song comprises thin whistling calls ending in descending scale; thin quiet 'tsip' call.

*adult*

*adult*

# ROCK PIPIT
## *ANTHUS PETROSUS*

**LENGTH** 16–17cm
**WINGSPAN** 22–27cm

During the breeding season, Rock Pipits favour cliffs and slopes within sight of the sea, nesting in rock crevices. Outside the breeding season, they favour beaches where small groups hunt for insects and sandhoppers.

**IDENTIFICATION** Larger and darker than Meadow Pipit, with strong bill and legs. Adult upperparts dark olive-grey with blackish mottled streaking. Pale-buff supercilium and pale-grey wingbars and tertial edgings relieve rather drab appearance. Tail dark brown with dirty-buff edges. Underparts creamy buff to darkish olive, with variable amounts of streaking across breast and on flanks. Some birds are so heavily streaked on underbody as to appear fairly uniform on upperparts and underparts. In winter paler birds become much darker with more blackish streaking. Bill dark grey-brown. Legs dull brown-grey. Juvenile similar to adult but appears more mottled. **HABITAT** Rocky sea cliffs and also coasts; salt-marshes in winter. **VOICE** Song is an accelerating series of loud, full, rattling notes; alarm call is a loud, metallic 'tsup'.

ABOVE AND BELOW: *summer adult*

17–18cm **LENGTH**
23–28cm **WINGSPAN**

# WATER PIPIT
### *ANTHUS SPINOLETTA*

**The Water Pipit is common in the Pyrenees, the Alps, the Apennines and the higher mountain ranges of central and eastern Europe. In winter it moves altitudinally but some eastern birds migrate to western Europe.**

**IDENTIFICATION** Medium-sized pipit, less streaked in summer than other pipits. Summer adult has grey-brown upperparts, brownest on back and closed wing. Prominent double wingbar formed by pale grey margins and tips to wing coverts, and panel caused by pale edgings to tertials gives strong pattern to closed wing. Tail brown-black with outer edges white. Underbody dull white with pinkish wash on breast. Winter adult loses grey cast to upperparts, and pink wash from breast becomes browner with streaked underparts. Bill dark grey-brown. Legs and feet dark brown-grey. Juvenile similar to winter adult but with cleaner appearance. **HABITAT** Montane short grasslands and heaths; lowland wetlands in winter. **VOICE** Melodious, abandoned, twinkling song; contact call is a full, almost grating 'tseep'.

winter
adult

spring
adult

spring
adult

# RED-THROATED PIPIT

*ANTHUS CERVINUS*

**LENGTH** 15cm
**WINGSPAN** 25–27cm

The Red-throated Pipit nests in open habitats north of the forest belt, preferring willow and birch swamps, where trees are widely spaced. It often creeps slowly through low vegetation, close to the ground.

**IDENTIFICATION** Smallish, short-tailed, stripy pipit with markedly different summer and winter plumage. Breeding adult has dark-brown upperparts, heavily streaked with black. Mantle often shows pale-buff braces. Yellowish-buff margins to blackish wing coverts show as double wingbars. Buff margins to tertials are distinct, contrasting with dark, heavily streaked rump. Tail dark with white edges. Face and chin plain pinkish-buff. Breast and flanks warm reddish-buff; flanks streaked black. Rest of underbody paler buff. Winter adult and juvenile more black and white than summer adult, with heavily streaked chest; reddish wash to face and throat absent. In all plumages, bill dark grey-brown with pinkish base, and legs and feet yellowish-buff.

*autumn adult*

**HABITAT** Arctic and sub-Arctic mossy tundra and swamps; muddy grazed pastures in winter.

**VOICE** Loud twittering and whistling song with bubbling trill; call is a loud, thin, buzzing note.

*juvenile*

*spring adult*

16.5cm **LENGTH**
25–28cm **WINGSPAN**

# TAWNY PIPIT
### *ANTHUS CAMPESTRIS*

The Tawny Pipit is a bird of warm, dry
lowlands, selecting sandy habitats, where it is
well camouflaged. It prefers scant vegetation
with bare ground in between clumps.

**IDENTIFICATION** Long, slim pipit, size of Yellow Wagtail.
Adult has crown, mantle, scapulars and rump sandy ochre,
mottled with dark brown on all but rump. Closed wing
darker sandy brown with noticeable line of dark spots
formed by blackish coverts with pale tips. Tail brown with
pale-cream edges. Face pale with long, cream supercilium
and narrow, black lores and moustachial stripe. Chest and
flanks sandy buff, usually
unstreaked; rest of
underbody whiter.
Longish fine bill, brown
with buff-pink base. Spindly
legs and feet yellowish with
long hind-claw. Juvenile much
more streaked than adult, with
some streaking on breast.
**HABITAT** Sunny, dry, sandy ground
with scant vegetation; grasslands
and coastal dunes. **VOICE** Monotonous
song of metallic repeated phrases; alarm
call like House Sparrow 'cherrup'.

*adult*

*adult*

*adult*

*The largest pipit breeding in
Europe, the Tawny Pipit
is found in open
habitats.*

*adult*

winter range uncertain

# WHITE WAGTAIL
## *MOTACILLA ALBA ALBA*

**LENGTH** 18cm
**WINGSPAN** 25–30cm

As a breeding species, the White Wagtail is the most common and widespread wagtail in Europe. In western and southern Europe the species is generally a year-round resident, while in the north and east of its breeding range it is a migrant.

**IDENTIFICATION** Breeding male has black cap and nape and black throat and upper breast. Back and rump grey, not black as on Pied Wagtail. Underparts white. Blackish wings show two white wingbars. Tail long and black with white outer feathers; constantly pumped up and down. On non-breeding male black on underparts is confined to upper breast band; plumage somewhat grubby but otherwise similar to breeding male's. Breeding female similar to male, but markings less well defined. In winter loses black cap, and face grubby. Juvenile similar to non-breeding female. **HABITAT** Farmland, wetlands, open country. **VOICE** Song is a twittering warble; call is a shrill 'tchissick'.

*adult male*

*adult male*

18cm **LENGTH**
25–30cm **WINGSPAN**

# PIED WAGTAIL
### *MOTACILLA ALBA YARRELLII*

The Pied Wagtail is the British and Irish race of the White Wagtail, and the striking plumage, active habits and bounding flight with loud calls all draw attention to it.

*adult male*

**IDENTIFICATION** Adult male in summer has black on crown, nape, chin and upper breast. Back, wings and tail black except for white fringes and tips to wings and white outertail feathers. Adult female in summer similar to male but with greyer back. Black throat absent in non-breeding adults, leaving narrow black breast band. Juvenile recalls non-breeding female but has dusky brown tinge to plumage, and buff fringes to wing feathers. **HABITAT** Mainly waterside habitats and bare areas created by human activity. **VOICE** Song is a hurried warbling twitter; main contact call loud 'chissik'.

*adult female*

*juvenile*

*Resembles slim black and white pipit with fast running action and wagging tail.*

*adult male*

*Pied Wagtails often gather together in large, communal roosts, partly for safety, partly for warmth.*

# GREY WAGTAIL

*MOTACILLA CINEREA*

**LENGTH** 18–19cm
**WINGSPAN** 25–27cm

The Grey Wagtail prefers fast-flowing rivers and streams and is found in upland regions of Europe, where it darts above streams in short sallies for insects, or stands on a rock in the water wagging its tail.

**IDENTIFICATION** Adult male has grey upperparts with olive-yellow rump. White supercilium and submoustachial stripe, contrasting with black bib. Closed wing shows yellowish-white fringes to tertials and inner secondaries; main flight feathers blackish. Underbody lemon yellow with greyish flanks. Female and non-breeding male show reduced black bib or white throat; underparts buffer. Legs and feet flesh-coloured in all birds and bill greyish-black. Juvenile resembles non-breeding adult but with buff fringes to wing feathers. **HABITAT** Running fresh water, particularly upland streams with rocky margins. **VOICE** Song is a series of shrill elements, getting louder; usual contact call is a shrill 'tchee'.

*adult male*

*In flight, upperwing shows white bar; underwing greyish with white centre.*

*winter female*

*Long, slim wagtail with a very long black tail with white outer feathers.*

*adult male*

# YELLOW WAGTAIL

17cm **LENGTH**
23–27cm **WINGSPAN**

*MOTACILLA FLAVA*

The Yellow Wagtail is widely distributed across lowland Europe. The species is represented in Europe by a spectrum of different geographical races, separable in adult male plumages.

*male*

*Smallest, most compact European wagtail, with pipit-like silhouette.*

*female*

**IDENTIFICATION** Adult males of the various geographical races separable in breeding plumage (*see* illustrations below). Females and juveniles duller yellow than males, with more uniform olive-buff plumage tones; geographical races essentially inseparable in field. **HABITAT** Lowland wetlands, particularly water meadows, salt-marshes and dune slacks. **VOICE** Song is a rhythmic series of twittering notes; usual call is shrill 'pseeep'.

*Adult males (*BELOW*) of all races have greenish-yellow mantle, greyish-green wings with whitish-yellow fringes to coverts and tertials, and dark greyish tail with outer feathers.*

*male*

*Adult male of race iberiae (Spanish Wagtail) shows blue-grey head, white supercilium and throat and black cheeks; breeds on Iberian peninsula.*

*Adult male of race thunbergi (Grey-headed Wagtail) shows slate-grey head, dark cheeks, white moustache and yellow throat; breeds in northeast Europe and Russia.*

*Adult male of race flava (Blue-headed Wagtail) shows blue-grey head, white supercilium and moustache, dark cheeks and yellowish throat; breeds across Central Europe and Scandinavia.*

*Adult male of race cinereocapilla (Ashy-headed Wagtail) shows blue-grey head, black cheeks and white throat; breeds in Italy.*

*Adult male of race feldegg (Black-headed Wagtail) shows entirely black head and yellow throat; breeds in southeast Europe and the Balkans.*

# WAXWING
## *BOMBYCILLA GARRULUS*

**LENGTH** 18cm
**WINGSPAN** 32–36cm

During the breeding season, Waxwings nest among old stunted conifers and are largely insectivorous. In winter they disperse south and west and seek out berry-laden trees and shrubs in gardens and parks.

**IDENTIFICATION** Adult plumage basically warm pinkish buff-brown with small areas of black and striking colours. Head has fluffy backward-pointing crest. Brown shades into chestnut around face, and pinkish on neck, breast and flanks. Narrow black eyestripe and wide black bib. Grey rump. Blackish tail has broad, yellow tip. Belly yellowish, contrasting with orange-brown vent. Closed wing shows remarkable pattern of white tips to primary coverts and secondaries with waxy red appendages. Dark primaries have white and yellow margins. Bill and legs black. Juvenile duller than adult, without rich plumage tones and wing decoration. **HABITAT** Northern spruce and pine forests; in winter irruptive into towns and gardens. **VOICE** Weak wheezing and twittering song; call is a thin, shrill whistle.

*Size and proportions of Starling, with similar flight action.*

*male*

*In winter, Waxwings are often indifferent to human presence as they gorge themselves on rowan or hawthorn berries.*

**Female** *tends to have less intense black bib than male and fewer red waxy tips to secondaries.*

9–10cm **LENGTH**
13–17cm **WINGSPAN**

# WREN
### *TROGLODYTES TROGLODYTES*

The Wren is usually found in scrub or rank herbage, close to ground level where it forages for insects and spiders, creeping and flitting among the stems. It is often very difficult to locate, as it stays in thick cover.

*adult*

*adult*

*In flight, whole appearance is of warm-brown, round, whirring, bee-like bird.*

**IDENTIFICATION** Adult has rufous-brown upperparts with paler buff-brown underparts, barred all over. Supercilium narrow and creamy, and throat pale buff. Closed wing shows lines of white barring on short, dark primaries. Undertail coverts and flanks also show some buffy-white barring. Bill long, thin and slightly decurved, dark grey-brown with yellowish lower mandible. Legs light brown. Juvenile like adult, but with even warmer brown tones to plumage. **HABITAT** Wide variety of habitats which offer some cover. **VOICE** Powerful, shrill, trilling song; ticking alarm call.

*Probably the shortest bird in Europe when holding short tail erect.*

*adult*

279

# DUNNOCK
*PRUNELLA MODULARIS*

The Dunnock is unobtrusive for much of the year, creeping along close to the ground, twitching its wings and tail nervously. It has a complicated breeding strategy, with both males and females often having multiple partners.

ABOVE AND RIGHT: *adults*

**IDENTIFICATION** Size of House Sparrow but slimmer. Adult head, neck, throat and breast slate grey with brown streaks on crown and greyish-white streaks on face. Mantle, scapulars and wing coverts rich brown, streaked with black. Closed wing dark with buff fringes forming wingbar. Rump unstreaked dull brown, tail blackish-brown. Slate-grey of breast shades into brown on flanks, and to whitish-grey on belly. Eye noticeably red-brown. Short, fine bill blackish with pale-brown base. Legs pinkish-brown. **HABITAT** Natural scrub in northern and upland coniferous forest; secondary scrub in western Europe. **VOICE** Song is a weak, truncated warble; call is a sharp 'tzchik'.

*The lively, warbling song is often delivered from an exposed perch.*

*Can be difficult to identify as it resembles a sparrow but has a warbler's bill.*

*adult*

18cm **LENGTH**
30–33cm **WINGSPAN**

# ALPINE ACCENTOR
### *PRUNELLA COLLARIS*

The Alpine Accentor is restricted in Europe to the highest mountain ranges of the central continent, preferring exposed but sunny short alpine grasslands and boulder fields. It feeds and nests on the ground and chooses habitats without any tall vegetation.

*Outside the breeding season, and especially in harsh winters, small numbers of Alpine Accentors are found on rocky coastal cliffs in southwest Europe.*

*adult*

*Bulky passerine recalling small lark.*

**IDENTIFICATION** Adult head, breast and belly ash-grey with brownish tinge in some lights. Chin whitish with neat black speckling. Mantle grey-brown with heavy black-brown streaking. Rump grey and uppertail coverts rufous, streaked black. Tail dark brown, tipped white. Closed wing patterned with black, white-tipped coverts forming noticeable panel against rufous-edged secondaries and dark primaries. Underwing mottled rufous and grey. Flanks boldly streaked and blotched chestnut. Undertail coverts have black and white arrowhead barring. Bill black with yellow base. Legs red-brown. Juvenile like adult but duller and scaly. **HABITAT** Montane habitats above tree-line. **VOICE** Musical chattering warble; ventriloquial rippling call.

*adult*

# DIPPER

*CINCLUS CINCLUS*

**LENGTH** 18cm
**WINGSPAN** 26–30cm

The Dipper has a patchy distribution throughout the continent, breeding only on fast-flowing streams and rivers. Most are resident, moving to lower valleys in winter, but some northern birds are partial migrants.

**IDENTIFICATION** Adult has dark-brown head and neck. Rest of upperparts, wings and tail very dark slate with blackish feather margins, giving mottled effect. Chin, throat and breast bright white. British and central European birds have reddish-brown belly grading to blackish-brown on rear of underparts. Birds from northern Europe have uniformly blackish-brown belly and rear of underparts. Underwing black-brown. Juvenile has all dark-slate upperparts, mottled by black feather margins. Underparts white, heavily mottled, spotted and barred with dusky feather tips. All ages show white eyelid when blinking and black-brown bill and legs. **HABITAT** Fast-flowing, rocky streams and rivers, usually in mountains; lower altitude in winter. **VOICE** Song is a pleasing rippling warble of mellow whistles; sharp 'tzit' call.

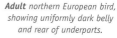

*Adult northern European bird, showing uniformly dark belly and rear of underparts.*

*juvenile*

*adult, British race*

Resembles a small, rotund thrush with short, rounded wings and cocked tail; British race has chestnut patch on anterior margin of dark underparts.

15cm **LENGTH**
21–26cm **WINGSPAN**

# RUFOUS BUSH ROBIN

*CERCOTRICHAS GALACTOTES*

The Rufous Bush Robin is likely to be first seen in flight, when it appears dashing and fluttering like a large warbler. However, when it is seen perched its similarities with chats are obvious.

**IDENTIFICATION** Adult Iberian race has rufous-brown upperparts and wings with brighter rump and bright reddish-chestnut tail, tipped black and white. Head shows long, cream supercilium and eyering, brown eyestripe and paler cheeks. On closed wing the pale-tipped coverts show as two wingbars. Chin and throat whitish, with rest of underbody sandy pink, brightest on breast and flanks; southeast European race greyer. All birds have strong bill, which is grey-brown with pale base. Legs and feet brown. Juvenile very similar to adult but has lightly speckled throat and breast.
**HABITAT** Southern steppes with planted scrub; also trees, parks, orange groves and gardens. **VOICE** Song is a jerky Robin-like warble; contact and alarm calls are short 'tsip' notes.

*Size of large warbler but with long, graduated tail.*

*adult*

*adults*

# ROBIN
## *ERITHACUS RUBECULA*

**LENGTH** 14cm
**WINGSPAN** 20–22cm

Robins choose shady habitats, usually with moist ground in which they can easily forage; they tend to stay away from open, dry and sunny locations. In Britain they live close to humans in gardens and parks.

*In the north of their range, Robins favour coniferous forests, while further south they prefer broad-leaved woodlands or even gardens and parks.*

ABOVE AND LEFT: *adult*

*juvenile*

**IDENTIFICATION** Small, round chat with large head. Sexes similar. Adult has olive-brown upperparts and tail. Often shows short, narrow wingbar formed by buff tips to greater coverts. Orange-red forehead, surround to eye, forecheeks, chin, throat and breast. Brown upperparts separated from orange face and chest by band of soft blue-grey. Flanks warm buff, belly and undertail coverts white. Bill dark brown and legs brown. Juvenile very different from adult, with brown upperparts and buff underparts all copiously spotted with pale buff. **HABITAT** Shady, undisturbed coniferous and broad-leaved woodland; also gardens and town parks. **VOICE** Both sexes sing series of mellow whistled warbles; call is a sharp 'tic'.

14cm **LENGTH**
20–23cm **WINGSPAN**

# BLUETHROAT
### *LUSCINIA SVECICA*

In the north of its range the Bluethroat prefers wooded tundra with marshy glades; further south it selects thick scrub by water. The red-spotted form is found in the north; birds south of the Baltic are mainly white-spotted.

**IDENTIFICATION** Adults of both sexes have buffish supercilium bordered by black above and brownish cheeks below. Tail dark brown with orange-chestnut base to outer feathers. Breeding male has metallic blue throat and upper breast with either a reddish or white central spot, depending on race; the spot is sometimes absent in some races. Blue throat is bordered below by narrow black, white and chestnut bands. Underbody off-white with greyish flanks. Non-breeding adult has pale throat and otherwise more subdued colours than breeding male. Female lacks male's blue throat; note dark 'moustache' and 'necklace'. Grey-brown bill and ochre-brown legs in both sexes. Juvenile spotted with pale buff, assuming female-like plumage in autumn. **HABITAT** Moist, wooded tundra with glades and scrub near water. **VOICE** Song mimics other species in loud, short, warbling phrases; contact call 'chuck'.

*Adult female usually lacks male's throat pattern but has black moustache joining brown-black necklace.*

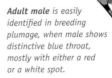

*Adult male is easily identified in breeding plumage, when male shows distinctive blue throat, mostly with either a red or a white spot.*

LEFT: *autumn male*

*juvenile*

THRUSHES

# NIGHTINGALE
*LUSCINIA MEGARHYNCHOS*

**LENGTH** 16.5cm
**WINGSPAN** 23–26cm

In Europe the Nightingale is the more westerly counterpart of the Thrush Nightingale. It prefers warmer climates, often dry, sunny hillsides on sandy soils. Woodland scrub is its preferred habitat.

**IDENTIFICATION** Adult has fairly uniform russet-brown upperparts with warmer tone to rump and uppertail coverts, and bright chestnut-brown tail with dark central feathers. Head has uniform brown face with buff eyering. Closed wing shows darker brown-centred flight feathers. Underparts are dull cream-white with brownish suffusion across breast and down flanks. Vent and undertail coverts brighter cream-buff. Bill dark grey-brown with pale base. Legs pale brown or flesh. Juvenile is very speckled, but when this plumage is lost, looks like adult with buff tips to wing coverts and tertials. **HABITAT** Scrub in woodland, along rivers or on dry, sunny hillsides. **VOICE** Beautiful, mellow, musical and varied song, with pure whistles and rattles.

*The long, broad tail with its bright chestnut colouring is the most obvious feature as the bird disappears into cover.*

*adult*

*May be confused with the Thrush Nightingale when trying to identify it by sight, but the more russet-toned plumage, brighter tail and cleaner underparts are all useful features.*

*adult*

*adult*

16.5cm **LENGTH**
24–27cm **WINGSPAN**

# THRUSH NIGHTINGALE
*LUSCINIA LUSCINIA*

The Thrush Nightingale and Nightingale are very similar. Plumage tone, contrast between the warm brown tail and the upperparts, and the mottled chest are important features in the Thrush Nightingale.

**IDENTIFICATION** Resembles a small thrush. Very difficult to separate from Nightingale on sight alone. Adult has dark olivaceous-brown upperparts with warmer brown uppertail coverts and dull rufous-brown tail. Underparts dull whitish-grey with clean throat bordered by brown malar stripe and breast. Chest and flanks mottled dusky brown. Bill dark grey-brown with pale base to lower mandible. Legs brown. Juvenile appears darker, with contrasting pale spots on tips of tertials and wing coverts. Legs pale flesh. **HABITAT** Open woodland and thicket scrub, often along rivers; also orchards and parks. **VOICE** Beautiful, long and varied warble with deep 'tchock' notes and rattles.

adult

adult

adult

*The rich and varied song with solemn, pealing bell-like notes, clipped phrases and rasping notes lacks only the crescendo elements of Nightingale's song.*

*The Thrush Nightingale is wholly migratory in Europe, overwintering in East Africa.*

287

# ISABELLINE WHEATEAR

*OENANTHE ISABELLINA*

**LENGTH** 16.5cm
**WINGSPAN** 27–31cm

**Identification of this pale wheatear is difficult. Subtle differences from other wheatear species should be noted: longer bill; rather shorter, broader tail with wider black and limited face pattern.**

*The Isabelline Wheatear's stance is more upright than that of other wheatears, its long legs making it look as though it is on stilts.*

**IDENTIFICATION** Largest and palest wheatear in the region. Sexes similar. Less contrast between upperparts and underparts than in other wheatears. Generally pale sandy brown above and buffish-white below, with brown wings showing broad creamy fringes to coverts and secondaries. Dirty-white supercilium, black lores and eyes. Tail white with broad, black terminal band and less noticeable vertical bar. Bill and legs long and black. Hard to distinguish from some female wheatears. Juvenile paler than adult but otherwise similar. **HABITAT** Bare hillsides and dry plains, all with sparse vegetation. **VOICE** Song is loud and mimetic, unlike other wheatears; call is 'tchok', 'click' and 'dweet'.

adult

adult

adult

18cm **LENGTH**
26–29cm **WINGSPAN**

# BLACK WHEATEAR
*OENANTHE LEUCURA*

The Black Wheatear is generally a sedentary bird. It is less solitary than most other wheatears, and three to five commonly feed together. They are territorial, probably pair for life and, although wary, are more approachable in the breeding season.

**IDENTIFICATION** Male black except for white rump and tail coverts, white tail with end marked by upside-down 'T', the end bar being narrower than the Northern Wheatear's. Black underwings contrast with greyish-white in fringes of flight feathers. Female separable at close range; more sooty brown than black, especially on face and underparts when feathers are worn. Bill and legs black in both sexes. Juvenile similar to female. **HABITAT** Gorges and rock-strewn places, quarries and screes. **VOICE** Call is a distinctive 'pee-pee-pee'; song is a quiet mixture of warbles and chatter.

adult
male

*The males are easily spotted from February onwards, when they perform the song-flight, rising up like a pipit and singing a more melodious song than most wheatears before gliding to a perch.*

adult male

# PIED WHEATEAR
*OENANTHE PLESCHANKA*

**LENGTH** 14–15cm
**WINGSPAN** 26–27cm

At the western edge of its range, the Pied Wheatear has a toe-hold in Europe, having bred in Turkey and the former Yugoslavia and nesting on a regular, if local, basis in Bulgaria.

*female*

*1st-winter male*

**IDENTIFICATION** Adult male has black face and throat linked by black feathering to black wings. Crown, nape and underparts essentially white. Superficially similar to black-throated form of Black-eared Wheatear. Tail pattern also similar to that of Black-eared Wheatear: white with black central feathers and trailing edge. Males in autumn and winter have pale-brown feather edges and so white elements of plumage look buff and black elements look greyish. Adult female has dark grey-brown head, throat and upperparts; underparts grubby white. During winter months pale feather margins reduce contrast in plumage. Bill and legs dark in all birds. **HABITAT** Stony hillsides and broken ground. **VOICE** Calls include a sharp 'tchek'; song includes rattling, buzzing and warbling phrases.

*male*

14cm **LENGTH**
23–25cm **WINGSPAN**

# CYPRUS PIED WHEATEAR

### OENANTHE CYPRIACA

**The Cyprus Pied Wheatear is the only wheatear species to breed on the island. It is migratory, overwintering in northeast Africa, and returning to Cyprus from late March.**

**IDENTIFICATION** Adult male has white crown and nape. Face, chin to upper breast, neck, back and wings black. Rump and uppertail coverts white. Tail white with black central feathers; all feathers black-tipped. Underparts from lower breast to undertail coverts black and flight feathers dusky. After autumn moult, plumage is browner with little contrast; breeding plumage acquired by wear. Female resembles dull male with dark olive-brown crown contrasting with pale-buff supercilium and nape. Juvenile dark with pale-spotted upperparts.
**HABITAT** Open, stony, arid areas and fallow fields.
**VOICE** Song is a continuous series of buzzing, sawing notes; various clicking calls.

*male*

*male*

# NORTHERN WHEATEAR

*OENANTHE OENANTHE*

The Northern Wheatear is the most widespread and best-known species of wheatear. This bouncy, ground-loving bird is found in a variety of open habitats from the Arctic to the Mediterranean.

*adult male*

*Male* (FAR RIGHT) *easily identified;* *female* (RIGHT) *and 1st-winter birds similar to other wheatears.*

**IDENTIFICATION**

Adult male has diagnostic grey crown and back, white supercilium, black mask through eye widening over cheek, and black wings; chin to breast pink-buff, rest of underparts white. Rump, uppertail coverts and tail white, the last with tip marked by broad, black upside-down 'T'. Adult female similarly patterned but wings, crown, cheek patch and back all brown-toned. Underparts usually buffer. Juvenile has dark upperparts with scaly appearance, and pale underparts with darker crescent-shaped markings. In many plumages similar to other wheatears; identification is best done by noting tail pattern and length, face pattern and colour tones of body plumage. This is the only wheatear breeding in north and northwest Europe. **HABITAT** Open, very diverse habitats; Arctic tundra, sand dunes, cliff-tops, moors, mountains. **VOICE** Song is an energetic, short warble; call is 'chak'; alarm call is 'weet-chak, chak'.

*juvenile*

14.5cm **LENGTH**
25–27cm **WINGSPAN**

# BLACK-EARED WHEATEAR
*OENANTHE HISPANICA*

The adult male Black-eared Wheatear is one of the smartest passerines in Europe. The richly coloured *O. h. hispanica* occurs in the west while the paler *O. h. melanoleuca* is found in the east.

**IDENTIFICATION** Males of both black- and pale-throated forms have sandy-buff crown, nape, mantle and underbody. Tail white with black inverted 'T' caused by black central feathers and narrow black tips. Forehead and supercilium creamy white. Throat either black or sandy as underbody. Underwing coverts black, contrasting with grey flight feathers. In autumn fresh buff feather margins reduce contrast between black and sandy

*female, eastern race*

*1st-autumn male*

plumage. Females of both races recall male but lack strong head pattern. Bill and legs black in both sexes. Juvenile resembles female but has buff spotted underparts and scaly, brown breast. **HABITAT** Warm Mediterranean and steppe open habitats with dry stony ground. **VOICE** Song is a rich warble interspersed with scratchy, buzzing phrases.

ABOVE: *Male of black-throated western form; both forms have black face and wings and white rump.*

*Adult male, black-throated eastern form*

# STONECHAT
## *SAXICOLA TORQUATA*

**LENGTH** 12.5cm
**WINGSPAN** 18–21cm

The Stonechat requires substantial vegetation cover. They are resident over much of their European range, but northern and eastern populations usually move south in winter.

**IDENTIFICATION** Adult male has dark-brown head and throat, with isolated white patches on sides of neck. Mantle and scapulars evenly dark brown. White rump streaked blackish. Closed wing shows white panel on coverts. Breast and flanks orange, shading to greyish-white on centre of belly and undertail coverts. Underwing dark. Adult female upperparts mottled brownish, and white areas replaced by buff. Juvenile greyer and heavily spotted, resembling bright but uniform buffish female by first autumn. **HABITAT** Dry, scrubby areas, particularly heaths and sand dunes; also young plantations. **VOICE** Shrill and fairly monotonous series of short, scratchy and whistled phrases; call is a harsh 'tchack'.

*female*

*male*

*male*

Smaller than Robin, with shorter, more rounded wings than Whinchat.

12.5cm **LENGTH**
21–24cm **WINGSPAN**

# WHINCHAT
### *SAXICOLA RUBETRA*

The Whinchat occurs most widely to the north and east of its close family relative, the Stonechat. A bird of the open country, it is found in tall grass, bracken or annual herbs, often on dry, stony ground.

*male*

**IDENTIFICATION** Smaller than Robin. Adult male has black-brown head with long, broad, white supercilium reaching nape, and similar white border to cheek, upturned at rear. Back dark brown with heavy blackish streaking. Rump paler with rufous tinge. Wing coverts black with bold, white bar extending onto tertials. Flight feathers brown-black with white bases to outer primaries. Tail black with white sides to base. Underbody uniform warm orange. Adult female similarly patterned to male but duller. Bill and legs black in both sexes. Juvenile recalls female but not as distinct; has buff underparts and less clear pattern to face. **HABITAT** Open grassland and scrub, particularly hay meadows; bracken on hills. **VOICE** Song is a long series of short units, varied with fluty and scratchy phrases; call is a harsh 'tzec'.

*Both sexes show distinctive white supercilium, but **female** (ABOVE) lacks black face mask of **male** (RIGHT).*

**295**

# REDSTART
*PHOENICURUS PHOENICURUS*

**LENGTH** 14cm
**WINGSPAN** 20–24cm

The Redstart inhabits fairly shady, wooded habitats with old trees, walls or banks to provide nest holes. Regular perches are often used as starting points for fly-catching or ground foraging sorties.

**IDENTIFICATION** Slimmer than Robin, with longer wings and tail. Adult male has white forehead and supercilium. Crown and back blue-grey. Wings blackish-brown with buffish fringes and tips to feathers. Rump, uppertail coverts and tail bright chestnut with dark-brown central feathers. Face, throat and upper breast black, contrasting with orange-red lower breast and flanks. Belly white and undertail coverts orange-red. Underwing coverts pale chestnut. Female plumage greyish-brown, darker on upperparts than underbody. White throat and eyering; chestnut tail. Bill and legs black in both sexes. Juvenile has tail like adult but rest of plumage speckled buff and brown. **HABITAT** Open, broad-leaved woodland and parkland or heaths, well-treed farmland. **VOICE** Melancholy song with sweet and rattling phrases; contact call is a soft 'tchuk'.

male

*Female* (ABOVE) *duller than* **male** (RIGHT) *but retains chestnut tail coloration.*

14.5cm **LENGTH**
23–26cm **WINGSPAN**

# BLACK REDSTART
### *PHOENICURUS OCHRUROS*

The Black Redstart is a common bird throughout much
of Europe. Its preferred habitat is open, rocky and
craggy terrain, often in mountain regions but it
is a village and city bird in some regions.

*female*

*Female has dull, grey-brown
body plumage with orange
areas less bright than on
male, and buff wing panel.*

*Male acquires his full breeding
plumage by abrasion of pale
feather tips over the winter.*

**IDENTIFICATION** In spring, adult male has dusky slate head, back, wing coverts and black face and
breast. Wings brown-black with off-white panel. Centre of belly greyish-white, vent and undertail
coverts orange. Rump and tail are chestnut with central tail feathers and tips dark brown. After
fresh moult in autumn, plumage colours are muted by pale feather edgings, and wing panel
is brighter white. For description of female, *see* caption. Bill and
legs black in both sexes. Juvenile resembles speckled female.
**HABITAT** Open, rocky and stony habitats in mountains; also
wasteland and buildings in cities. **VOICE** Song is a quick,
scratchy warble; contact call 'sit'.

*male*

# ROCK THRUSH
## *MONTICOLA SAXATILIS*

The Rock Thrush is a very shy and solitary bird in its breeding grounds, seeking cover among the rocks when disturbed – it is more likely to be heard than seen.

*Resembles large wheatear, with erect posture and characteristically wagging tail.*

*female*

*male*

*male*

**IDENTIFICATION** Adult summer male unmistakable, with slate-blue head and throat, white back, blue rump and brownish-black wings. Uppertail coverts, tail, underparts and underwing orange; striking in flight. In winter male appears more scaly owing to pale feather fringes. Adult female resembles non-breeding male but lacks blue in plumage. Head, throat and back mottled brown and buff. Lacks male's white patch on back. Underparts buff with brown, crescent-shaped markings. Tail orange. Bill and legs of both sexes dark brown. Juvenile similar to female but even more strongly marked.

**HABITAT** Sunny, dry, stony terraces with scattered trees.

**VOICE** Song is a mellow, flute-like warble; call is 'chack, chack'.

20cm **LENGTH**
33–37cm **WINGSPAN**

# BLUE ROCK THRUSH
### *MONTICOLA SOLITARIUS*

**Some European Blue Rock Thrushes are resident; most are migrants, or at least disperse from their breeding grounds in winter. They are territorial and shy.**

**IDENTIFICATION** Adult male is the only all-blue songbird in the region. Plumage mostly dull slate-blue but with black tone on wings and tail. Whole bird looks black in poor light. Female dark grey-brown, with no blue tone; sides of head and throat spotted brown, rest of underparts covered with scaly, buff markings. Bill dark grey-brown and legs black in both sexes. Juveniles similar to female. **HABITAT** Rocky coastlines, rocky mountain valleys, big buildings. **VOICE** Call and alarm deep 'tak, tak'; song loud and melodious, of simple phrases.

*Larger than any wheatear and nearly as big as a Redwing, but stockily built.*

*female*

*male*

# BLACKBIRD
## *TURDUS MERULA*

**LENGTH** 24–25cm
**WINGSPAN** 34–38.5cm

**The Blackbird is basically a woodland bird but inhabits many places, from wooded mountain sides to city centres. Northern populations are migrants; others are resident.**

**IDENTIFICATION** Male is only small all-black bird in Europe with bright golden-yellow bill and long, broad tail. Black is glossy but not iridescent. Orange-yellow eyelids form an eyering. Legs dark brown. Immature male's bill is dark grey-brown, turning golden through the first winter, and plumage is dull black. Female head and body dark brown. Underparts often have rufous tone and dark thrush-like mottling on breast; some birds more marked than others. Legs dark brown and in parts of northwest bill dark but yellow at base of lower mandible. Juvenile like female, but more rufous and more spotted below. **HABITAT** In most places where trees are present, but also on moors and in towns. **VOICE** Call sounds like 'see'; alarm is a shrill chatter; song is a variety of flute-like, musical phrases.

*Female is much darker than Song Thrush.*

*Juvenile more spotted than female.*

*Adult male unlikely to be confused with any other bird.*

24cm **LENGTH**
38–42cm **WINGSPAN**

# RING OUZEL
### *TURDUS TORQUATUS*

**The Ring Ouzel has a restricted breeding range in Europe, preferring wild and remote upland areas for nesting. Ring Ouzels arrive on breeding territory by mid-April and leave again by August and September.**

**IDENTIFICATION**

Male has blackish plumage with pale fringes to feathers on wings and underparts. Conspicuous white crescent on breast is diagnostic. Legs dark flesh in colour, and bill yellow with black tip. Female has brownish plumage, with more noticeable pale fringes to feathering giving scaly appearance. Pale crescent of female has dark feather edging. Juvenile is similar to female but crescent band is usually faint. Closed wings of both sexes show pale panel. **HABITAT** Mountains and moorland; winters on Mediterranean slopes. **VOICE** Song simple and fluty; chattering alarm call.

*male*

*Flight pattern recalls that of other thrushes, although it is noticeably deep-winged and powerful.*

*female*

*Bright white breast crescent and grey wing-panel obvious on **adult male**.*

# REDWING
### *TURDUS ILIACUS*

**LENGTH** 21cm
**WINGSPAN** 33–34.5cm

The Redwing is the smallest of the European thrushes. The species is mostly migratory, many millions of birds moving to western and southern Europe for the winter.

**IDENTIFICATION** Plumage recalls Song Thrush but adult recognisable by red flanks and long, creamy supercilium contrasting with dark-brown cheeks and brown crown. Sexes alike. Dark-brown streak runs from base of bill. Breast yellowish-buff on sides, dark-brown streaks spreading out to form a gorget. Undertail coverts white. Belly white, streaked with lighter brown on side. Underwing chestnut-red. Bill blackish-brown. Legs yellowish or flesh-brown. Juvenile recalls adult but shows darker streaking and spotting with buffish wash to face and flanks. **HABITAT** Open woods, thickets, birch scrub; winters on grassland, stubble, and in open woodland. **VOICE** Call far-carrying 'see-ip'; song variable, 4–6 fluty notes plus warbling.

*In flight, tawny-red underwing is diagnostic.*

*Adult upperparts uniformly dark warm brown, darkest on flight feathers.*

*adult*

25.5cm **LENGTH**
39–42cm **WINGSPAN**

# FIELDFARE
## *TURDUS PILARIS*

The Fieldfare breeds widely across northern Europe. Northern and eastern populations are migratory, although birds reach southern Europe only in the hardest winters. Emigration from Scandinavia is linked to the success or failure of the Rowan crop.

**IDENTIFICATION** Adults of both sexes have slate-grey head, nape and rump contrasting with chestnut back and black tail. Throat and breast golden-brown, streaked black. Bill yellow on breeding male; has dusky tip and culmen in winter male, females in all plumages and juveniles. Juvenile plumage recalls Mistle Thrush but shows pale streaks on back. **HABITAT** Open woodland, and beyond tree-line, gardens and parks. **VOICE** Call 'tchak, tchak'; song weak warble with some wheezes and chuckles.

*adults*

On ground, shows upright stance and hopping run typical of all thrushes.

*Large thrush with unmistakable plumage pattern. Combination of white underwing, grey rump and black tail diagnostic.*

303

# SONG THRUSH
*TURDUS PHILOMELOS*

| LENGTH | 23cm |
| WINGSPAN | 35–36cm |

Many Song Thrush populations are resident, but northern birds are migratory. It is found wherever grassland and nearby trees and bushes provide a plentiful supply of invertebrate food.

**IDENTIFICATION** Sexes similar. Adults have warm-brown upperparts. Rump and uppertail coverts more olive, crown and tail with a rufous tone. Indistinctly marked face has whitish eyering, pale-cream moustachial stripe and blackish-brown streak from base of bill, which contrasts with white throat. Underparts white with golden-brown wash on sides of breast and flanks, breast marked with blackish-brown spots that fade out on belly; spots arranged more in streaks than random spots of Mistle Thrush. Underwing coverts and axillaries golden-buff. Bill blackish-brown; legs pale flesh. Juvenile similar to adult but with pale streaks on back. **HABITAT** Parks, woods, hedges, even in towns and cities. **VOICE** Call 'tsip'; alarm rattle 'tic-tic-tic'; song loud, repetitive, musical.

*Creamy-buff underwing shows well in flight.*

Familiar song comprises two or three syllables repeated two to four times.

*This **juvenile** shows the long-legged, upright stance typical of all ground-feeding thrushes.*

*adult*

27cm **LENGTH**
42–47.5cm **WINGSPAN**

# MISTLE THRUSH
### *TURDUS VISCIVORUS*

The Mistle Thrush breeds widely across the region, but is scarce in Norway and southeast Europe. Birds in the south are mostly sedentary but northern and eastern populations move south and west in winter.

*Gleaming white underwing obvious in flight.*

*Juvenile shows white spotting on back and wings.*

**IDENTIFICATION** Sexes similar. Adult recalls Song Thrush but is larger, with whitish underparts covered with large, wedge-shaped black spots; flanks and breast marked with buff. Upperparts and wings greyish-brown with conspicuous greyish-white fringes to tertials and wing coverts. Tail grey-brown with diagnostic white tips to outer feathers noticeable when bird flies away. White underwing striking in distinctive, powerful flight; it closes its wings after each burst of wingbeats but the flight path is still direct, not undulating. Upright stance on ground emphasised by long tail. Juvenile similar to adult but spotted white on head, mantle and wing coverts. **HABITAT** Orchards, woods, farmland, parks and gardens. **VOICE** Call harsh, distinctive rattle; song loud, short, fluty phrases.

*Overall appearance very grey when compared to Song Thrush.*

*adult*

# CETTI'S WARBLER
*CETTIA CETTI*

**LENGTH** 13.5cm
**WINGSPAN** 15–19cm

The Cetti's Warbler's song is its most distinctive feature: a sudden explosion of sound, usually 2.5 to 5 seconds long, composed of clear-cut, rhythmic phrases, rendered 'CHE–che-weechoo-weechoo-wechoo-wee'. Each male has an individual song pattern.

adults

*Song has been described as the loudest song among small European birds.*

**IDENTIFICATION** Sexes similar but male larger and heavier than female. Adult upperparts and wings uniform chestnut brown. Face broken only by off-white eyering and short, grey supercilium. Chin and central underparts off-white, rest grey-brown or darker brown, especially on flanks and undertail coverts; dull-white tips of undertail coverts usually obvious when bird cocks its tail in excitement. Bill short and fine, dark brown. Legs strong, brown-flesh. Juvenile similar to adult. **HABITAT** Bushy places giving shelter by swamps, watersides, marshes. **VOICE** Call is a sharp 'chip'; song is very distinctive, loud and abrupt.

10cm **LENGTH**
12–14.5cm **WINGSPAN**

# FAN-TAILED WARBLER
### *CISTICOLA JUNCIDIS*

The Fan-tailed Warbler is a skulking bird, but may perch on grass stems. The male's song-flight is long and undulating, each bounce synchronised with the song-note 'zit'.

**IDENTIFICATION** Adult has warm buff upperparts streaked blackish-brown on crown, mantle and wings. Nape, rump and uppertail coverts almost unstreaked. Paler face has short, creamy supercilium and pale circle around eye. Breast and flanks buff. Tail brown with underside marked with black sub-terminal band and white tip. Bill brown above and grey below, with dark tip on breeding male and flesh-pink tip on other males and females. Juvenile similar to adult female. **HABITAT** Rough, grassy plains, grain fields, marshes, rice fields. **VOICE** Call is persistent 'zip'. Song is high-pitched, sharp 'tsip-tsip- ...' or 'zit-zit- ...'.

*Chin, throat, belly and undertail coverts white.*

*adult*

*May be seen flitting across the grass with whirring wings and short, spread tail like a big, buff bee; most conspicuous on male's song-flight.*

*adult*

**307**

# GRASSHOPPER WARBLER

*LOCUSTELLA NAEVIA*

**LENGTH** 12.5cm
**WINGSPAN** 15–19cm

The Grasshopper Warbler is the commonest and most widespread *Locustella* in Europe. Its winter quarters are in West Africa, and most European birds return to their breeding grounds in late April.

*adult*

*adult*

**IDENTIFICATION** Small, uniformly coloured warbler. Adult upperparts olive-brown, spotted and streaked with dark brown from crown to rump. Wings darker brown with buff to reddish fringes to feathers, visible at close range. Streaks on rump fade out on reddish-brown uppertail coverts. Tail reddish-brown, softly barred darker. Underparts mostly buff, but almost white on chin, throat and centre of breast and belly. Undertail coverts streaked with brown. Bill blackish brown with bright-yellow base. Legs pale, yellowish-brown to pink. Sexes alike. Juvenile very similar to adult. **HABITAT** Undergrowth in marshes, thick hedges, heathland, new plantations. **VOICE** Short quiet 'pitt' call; song is a high-pitched, monotonous trill.

*adult*

Mouse-like bird in its movements, preferring to run and creep rather than fly if disturbed.

13cm **LENGTH**
19–22cm **WINGSPAN**

# RIVER WARBLER
### *LOCUSTELLA FLUVIATILIS*

The River Warbler is a bird of central and eastern Europe, though it has spread westwards since the 1950s. It favours areas of very dense vegetation up to 2m tall among trees, such as bogs, carr, and damp forest clearings.

*adult*

**IDENTIFICATION** Unstreaked small-to medium-sized warbler. Upperparts, wings and tail olive-brown, darker on uppertail coverts and tail, slightly greyer on head and back. Underparts dull white with olive-brown wash on flanks and sides of breast. Undertail coverts long, to tip of tail, buff-brown with broad, white tips. Bill dark brown with pale base. Legs flesh to brown. Sexes similar but female greyer above. Juvenile similar to adult. **HABITAT** Dense vegetation in backwaters, bogs, carr, flooded woods. **VOICE** Sharp 'tsick' call; song is a curious, rhythmic 'chuffing' sound.

*Combination of unstreaked upperparts and faint mottling on chest is best distinguishing feature.*

14cm **LENGTH**
18–21cm **WINGSPAN**

# SAVI'S WARBLER
### *LOCUSTELLA LUSCINIOIDES*

Savi's Warbler is a bird of unbroken swamps and reedbeds, and the nest site can usually only be approached by wading. Its habitat preference gives the species a very fragmented distribution.

*adult*

**IDENTIFICATION** Similar to other plain warblers. Sexes similar. Adult distinguished by dark, unstreaked, reddish-brown head and upperparts, with faint, buff supercilium fading out behind the eye. Underparts brownish-white with rufous-brown along sides of breast and flanks to undertail coverts. Wings and tail uniform reddish-brown like upperparts. Tail broad and graduated towards the tip. Bill dark grey-brown. Legs pale brown. Juvenile similar to adult. **HABITAT** Reedy swamps and fens, overgrown fringes of lakes. **VOICE** Call 'pit'; alarm sharper rattle; song accelerating ticking sound.

*Bird turns its head as it sings, making its position very difficult to pinpoint.*

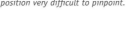

**309**

# MOUSTACHED WARBLER

*ACROCEPHALUS MELANOPOGON*

**LENGTH** 12–13cm
**WINGSPAN** 15–16.5cm

The Moustached Warbler has a scattered distribution across southern Europe, being dependent on suitable wetland habitats. It is noted for skulking, but it can be approached closely on occasions.

**IDENTIFICATION** Similar to Aquatic and Sedge Warblers, but separable with care; note the head pattern, upperparts, duller wings, behaviour and diagnostic song. Sexes similar. Adult and juvenile have nape and mantle rufous brown, nape unmarked but mantle streaked black. Unstreaked rump almost same colour as dark-brown tail. Wings olive-brown with paler feathers. Underparts whitish with rusty flanks, vent and sides to breast. Head has distinctive pattern of blackish crown and broad, white supercilium – square-ended behind eye – highlighted by dusky lore and eyestripe. **HABITAT** Swamps of sedges, reeds and reedmace. **VOICE** Call is a soft 't-rrrt'; alarm is 'churr'; song is a distinctive musical medley.

*adult*

*The southerly counterpart of the Sedge Warbler, the Moustached Warbler prefers emergent vegtation over water, where its large feet and claws enable it to move easily among the reed stems when searching for food.*

# AQUATIC WARBLER

*ACROCEPHALUS PALUDICOLA*

**LENGTH** 13cm
**WINGSPAN** 16.5–19.5cm

The Aquatic Warbler is a summer visitor to lowland marshes in eastern Europe. Its distribution has probably always been broken because of its preferred habitat; it is now one of Europe's rarest passerines.

**IDENTIFICATION** Sexes similar. Adult upperparts more sandy than Sedge Warbler's, with long, dark-brown streaks highlighted by paler stripes. Rump rusty, streaked with brown. Underparts creamy buff, becoming whiter with wear, with fine, brown streaks on side of breast and on flanks. Head pattern diagnostic: pale-buff crown stripe and supercilium, separated by dark-brown stripe at side of crown; supercilium highlighted by brown eyestripe from behind eye. Tail is dark with tawny fringes and pointed feathers. Bill dark brown and legs orange-yellow. Juvenile is brighter than adult. **HABITAT** Marshes of sedge and iris, with low vegetation. **VOICE** Call is a harsh 'churr'; song incorporates short rattles, with some fluty notes.

*Very similar to Sedge and Moustached Warblers, but with sharp crown stripe.*

*adult*

# SEDGE WARBLER
### *ACROCEPHALUS SCHOENOBAENUS*

13cm **LENGTH**
17–21cm **WINGSPAN**

The Sedge Warbler is the most common and widespread *Acrocephalus* warbler in Europe; it is also the easiest to observe. The species favours low vegetation in moist habitats from the high Arctic to Southern Europe.

**IDENTIFICATION** Adult upperparts and head strongly marked. Shows olive-brown nape, mantle and scapulars with dark streaks. Rump tawny and unstreaked, tail dark brown. Wings buff-brown with lighter edges to tertials and greater coverts. Underparts off-white, washed whitest on throat and belly, more rufous on flanks. Head has black-streaked crown and long, creamy white supercilium above dusky olive lores. Bill blackish, paler at base; legs greyish. Juvenile separable from adult by creamier supercilium, yellower underparts and distinct brown spots across breast. **HABITAT** Reedbeds and other lush vegetation near water. **VOICE** Call 'tuc'; alarm 'churr'; song is a loud and varied mix of harsh and musical notes.

*Inquisitive birds often sidle up vertical stems to investigate an intruder or noise.*

*Sedge Warblers are territorial in winter and summer, defending feeding and breeding areas.*

*adults*

# REED WARBLER
*ACROCEPHALUS SCIRPACEUS*

**LENGTH** 13cm
**WINGSPAN** 18–21cm

The Reed Warbler is a skulking but not especially shy bird of reedbeds. It is common and widespread throughout much of Europe, wherever suitable habitats occur. It is a summer visitor, present mainly from May to August.

**IDENTIFICATION** Medium-sized warbler. Sexes similar. Adult upperparts uniform olive-brown, with often noticeably more rufous rump and uppertail coverts, and darker-brown primaries and tertials. Underparts white with buff undertail coverts and sides of breast. Bill dark grey or greyish-brown with pale base. Legs sturdy, variable, but usually greyish. Juvenile brighter and rustier than adult, but face pattern less distinct. Similar to juvenile Marsh Warbler. **HABITAT** Edges of reedbeds with strong stems, and nearby vegetation. **VOICE** Call 'churr-churr'; alarm harsher; song low, guttural churring, with long phrases.

*adults*

This very agile bird clings to reed stems with both feet, or to adjacent stems; moves up and down in jerks, or hops from one plant to another.

13cm **LENGTH**
18–21cm **WINGSPAN**

# MARSH WARBLER
*ACROCEPHALUS PALUSTRIS*

The Marsh Warbler is a summer visitor to Europe. The song is an outstanding warbling, lively chatter, with a remarkable amount of mimicry and variety of tones and pitches. The song is often sung after dark.

**IDENTIFICATION** Medium-sized warbler, very hard to separate from Reed and Blyth's Reed Warblers (latter breeds from Baltic eastwards). Sexes similar. Adult usually has more olive-brown upperparts than Reed Warbler and lacks rufous rump. Has short, wide-based bill, round head, long wings showing eight to nine primary tips, pear-shaped or pot-bellied appearance and long undertail coverts. Less agile than Reed Warbler. Juvenile similar to adult. **HABITAT** Dense low vegetation, osier beds, other rank vegetation. **VOICE** Call 'tchuc'; alarm 'chirrr'; prolonged, very musical song.

*adult*

***Adult:*** *Fuller-bodied and heavier than Reed Warbler, with slightly shorter bill and more rounded crown.*

*Sings in an upright posture, often raising and fanning wings.*

313

# GREAT REED WARBLER

*ACROCEPHALUS ARUNDINACEUS*

**LENGTH** 19–20cm
**WINGSPAN** 25–29cm

The Great Reed Warbler breeds widely across Europe from Iberia to Russia. The male sings more or less throughout the day, from arrival in spring until a mate is found.

**IDENTIFICATION** Similar in appearance to Reed Warbler but clearly larger, with longer, stouter bill. Adult upperparts warm olive-brown, crown darker, rump fawnier, wing coverts edged rufous. Shows creamy supercilium, dusky eyestripe and pale-cream eyering. Underparts mainly creamy buff but more buff on flanks, and chin and throat off-white. Bill grey-brown, with bright pinkish base to lower mandible. Legs pale brown. Singing bird reveals bright orange-yellow mouth. Female tends to be brighter above and less white below than male. Sexes otherwise similar. Juvenile similar to adult. **HABITAT** Mostly lowland in aquatic vegetation, especially dense reedbeds. **VOICE** Call 'chak'; alarm harsh chatter; song very loud, harsh 'churrs' and rattles.

*Large warbler, nearly as big as a small thrush.*

**adults**

WARBLERS

12–13.5cm **LENGTH**
18–21cm **WINGSPAN**

# EASTERN OLIVACEOUS WARBLER

*HIPPOLAIS PALLIDA*

**Eastern Olivaceous Warblers favour a range of habitats and are not especially shy. However, their dull appearance and preference for shrubby places can make observation tricky.**

*adults*

**IDENTIFICATION** Medium-sized warbler. Sexes are similar; adults and juveniles are similar. Plumage recalls Garden Warbler: dull grey-brown above, creamy white below with pale buff wash on sides of breast and flanks; yellowish wash sometimes seen in spring. Note dull white supercilium, pale lores and square-ended tail. Face dominated by flat crown, rather long, prominent bill and dark eye with whitish eyering. Rump washed buff, faintly distinct from tail. Wings short relative to body size. Legs very variable, brown to bluish-grey.
**HABITAT** Shrubs, orchards, gardens, palm groves, lowlands and bushy hills.
**VOICE** Call 'tack'; alarm repeated ticking; song high-pitched, rapid, scratchy warble.

*Eastern Olivaceous Warblers are found in a variety of habitats: tree-lined roads, thickets with scattered trees, coppices and thick hedges around cultivation.*

315

# WESTERN OLIVACEOUS WARBLER

**LENGTH** 12–13.5cm
**WINGSPAN** 18–21cm

*HIPPOLAIS OPACA*

**Similar to Eastern Olivaceous and the two were treated as conspecific until recently. A summer visitor to Iberia and North Africa, it breeds from May onwards.**

**IDENTIFICATION** Medium-sized warbler. Sexes are similar; adults and juveniles are similar. Plumage recalls Garden Warbler: dull brown above, creamy white below with pale buff wash on sides of breast and flanks; yellowish wash sometimes seen in spring. Note dull white supercilium, pale lores and square-ended tail. Face dominated by flat crown, rather long, prominent bill and dark eye with whitish eyering. Rump washed buff, faintly distinct from tail. **HABITAT** Shrubs, orchards, gardens, palm groves, lowlands and bushy hills. **VOICE** Call 'tack'; alarm repeated ticking; song high-pitched, rapid, scratchy warble.

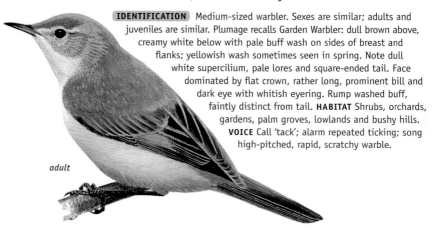

*adult*

# OLIVE-TREE WARBLER

**LENGTH** 15cm
**WINGSPAN** 24–26cm

*HIPPOLAIS OLIVETORUM*

**The Olive-tree Warbler is an arboreal species, favouring oak woods, orchards and olive groves. It is a more skulking, secretive species than other *Hippolais* warblers, feeding mostly in the canopy of the trees.**

**IDENTIFICATION** Large, greyish, long-winged warbler with dagger-like bill. Sexes similar. Adult upperparts and wings brownish-grey, with whitish edges to greater coverts, secondaries and tertials, forming wing panel. Has buff-white supercilium and whitish eyering. Bill's large size

accentuated by long, flat crown. Tail grey with white edges. Underparts dirty white with grey wash on breast, flanks and neck. Late summer plumage looks duller and wing panel is obscured. Juvenile as adult but upperparts more olive. **HABITAT** Coastal, insular, open-canopy woods, groves and orchards. **VOICE** Call 'tuc'; song distinctly lower-pitched and slower than its relatives'.

*adult*

# ICTERINE WARBLER

13.5cm **LENGTH**
20.5–24cm **WINGSPAN**

*HIPPOLAIS ICTERINA*

The Icterine Warbler is a robust bird with a dramatic song, and is the northeastern counterpart of the Melodious Warbler. This warbler is a summer visitor to the region.

*adults*

**IDENTIFICATION** Medium-sized warbler, with long bill accentuated by rather flat crown and long wings reaching at least to end of uppertail coverts. Sexes similar. Adult basically green above and yellow below. Area between bill and below eye yellow, giving a pale-faced effect. Wings have distinct pale panel formed by yellow edges to dark-olive tertials and secondaries. Legs bright blue-grey. Late-summer adults in worn plumage are browner above and whiter below. Juveniles usually flushed with yellow. **HABITAT** Mainly sunny wooded lowlands, cultivated lands and gardens, even in towns. **VOICE** Call 'tec' and, in spring, diagnostic 'deeteroo', song loud and mimetic.

*adult*

# MELODIOUS WARBLER

*HIPPOLAIS POLYGLOTTA*

| | |
|---|---|
| **LENGTH** | 13cm |
| **WINGSPAN** | 17.5–20cm |

The Melodious Warbler is the western counterpart of the Icterine Warbler, and like its relative is a summer visitor to Europe, overwintering in West Africa. It is very vocal in spring.

**IDENTIFICATION** Medium-sized, long-billed warbler. Sexes similar. Adult upperparts brownish-green (less bright than Icterine), underparts rich yellow. Wings and tail olive-brown; wings without pale wing panel (cf Icterine). Head round-crowned, brownish-green with yellow supercilium from bill to just behind eye, which has yellow eyering. Late-summer adults in worn plumage are bleached and appear dun-coloured above and whitish below. Juvenile in fresh plumage sometimes bright yellow or yellowish-green.

**HABITAT** Principally on wooded lowlands, often near water. **VOICE** Call 'hooeet'; alarm harsh 'tchurrrr'; song sustained, varied and musical.

*adults*

12.5cm **LENGTH**
13.5–17cm **WINGSPAN**

# SPECTACLED WARBLER
### SYLVIA CONSPICILLATA

The Spectacled Warbler is typically shy and skulking but, like a Whitethroat, it scolds intruders from a prominent perch, cocking its tail and showing off its white outertail feathers.

**IDENTIFICATION** Adult male grey to sandy brown above with striking orange edges to wing feathers forming glowing patch. Black tail clearly edged white. Underparts pink except for white chin, grey throat and buffish-grey head, which in some lights appears black between bill and below eye. Female browner on head and upperparts than male with no black on face; underparts less pink, more buff. Chin white. Female looks more like Whitethroat than male. Juvenile similar to female but with buffish suffusion to plumage. **HABITAT** In low scrub and rough ground beside cultivation; also in glasswort in wet lowlands with salt-laden soils. **VOICE** Call high 'tseet'; song short, sweet, rapid, variable warble.

*Recalls small Whitethroat or Subalpine Warbler without moustache but with striking white eyering.*

TOP: *juvenile*; ABOVE; *female*; BELOW: *male*

# DARTFORD WARBLER

*SYLVIA UNDATA*

**LENGTH** 12.5cm
**WINGSPAN** 13–18.5cm

**The Dartford Warbler is easy to separate from all other warblers except Marmora's and Balearic. It is a skulking bird and patience is needed to see it well.**

female

**IDENTIFICATION** Adult male is dark slaty brown above with greyer head, and wine-red below. Wings almost uniformly brownish-black. Tail grey-black with narrow, white edges. Throat white-spotted in fresh plumage but spots wear off by June or July. Bill dark brown. Legs brownish-yellow. Eye and eyering orange to red. Female duller than male. Juveniles are browner on upperparts and may be all grey below. **HABITAT** Low, dense cover on coastal scrub, heathland or maquis. **VOICE** Call 'tuc' and grating alarm 'tchirrr'; song musical chatter, some liquid notes.

*The Dartford Warbler is emblematic of southern English heathlands – its favoured habitat. Its fate is inextricably linked to that of these fragile heathlands themselves.*

male

male

12cm **LENGTH**
13–17.5cm **WINGSPAN**

# MARMORA'S WARBLER

*SYLVIA SARDA*

Marmora's Warbler is confined in the breeding season to the western Mediterranean islands between Corsica and Pantelleria (southwest of Sicily). Some birds migrate to northwest Africa in winter.

**IDENTIFICATION** Adult male dull blue-grey above and below. Wings and tail dull black, latter with dusky-white edges, often not noticeable. Legs yellow-brown. Female's plumage drabber and browner than male's. Juvenile even browner than female with dull-yellow eyes. **HABITAT** Heath and low scrub on dry hillsides and coastal slopes. **VOICE** Call explosive 'crrip' or 'tsig'; song weak, high-pitched warble.

*male*

> *Marmora's Warbler is found in the lowest vegetation layer and, unusually for a warbler, it spends up to one-third of its time on the ground. It often sings from the tops of bushes or in a song-flight, which is a steady ascent between 4m and 7m, followed by a dive into cover.*

12cm **LENGTH**
13–17.5cm **WINGSPAN**

# BALEARIC WARBLER

*SYLVIA BALEARICA*

Tiny, skulking warbler, restricted to Balearic islands (except Menorca) where it is resident. Easiest to see in spring when territorial males sometimes sing from exposed perches.

**IDENTIFICATION** Adult male is mostly dull blue-grey but with whiter throat than on Marmora's. Legs are orange and eye is orange-red. Female is duller than male with overall more brown tone to plumage. Juvenile is similar to female but browner and with dull yellow eyes. **HABITAT** Low Mediterranean scrub. **VOICE** Harsh alarm rattle; 'treek, treek' call; song rapid medley, harsh and musical.

> *Balearic Warbler was formerly considered to be conspecific with Marmora's Warbler, but it is now treated as a separate species. Outside the breeding season, when males in particular are sometimes inquisitive about human intruders into their territories, its skulking habits mean it is hard to find.*

*male*

# SARDINIAN WARBLER

*SYLVIA MELANOCEPHALA*

**LENGTH** 13.5cm
**WINGSPAN** 15–18cm

**The Sardinian Warbler breeds across the Mediterranean. Its song is more tuneful than the Whitethroat's, but uttered similarly from a perch or in flight.**

**IDENTIFICATION** Adult male has black hood extending well below eyes to lores and ear coverts; sharp division between cap and pure white chin and upper throat. Steep forehead helps to accentuate red eye and eyering. Rest of upperparts grey; rest of underparts off-white, fading to grey on flanks. Bill buffish-brown with black tip. Legs reddish. Wings blackish with feathers edged grey. Tail black, edged white. Female has same pattern on head as adult male but black replaced by dusky grey. Upperparts dirty brown; underparts and breast pinkish-brown, flanks dull brown; otherwise white. Juvenile similar to female. **HABITAT** From scanty undergrowth, scattered shrubs and thickets to open woodland. **VOICE** Harsh alarm rattle; 'treek, treek' call; song rapid medley, harsh and musical.

*Like male, **female** has red eye and eyering; dark-brown tail has same white edges as male's.*

***Adult male** distinctive but needs some care at first to separate from other black-headed warblers.*

12cm **LENGTH**
15–19cm **WINGSPAN**

# SUBALPINE WARBLER
*SYLVIA CANTILLANS*

The Subalpine Warbler is a summer visitor to the region, overwintering in Africa. It is most often seen in garrigue where broom, cistus and fragrant shrubs bloom.

**IDENTIFICATION** Adult male has pale blue-grey upperparts, dark pink-chestnut breast and unmarked throat, and conspicuous white 'moustache'. Rest of underparts and belly white, undertail coverts buff. Wings and tail dark grey-brown with pale-grey fringes to wing feathers and white outertail feathers. Bill blackish-brown, legs yellowish-brown. Rich red eye in red eyering. Adult female is pale grey-brown above, with clear but duller moustache. Underparts pinkish-buff; white area more extensive than on male and wings browner. Juvenile has washed-out colours but usually a hint of a white 'moustache'. Often hard to separate this species from Spectacled Warbler in autumn.

**HABITAT** Woodland glades, thickets, stream banks.

**VOICE** Call 'tec'; alarm oft-repeated 'tec'; song like Whitethroat's, but more musical.

ABOVE: *male*
BELOW: *female*

# CYPRUS WARBLER

*SYLVIA MELANOTHORAX*

**LENGTH** 13.5cm
**WINGSPAN** 15–18cm

As a breeding bird, the Cyprus Warbler is entirely restricted to Cyprus; it is widespread and common in suitable habitats. It tends to be shy and skulking.

**IDENTIFICATION** Adult male easily separated from other *Sylvia* warblers by black and white mottled underparts, from chin to undertail coverts, and pale fringes to innerwing feathers. Pronounced white moustache. Black tail with white edges contrasts with grey mantle, back and rump. Yellow to chestnut eye in yellowish to red eyering. Female similar to male but much duller and browner; moustachial stripe dull white. Eye and eyering duller than male's. Juvenile similar to female but markings on throat less pronounced; difficult to distinguish from juvenile Sardinian Warbler.
**HABITAT** Maquis scrub, especially among *Cistus*; also scrub forest edge.
**VOICE** Call is a grating 'tchek'; song vigorous rattle of high and low notes.

*Bill buffish-yellow and legs vary from flesh-yellow to reddish-brown.*

# ORPHEAN WARBLER

*SYLVIA HORTENSIS*

**LENGTH** 15cm
**WINGSPAN** 20–25cm

The Orphean Warbler is a summer visitor to the region. Eastern birds are often treated as separate species (*S. crassirostris*) from Western Orphean Warbler (*S. hortensis*).

**IDENTIFICATION** Robust warbler resembling a large Blackcap but easily distinguished by white outertail feathers and adult's pale yellow-white eyes. Adult male has dark cap extending to lores and ear coverts. Nape and upperparts grey-brown; wings and tail dusky brown. Pale-grey fringes to tertials and larger coverts. Underparts basically white but with pinkish flush on breast in breeding season. Bill long, blackish. Female closely resembles male but duller with more grey on upperparts. Juvenile even browner than female and lacks adults' dark head.
**HABITAT** Forest and scrub; also orange and olive groves, and gardens. **VOICE** Call 'tac, tac' or 'trrrr' alarm; song pleasant, thrush-like warble.

ABOVE LEFT: *adult Eastern*
LEFT: *adult Western*

14cm **LENGTH**
18–21cm **WINGSPAN**

# RÜPPELL'S WARBLER
### *SYLVIA RUEPPELLII*

Rüppell's Warbler is a summer visitor to its eastern Mediterranean breeding range. It has a splendid song-flight, with the bird rising to a height of 10 to 20m.

**IDENTIFICATION** Adult male has forehead, crown, lores, chin, throat and upper breast black, relieved by bright-red eye and eyering and conspicuous white moustache. Rest of upperparts grey and underparts greyish-white, greyer on flanks and whiter on belly. Tail black with white outer feathers. Bill quite long, blackish with paler, yellowish base to lower mandible. Female and juvenile duller and browner than adult male, with most showing faint impression of male's head markings.
**HABITAT** Thorny scrub, maquis, on rocky slopes and in gullies; also undergrowth in old woods.
**VOICE** Hard 'tak, tak', song rapid, chattering, with some call notes and pure tones.

Wings mainly black with striking whitish fringes and tips to tertials.

*female*

*male*

# BARRED WARBLER
*SYLVIA NISORIA*

**The Barred Warbler is a summer visitor to Europe and is the largest and among the most secretive of the *Sylvia* warblers. The males are best observed when displaying.**

**IDENTIFICATION** Robust warbler, all plumages of which show pale wingbars, pale-edged tertials and white-tipped tail. Adult male's head, face and upperparts grey. Pale-yellow eye. Wings dark brown-grey with pale bar on greater coverts, less clear bar on median coverts and pale, bright-grey edges and tips to tertials. Underparts dull white from chin to undertail coverts, liberally barred with dark grey-brown crescents, emphasised by white tips. Tail long and broad, dark brown with white edges. Adult female like male but duller and browner above with barring less clear below and paler eye. Juvenile recalls Garden Warbler, being unbarred and dark-eyed. **HABITAT** Often thorn thickets, riverine woodland or orchards. **VOICE** Call harsh 'charr'; song short, rich warble with harsh call notes mixed in.

RIGHT: *juvenile*
BELOW: *male*

14cm **LENGTH**
20–24.5cm **WINGSPAN**

# GARDEN WARBLER
### *SYLVIA BORIN*

The Garden Warbler is a bird of broad-leaved woodland with thick undergrowth. Its skulking habits and the similarity of its song to the Blackcap's mean that it may be a long time before an observer sees one and confirms its identity.

**IDENTIFICATION** Sexes similar. Adult has plain, brown plumage on upperparts, darker brown wings and pale-buff underparts (latter feature separating it from *Phylloscopus* warblers); belly and undertail coverts white. Eyering pale. Rounded head and stubby bill help distinguish it from *Hippolais* warblers. Juvenile more strongly marked buff below and tawny above. **HABITAT** Open deciduous or mixed woodland with thick undergrowth. **VOICE** Call soft, nasal 'check'; song rich, sustained, flowing warble.

*Plainest of the* Sylvia *warblers and medium- to large-sized.* **Adults** *shown here.*

*Song lacks Blackcap's flourish and wider range of pitch, but this is compensated for by greater persistence and richness of sound.*

327

# LESSER WHITETHROAT

*SYLVIA CURRUCA*

**LENGTH** 12.5–13.5cm
**WINGSPAN** 16.5–20.5cm

**A summer visitor, the Lesser Whitethroat arrives in the region from late April to early May. It frequents thickets, woodland edge and areas with scattered trees and thick cover.**

**IDENTIFICATION** Adult greyer above and whiter below than Whitethroat and lacks the contrasting rufous wing panel, so upperparts look dull grey-brown and underparts are dull white. Dark face mask formed by black lores and ear coverts against slate-grey on rest of head. Primaries and tail browner and darker than rest of upperparts. Outertail feathers white. Unusually for this genus, sexes similar but when seen side by side, male sometimes has blacker mask and paler pink flush on breast than female. **HABITAT** Woodland edge, thick hedges, shrubberies with thick, dark cover. **VOICE** Hard 'tack' or 'churr'; song loud rattle often preceded by quiet warble.

*Song is quite unlike Whitethroat's but can be misidentified as that of Cirl Bunting or Bonelli's Warbler.*

*adults*

14cm **LENGTH**
18.5–23cm **WINGSPAN**

# WHITETHROAT
### *SYLVIA COMMUNIS*

The Whitethroat is the most widespread *Sylvia* warbler in Europe, and the commonest on farmland. It is a bold bird, often scolding the observer from its vantage point on a bramble or bush.

*Female and **juvenile** (ABOVE) similar to **male** (RIGHT) but white throat is duller and rest of plumage browner; bill and leg colour as male's.*

**IDENTIFICATION** Adult male has grey cap extending to below eye, whitish eyering and brown eyes. Chin and throat pure white. Breast pale pinkish-buff and rest of underparts white. Upperparts dull brown, suffused with grey in spring plumage. Very distinctive panel on wing formed by rufous edges to wing coverts, secondaries and tertials. Tail dark brown with white outer feathers. Bill buffish-brown with dark tip; legs pale to flesh brown. For description of female and juvenile, *see* caption. **HABITAT** Most open habitats with thickets and shrubs. **VOICE** Scolding 'charr', sharp 'tac'; song short, rapid, chattery warble.

*adult male*

*Male has rather jerky song-flight, as if being bounced on invisible piece of elastic.*

# BLACKCAP
## *SYLVIA ATRICAPILLA*

**LENGTH** 13cm
**WINGSPAN** 20–23cm

**Across most of Europe the Blackcap is a summer visitor from Africa. Birds from the Mediterranean region are generally resident, however, and small numbers overwinter in northwest Europe.**

**IDENTIFICATION** Adult male has diagnostic black forehead and crown (cap) above ash-grey nape and face. Upperparts ashy brown, darker on tail and primaries (although wing coverts and tertials edged paler). Chin, breast and flanks grey, the first two silvery when plumage is fresh; belly and undertail coverts white. Bill dull black, legs slate. Adult female similar to male but cap bright red-brown and upperparts browner. Juvenile very like female but cap duller brown. **HABITAT** Open woodland and copses with thick undergrowth; in towns. **VOICE** Call loud repeated 'tac'; song loud, rich warble, rising in pitch.

*female*

*Unlike Marsh Tit's cap, male's black crown only extends as far as eye, not below; red-capped female unmistakable.*

*male*

12cm **LENGTH**
19.5–24cm **WINGSPAN**

# WOOD WARBLER
### *PHYLLOSCOPUS SIBILATRIX*

The Wood Warbler arrives on its breeding grounds in early May. On arrival the male vigorously defends a territory.

*adult*

*adult*

*First part of the song often delivered in flight, but trill invariably comes from a perch.*

**IDENTIFICATION** The most distinctive *Phylloscopus* warbler; larger than others, with relatively longer wings and shorter tail. Sexes alike. Adult appears to be a three-colour bird: yellowish-green upperparts; bright-yellow supercilium, throat and breast; pure white belly and undertail coverts. Tail, flight feathers and tertials brown, outer edges of first two edged yellowish-green, but tertials edged white or yellowish-white. Bill has dark-brown upper mandible, pale-flesh lower mandible. Legs pale yellowish-brown. Juvenile similar to brightly coloured adult. **HABITAT** Prefers hilly terrain, and woodland with good canopy (beech and oak especially). **VOICE** Usual call plaintive 'pew, pew'; song in two phases, mainly a trill.

*adult*

# WILLOW WARBLER

**LENGTH** 10.5–11.5cm
**WINGSPAN** 16.5–22cm

*PHYLLOSCOPUS TROCHILUS*

The Willow Warbler arrives in Europe in April.
It is the commonest *Phylloscopus* warbler in
the region and one of the most numerous
of Europe's summer visitors.

**IDENTIFICATION** Delicate little warbler, size of
a Blue Tit but slimmer. Adult olive-green above,
yellowish-white below; has cleaner colours
than very similar Chiffchaff. Has pale-yellow
supercilium, brown bill and orange-brown legs
(the latter reliably distinguish it from Chiffchaff).
Adults become browner above and whiter below
during summer from feather abrasion. Juvenile
in autumn has much yellower supercilium, throat
and breast than adult. **HABITAT** Woods, forests;
mostly coppices, scrub, anywhere with a few
trees. **VOICE** Call plaintive, disyllabic 'hoo-eet';
song lovely cascade of pure notes.

TOP AND ABOVE: *adult*
LEFT: *juvenile*

Like Chiffchaff, Willow Warbler
constantly inspects twigs and
foliage for tiny insects; frequently
flicks its wings and sings while
foraging.

10–11cm **LENGTH**
15–21cm **WINGSPAN**

# CHIFFCHAFF
*PHYLLOSCOPUS COLLYBITA*

*adult*

The Chiffchaff is a summer visitor and usually the first warbler to arrive; migrants first appear in early March. Most overwinter around the Mediterranean but a few overwinter in Britain.

*adult*

**IDENTIFICATION** Adult is dull brownish-olive above and dull, pale yellow below, shading to buff flanks. Browner above and more buff below than Willow Warbler, with much less yellow tint (although this is more noticeable on autumn juveniles). Eastern forms greyer above and whiter below than western forms, with whitish wingbar not normally found on western and southern forms. Otherwise all forms lack distinctive features except for pale-yellow supercilium, pale eyering, contrasting dark eyes and dark legs (distinguishing it from Willow Warbler). Juveniles and first-winter birds have warm-brown upperparts and yellowish underparts. **HABITAT** Woodland, but not deep forest or coniferous plantations; also copses, hedgerows. **VOICE** Call monosyllabic 'hweet, hweet'; song diagnostic 'chiff-chaff-chiff'.

10–11cm **LENGTH**
15–21cm **WINGSPAN**

# IBERIAN CHIFFCHAFF
*PHYLLOSCOPUS IBERICUS*

Previously treated as a subspecies of Chiffchaff, Iberian Chiffchaff has been elevated to species status. It is a summer visitor to uplands in central Spain and winters in Africa.

**IDENTIFICATION** Adult is similar to adult Chiffchaff but greener on the rump and yellower on the underparts. Note the pale supercilium and eyering, and dark eyes and legs. **HABITAT** Upland woodlands and scrub. **VOICE** Song is a sweet 'tsit-tsit-tsit-tswee-tswee', quite different from that of Chiffchaff.

*adult*

# GREENISH WARBLER

*PHYLLOSCOPUS TROCHILOIDES*

**LENGTH** 10cm
**WINGSPAN** 15–21cm

The Greenish Warbler is always on the move, usually in the forest canopy. It is like Willow and Arctic Warblers and Chiffchaff, but has a distinctive call and song.

**IDENTIFICATION** Small and superficially similar to Willow Warbler. Plumage pale greyish-olive above, dull white below. Shows long, yellowish-white supercilium reaching nearly to the nape (often upturned at the end), dark eyestripe and pale wingbar (in fresh plumage). Bill has pale lower mandible; legs variable shade of brown, distinguishing bird from Arctic Warbler. Juvenile in first-winter plumage similar to adult but sometimes shows faint second wingbar. **HABITAT** Open woodland (coniferous or broad-leaved) copses, overgrown orchards. **VOICE** Call distinctive 'chee-wee', the second note lower; song Wren-like medley.

*Small, slim, graceful warbler; continually active.*

**adult**

# ARCTIC WARBLER

*PHYLLOSCOPUS BOREALIS*

**LENGTH** 10.5–11.5cm
**WINGSPAN** 16.5–22cm

The Arctic Warbler is a common breeding bird within its range. At the start of the breeding season, the male's display includes a remarkable wing-rattling as he flies between song-posts.

**IDENTIFICATION** Superficially similar to several other members of the genus *Phylloscopus* (especially Willow and Greenish Warblers, and Chiffchaff) but bulkier in the body. Adult largely greenish above and off-white below. Best features are obvious creamy wingbar and yellowish-white supercilium from bill to nape, often upturned at hind end. Shows dark eyestripe, noticeably pointed brown bill and pale yellowish-brown legs. Juvenile similar to adult but with brighter colours. **HABITAT** Taiga forest, willow and birch forest, often near water or damp ground. **VOICE** Calls 'tzic' and 'tseep'; song loud, energetic but monotonous trill.

**adult**

*Robust and active*
Phylloscopus *warbler.*

11.5cm **LENGTH**
16–20cm **WINGSPAN**

# WESTERN BONELLI'S WARBLER

*PHYLLOSCOPUS BONELLI*

Formerly treated as a race of Bonelli's Warbler, Western Bonelli's Warbler has been split from its eastern cousin and elevated to species status. It is widespread in western southern Europe.

**IDENTIFICATION** Distinctly pale leaf warbler with light grey-brown upperparts, washed with pale olive-green. Head and nape often look particularly pale and note the silky white underparts and pale yellowish rump. Legs are dull brown. Sexes and ages are similar.
**HABITAT** Forests, usually 700–2,000m above sea level.
**VOICE** Call 'hu-eet'; song is a trill, recalling Wood Warbler.

*Western Bonelli's Warbler has 'warmer' more yellow-buff tones to the upperparts than its eastern cousin (see below).*

*adult*

11.5cm **LENGTH**
16–20cm **WINGSPAN**

# EASTERN BONELLI'S WARBLER

*PHYLLOSCOPUS ORIENTALIS*

The eastern counterpart of Western Bonelli's, this species is found mainly in Greece and Turkey. Like its western cousin it is an unobtrusive bird of the upper leaf canopy of forests.

**IDENTIFICATION** Distinctly pale leaf warbler with light grey-brown upperparts. Head and nape often look particularly pale and note the silky white underparts and pale yellowish rump. Legs are dull brown. Sexes and ages are similar. **HABITAT** Forests, usually 700–2,000m above sea level. **VOICE** Call 'chirp'; song is a trill, recalling Wood Warbler.

*Most birds arrive at the breeding grounds by mid-April and the eggs are laid by mid-May.*

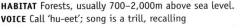

*adult*

335

# GOLDCREST
### REGULUS REGULUS

**LENGTH** 9cm
**WINGSPAN** 13.5–15.5cm

In the breeding season Goldcrests are mainly found in conifer woodlands, but will inhabit cemeteries and parks if some suitable conifers are present. In winter they often move with tits and treecreepers.

*Whilst foraging for food, Goldcrests are often seemingly indifferent to human observers.*

*male*

*female*

**IDENTIFICATION** Tiny: Europe's smallest bird. Adults have dull, greenish upperparts, pale olive-green underparts, darker on the flanks. Wing coverts greenish; paler wing panels and wingbar. Appears to be large-eyed, black on a plain face. Crown of male orange-yellow, lined each side with black, often not noticeable in the field; in display male raises crest to reveal startling orange centre. Crown centre of female yellow. Juvenile lacks adults' crown markings. **HABITAT** Coniferous woods for breeding; wanders widely in winter. **VOICE** Calls frequently; song repeated double note and trill; all very high pitched.

*male*

9cm **LENGTH**
13–16cm **WINGSPAN**

# FIRECREST
### *REGULUS IGNICAPILLUS*

*juvenile*

The Firecrest is much less widespread than the Goldcrest, breeding only in warmer parts of Europe. Northern and eastern populations are migratory.

**IDENTIFICATION**  Adult is more brightly coloured than Goldcrest. Most striking feature is striped head: male has golden-orange crown stripe, lined each side with black; crown stripe of female yellow. Both sexes show white supercilium underlined by black eyestripe. Mantle to uppertail coverts bright olive-green, tail darker and browner; all underparts greenish-white. Striking bronze patch on side of neck. Bill black, legs brown. Juvenile plumage shows pale supercilium but crown and shoulder are plain greenish. Immatures acquire adult-like plumage before autumn migration.

**HABITAT** Less restricted to conifers than Goldcrest; gardens, scrub, tree heath.
**VOICE** Very high-pitched; 'zit, zit,' call, lower than Goldcrest; song rapid string of calls.

*Greener above and whiter below than Goldcrest, and shows bright-orange shoulder patches.*

ABOVE AND BELOW: *male*

# PIED FLYCATCHER
*FICEDULA HYPOLEUCA*

**LENGTH** 13cm
**WINGSPAN** 21.5–24cm

Pied Flycatchers are summer visitors to Europe and winter in Africa. Males arrive before females and select a nest hole. They sing until they have attracted a mate. After nesting, most adults migrate south in August, stopping off in southern Europe for a week or so to feed.

**IDENTIFICATION** Very similar to Collared and Semi-collared Flycatchers. Breeding male black above and unmarked white below, but black is relieved by white forehead (often divided into two spots), white-edged tertials, which meet white bar on greater wing coverts and white basal half of outertail feathers. From central Europe eastwards males are increasingly grey-brown, not black. After breeding, male moults and black elements of plumage replaced by brown or grey, so white wing panel not so striking. Female resembles non-breeding male but tail and rump not as black. Bill and legs black in all plumages. Juvenile looks like non-breeding adult with buff-spotted crown, mantle and breast. **HABITAT** Deciduous and mixed open woodland; has spread to orchards, gardens. **VOICE** Call loud 'whit' or 'wee-tic'; alarm 'phweet'; song a rapid sequence of high and low notes.

ABOVE: *Adult female has black elements of male's plumage replaced by brown.*
BELOW: *male*

13cm **LENGTH**
22.5–24.5cm **WINGSPAN**

# COLLARED FLYCATCHER
### FICEDULA ALBICOLLIS

The Collared Flycatcher returns to Europe to breed from late April to mid-May. It feeds mainly in tree canopies. The best chance of finding one in a wood comes with recognising the call and song.

ABOVE: *female*
RIGHT: *male*

**IDENTIFICATION** Very like Pied and Semi-collared Flycatchers; breeding male unmistakable but other plumages hard to separate from these two species. Breeding male white below and black above. Note white forehead, broad white collar, white wing panel from tertials to flight feathers, whitish patch on lower back and rump, and black (or mottled white) outertail feathers. Female, immature and winter male lack collar and have black elements of male's plumage replaced by brown. **HABITAT** Sunny, deciduous woodland and forest, well-timbered parks, orchards. **VOICE** Call 'seep'; song like Pied Flycatcher's, a series of high and low notes and whistles.

13cm **LENGTH**
23.5–24cm **WINGSPAN**

# SEMI-COLLARED FLYCATCHER
### FICEDULA SEMITORQUATA

The Semi-collared is the rarest flycatcher in the region, restricted to oak or Hornbeam forest in its main range, and beech forest in Greece. Males arrive at their breeding grounds several days before females.

**IDENTIFICATION** Breeding male black above and white below; has white patch on forehead. Note white half-collar, white wing panel where tertials meet white-tipped greater coverts and bases to flight feathers. Short white bar on median coverts is not found in other flycatchers. Has greyish lower back and rump, and more extensive white in outertail feathers than Pied or Collared Flycatchers. Female has black elements of male's plumage replaced by grey-brown. **HABITAT** Deciduous forest on mountain slopes up to 2,000m above sea level, and riverine forest. **VOICE** Calls include a loud 'whit'; song a rapid sequence of high and low notes; hard to distinguish from related flycatchers.

*male*

# SPOTTED FLYCATCHER

*MUSICAPA STRIATA*

**This drably coloured flycatcher is the most widespread flycatcher in the region. It obtains most of its food in flight and uses an open perch from which it sallies forth.**

**IDENTIFICATION** Largest flycatcher in the region and the only one with streaked underparts. Adult has all upperparts, wings and tail grey-brown, appearing unmarked at long range. Sexes similar. Forehead and crown streaked black, outlined in white. Underparts white, washed with brown on side of breast and flanks. At close range, throat, side of breast and flanks show dull-brown streaks. Bill dull grey-brown. Legs brown or black. Juvenile superficially similar to adult but upperparts buffer than adult's; feathers of head, back, rump, lesser and median coverts have pale, round, buff-white spots; underparts not streaked like those of adult but spotted dark brown. **HABITAT** Woodland edge, glades, parks, orchards, gardens. **VOICE** Call 'tzee-zuk-zuk'; song quiet, short, squeaky.

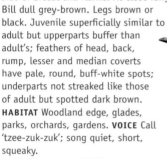

*adults*

11.5cm **LENGTH**
18.5–21cm **WINGSPAN**

# RED-BREASTED FLYCATCHER
### *FICEDULA PARVA*

*1st autumn*

The Red-breasted Flycatcher is a forest bird, preferring tall trees, especially beech. It is a summer visitor and usually arrives in Europe in early May.

*Male's song is a loud, silvery run of mostly pure notes, reminiscent of Willow Warbler; he only sings until incubation starts.*

*summer male*

**IDENTIFICATION** Adults of both sexes ashy brown above; flanks washed with buff; wings and tail dark brown. Tail has diagnostic long, white patches each side at the base, noticeable in flight and when bird flicks its tail. Male has orange-red chin, throat and upper breast, and looks like diminutive Robin, but female has buff throat and breast. Juvenile is spotted, but retains the white tail patches. First-winter plumage similar to female. In all plumages, dark eye is highlighted by white eyering, more noticeable in the male. **HABITAT** Mixed and deciduous forest with much undergrowth. **VOICE** Call short, harsh 'trrt'; song cadence, descending in pitch.

341

# CRESTED TIT
## *LOPHOPHANES CRISTATUS*

**LENGTH** 11.5cm
**WINGSPAN** 17–20cm

**The Crested Tit is the only small European bird with a crest. It is a very sedentary bird, only very rarely wandering as far as 50km.**

**IDENTIFICATION** Small tit with backward-pointing black crest, with the feathers tipped white. Sexes similar. Adult has very distinctive face pattern of black line on a white face, running behind eye and around rear of ear coverts; another black line starts at end of crest and runs down side of neck to join black bib. Upperparts buff-brown, wings and tail grey-brown. Bill black, quite long for a small tit. Legs olive-grey. Juvenile has shorter crest than adult but otherwise similar. **HABITAT** Pine forest in the north; mixed woods; also in beech or cork oak woods in south. **VOICE** Call low-pitched purring trill; song makes repeated use of calls.

*The Crested Tit's range is limited by its need for rotten wood in which to excavate its nest hole.*

*Crest can be very difficult to see, particularly if bird is overhead.*

*adult*

*adult*

11.5cm **LENGTH**
17–21cm **WINGSPAN**

# COAL TIT
*PERIPARUS ATER*

The Coal Tit is often considered the most typical tit of coniferous woods, but in southern and western Europe it is more often found in mixed and deciduous forest. It readily comes to bird tables in winter.

*Distinctive double wingbar is often easier to see than nape patch; at close range wingbars show as separate white spots.*

*adult*

*adult*

**IDENTIFICATION** Slightly smaller and shorter-tailed than Blue Tit. Adult has glossy black cap and white cheeks; large, white patch on nape is diagnostic. Cap extends down to level of eye; chin, throat, upper breast black, joined to cap by black collar. Underparts buff, paler towards the centre. Upperparts, wings and tail olive-grey. Median and greater wing coverts have white tips, forming two wingbars. Bill rather fine, black. Legs lead-blue. Sexes similar but female has less extensive bib. Juvenile similar to adult but markings less distinctive. **HABITAT** Typically coniferous forest and woodland, but now anywhere with firs, including cemeteries and parks. **VOICE** Call piping 'tsee'; song loud and clear 'teechu, teechu, teechu'.

*adult*

# LONG-TAILED TIT

*AEGITHALOS CAUDATUS*

**LENGTH** 14cm
**WINGSPAN** 16–19cm

Long-tailed Tits are territorial in the breeding season, after which they are gregarious, forming small flocks. A flock keeps together with the help of a constant 'conversation' of 'tsirrrup' calls.

**IDENTIFICATION** Sexes similar. Adult birds from most of Europe have head and underparts whitish, washed with dusky pink on nape, and from belly to undertail coverts; black bands extend from bill, above the eyes to the mantle. Upperparts, wings and tail dull black, with pink scapulars and rump, and white tips and edges to graduated tail feathers. Pink tones wear off. Adult of subspecies from northern and eastern Europe has pure white head and noticeably white-edged tertials and secondaries; birds of southern subspecies have grey backs, darker faces, and little or no pink. Eyering reddish in all birds. Juvenile shorter and darker than adult, with dusky mask and drab upperparts.
**HABITAT** Deciduous woodland; for nesting, thick scrub like gorse, bramble or briar.
**VOICE** Call low, repeated 'tsupp'; alarm trilled 'tsirrrrup'; song rapid repetition of calls.

*Adult* of western European race.

*Tiny-bodied, long-tailed bird, not related to true tits.*

*Adult* of Scandinavian race.

*Adult* of Western European race.

14cm **LENGTH**
22.5–25.5cm **WINGSPAN**

# GREAT TIT
*PARUS MAJOR*

The Great Tit has the widest distribution
in the world of all the tits. In winter
they regularly come to bird
tables and feeders.

*adult
male*

*Song is vary varied,
often leading to
misidentification.*

***Juveniles*** (LEFT) *look very
washed out and have yellow
cheeks rather than white.*

*adult
male*

*Large size and
striking combination
of colours make Great
Tit unmistakable.*

**IDENTIFICATION** The largest common
tit, with quite a long tail. Adult is
basically yellow-green above and
yellow below. Wings have black
flight feathers, blue-grey coverts and
black tertials, tipped white. Shows white wingbar and white outertail feathers. Distinctive head
pattern comprises glossy blue-black cap with triangular white cheek patch. Black on chin and
throat extends into bold, black stripe down centre of underparts, forming a wide black patch
between legs on male, and much narrower one on female. Bill strong and black. Legs blue-grey.
Juvenile similar to adult but has sooty crown, browner back, cheeks washed yellow and underparts
duller yellow. **HABITAT** Almost anywhere with trees, except coniferous forest; even in cities.
**VOICE** Call loud 'tink, tink, tink'; song far-carrying 'teacher, teacher, teacher'.

# BLUE TIT
*CYANISTES CAERULEUS*

**LENGTH** 11.5cm
**WINGSPAN** 17.5–20cm

The Blue Tit is abundant in most habitats with trees, although it avoids conifers. It tends to feed high up in broad-leaved trees, but will visit bird tables in winter.

### IDENTIFICATION

Adult is the only European tit with bright-blue crown, bordered with white. Has dark lines from bill through eye, around back of head and around otherwise white cheeks. Upperparts yellowish-green, underparts sulphur-yellow, with small blackish central streak. Wings dark blue with white wingbar. Tail dark grey-blue. Bill short, black. Legs dusky blue. Female very similar to male but colours less bright. Juvenile washed yellow and lacks blue in plumage but similar to adult in other respects.
**HABITAT** Anywhere with trees, even inner-city parks and gardens. **VOICE** Call 'tsee-tsee'; alarm 'chirr.r.r'; song tremolo 'tsee-tsee-tsee-tsuhuhuhu'.

*Male glides slowly towards a possible nest site to attract females to it; at other times flight action is fluttery.*

*Blue Tits are extremely acrobatic and, unlike Great Tits, are light enough to forage at the tips of even the thinnest twigs.*

*adults*

14cm **LENGTH**
21.5–23cm **WINGSPAN**

# SOMBRE TIT
*POECILE LUGUBRIS*

**Although as large as a Great Tit and easy to identify, the Sombre Tit is hard to find because it spends so much time in the foliage of the woods and open forests it inhabits.**

*Has heavy bill to split large seeds.*

**IDENTIFICATION** Dull plumage pattern similar to Marsh Tit's. Adult has sooty black, long cap. Sooty black chin and throat appear as large bib. Cheeks, ear coverts and sides of neck white. Upperpart, wings and tail ashy brown, with distinct greyish-white fringes to tertials and inner secondaries. Underparts dull, creamy white with ash-brown wash on the sides. Bill strong, black. Legs grey. Female similar to male but with less contrasting cap. Juvenile is similar to adult female, with grubby cheeks. **HABITAT** Open forest, orchards, vineyards, conifers, scrub. **VOICE** Call loud 'churrrr'; song unmusical repetition of a single note.

*adult*

11cm **LENGTH**
16–17.5cm **WINGSPAN**

# SIBERIAN TIT
*POECILE CINCTUS*

**The Siberian Tit is a rather sedentary resident. In winter it visits the houses of foresters to feed on bird tables and rubbish-tips.**

*Very confiding, even at nest site.*

**IDENTIFICATION** Large, often fluffy-looking tit. Sexes alike. Adult and juvenile have sooty-brown cap and nape, with darker line through eye. White face. Large sooty-black bib with broken edge. Upperparts warm brown. Wings dark brown, flight feathers edged with greyish-white, creating strong contrast between wings and back. Tail grey-black with dull-white outer feathers. Breast and belly are dull white, sides of breast and flanks are rusty red. Bill black. Legs grey. **HABITAT** Coniferous taiga, tree-lined river banks, virgin coniferous forest. **VOICE** Call 'sip' and 'tchay' similar to Willow Tit; song unmusical repetition of calls.

*adult*

# WILLOW TIT
*POECILE MONTANA*

**LENGTH** 11.5cm
**WINGSPAN** 17–20.5cm

The Willow Tit favours different habitats across its range. Conifers are preferred on southern mountain slopes while lowland river valleys and trees on damp ground are chosen at lower altitudes. Northern birch and conifer woodlands are the species' haunt at northern latitudes.

**IDENTIFICATION** Very similar in size and appearance to Marsh Tit, but looks less smart than that species. Adult has black cap extending down to mantle. Black bib quite extensive, with poorly defined borders. Tail is slightly round-ended, not square or slightly forked. Best plumage difference is this species' light patch on secondaries in closed wing (not always conspicuous, however). Scandinavian and central European birds much greyer on back and whiter on face than British birds, which are closest in appearance to Marsh Tit. Juvenile very similar to adult of any given race. Always note call notes as well as plumage details to separate this species from Marsh Tit. **HABITAT** Montane, coniferous forest; trees on damp ground; mixed woodland. **VOICE** Calls 'eez-eez-eez' and characteristic, nasal 'tchay, tchay'; song a single note, repeated lugubriously.

The nest hole is excavated by both male and female but only the female builds the nest.

*Adult of British race very similar to Marsh Tit; has plumper appearance, duller black cap and buffish flanks.*

*adult*

11.5cm **LENGTH**
18–19.5cm **WINGSPAN**

# MARSH TIT
*POECILE PALUSTRIS*

**The Marsh Tit is separable from the Willow Tit only with difficulty: note its glossy black cap, small bib, paler underparts, lack of a pale wing panel and its distinct calls and song.**

*adult*

**IDENTIFICATION** In Europe, one of four dark-capped tits with similar plumage pattern (*see also* Willow, Siberian and Sombre Tits), though each has clear size and colour differences. Sexes similar. Adult has glossy black cap from bill to nape. Small black chin and centre of throat, rest of face white. Wings, tail and upperparts greyish-brown, with dark-brown centres to tail feathers. Underparts dull white, with pale-buff tinge on flanks and undertail coverts. Bill short and black. Legs dark blue-grey. Juvenile very similar to adult but cap not glossy. Acquires adult plumage by September. **HABITAT** Deciduous woodland, especially oak and beech, not marshes. **VOICE** Calls 'pitchoo' and nasal 'ter-char-char-char'; song repetition on one note.

*adult*

*Neck is slimmer and bib neater than on Willow Tit.*

# PENDULINE TIT
## *REMIZ PENDULINUS*

**LENGTH** 11cm
**WINGSPAN** 16–17.5cm

The Penduline Tit is migratory in the north of the range, and resident in the south. The migrants winter in southern Europe within the species' overall breeding range. Small groups are sometimes seen outside the breeding season.

**IDENTIFICATION** Smaller than Blue Tit, but with relatively longer tail. Adult has pale-grey head with black mask. Mantle, scapulars and wing coverts chestnut. Flight feathers black, fringed with buff. Back and rump greyish, contrasting with nearly black tail, which has off-white feather margins. Underparts off-white with chestnut smudges on sides of breast and flanks. Bill black. Legs bluish-black. Sexes similar, but female less bright than male. Juvenile lacks black face mask of adult and has cinnamon back. **HABITAT** Luxuriant vegetation by fresh or brackish water. **VOICE** Call soft drawn out 'tseeoo' and tit-like 'tsi-tsi-tsi'; song finch-like trill.

*Plant fibres of hop and nettle are the main nest materials, woven tightly to a felt-like consistency with plant down and wool.*

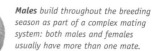

*Males build throughout the breeding season as part of a complex mating system: both males and females usually have more than one mate.*

12.5cm **LENGTH**
16–18cm **WINGSPAN**

# BEARDED TIT
### *PANURUS BIARMICUS*

The Bearded Tit is very dependent on reedbeds and its patchy distribution reflects its precise habitat requirements. It is a species that suffers badly in hard winters. Birders often refer to it as a 'pinger' because of its distinctive call.

**IDENTIFICATION** Short-winged, very long-tailed, unmistakable bird with predominantly tawny russet plumage at all times. Adult male has grey head and striking black 'moustaches' of loose feathers highlighted by white chin and throat. Tail graduated, with white tips to feathers forming ladder effect. Undertail coverts black. Closed wing appears banded: white on outer flight feathers, rufous centre panel, black and white tertials. Stubby yellow bill, orange eye, black legs. Female lacks male's head pattern, is duller and less russet; undertail coverts warm buff but similar to male in other respects. Juvenile resembles female but has obvious black back and wing coverts. **HABITAT** Large reedbeds. **VOICE** Call explosive, metallic 'ping'; song quiet and easy to miss.

*adult male*

*adult female*

# NUTHATCH
*SITTA EUROPAEA*

**LENGTH** 14cm
**WINGSPAN** 22.5–27cm

The Nuthatch is the only widespread member of its family in Europe. It is a resident and very sedentary. All ages are tolerant of humans and regularly visit bird tables in winter.

*Scandinavian race **adult***

**IDENTIFICATION** Easily recognised by plump body, short tail, long head and woodpecker-like bill. Only male has darker chestnut patch on flanks. Adult upperparts all blue-grey. Cheeks and throat white. Rest of underparts orange-buff merging into orange in birds from central, southern and western Europe but much paler in Scandinavian race. Has white-centred chestnut undertail coverts. Broad, black eyestripe. Outertail feathers black with white subterminal spots. Bill long, pointed, greyish-black. Legs yellowish-brown. Juvenile similar to adult but duller below. **HABITAT** Broad-leaved and mixed woods, open parkland, avenues of older trees.
**VOICE** Call loud 'chwit-chwit'. Song rapid 'chu-chu-chu', slow 'pee, pee, pee'.

*This small, woodpecker-like bird is always on the move.*

*British race* **adult**

Nuthatches are the only European birds that can move head first down a tree-trunk in search of food.

12cm **LENGTH**
21–22cm **WINGSPAN**

# CORSICAN NUTHATCH
*SITTA WHITEHEADI*

The Corsican Nuthatch is one of Europe's rarest birds. It is chiefly sedentary, although snow in the mountains will force birds down below 1,000m.

**IDENTIFICATION** Noticeably small nuthatch. Finest bill, longest-looking head and shortest tail of the European nuthatches. Adult essentially grey-blue above, dull white below. Male has head pattern of jet-black crown and long, white supercilium, underlined with long, black eyestripe. Female has black crown replaced by dusky blue. Both sexes show dark primaries. Outertail feathers black with white tips. Bill black, greyish at base. Legs lead-grey. Juvenile similar to adult female but with buff wash to all underparts except throat. **HABITAT** Tall, old, unmixed, unmanaged pine forest at 1,000–1,500m above sea-level. **VOICE** Call quiet 'yip'; song trill of short notes, ascending in pitch.

*adult*

12cm **LENGTH**
21–22cm **WINGSPAN**

# KRÜPER'S NUTHATCH
*SITTA KRUEPERI*

Krüper's Nuthatch has a limited global range – mainly coastal Turkey and the southern fringes of the Black Sea. In Europe, it is also found on the Greek island of Lesvos.

**IDENTIFICATION** Small nuthatch with an extremely slender bill. Adult male is essentially grey-blue above, with white face and throat and pale blue-grey underparts showing striking red chest patch and reddish undertail coverts; note the dark eyestripe, white supercilium and blackish cap. Female is similar to male but with less intense dark cap and paler chest band. Bill is greyish with dark tip. Legs are lead-grey. Juvenile similar to adult female. **HABITAT** Mature, unmanaged pine forests. **VOICE** Call quiet 'tiuu'; song is a trilling series of nasal notes.

*adult*

# ROCK NUTHATCH
*SITTA NEUMAYER*

**LENGTH** 13.5–14.5cm
**WINGSPAN** 23–25cm

Rock Nuthatches mostly hunt on the ground and in rock crevices. When feeding, one of the pair will continually break off from foraging to check for predators.

**IDENTIFICATION** Similar in appearance to Nuthatch but much paler. Adult is basically blue-grey above from forehead to tail, and dirty white below. Underparts change from white on face and throat, to buff belly; darkest on undertail coverts. Long, broad, black eyestripe separates grey crown and white face. Grey tail is unmarked. Bill black with paler base to lower mandible.
**HABITAT** Sunny, rocky slopes with poor shrub vegetation up to 1,000m. **VOICE** Call excited trill; song is a loud trill, variable in tempo.

adult

adult

adult

354

16.5cm **LENGTH**
27–32cm **WINGSPAN**

# WALLCREEPER
### *TICHODROMA MURARIA*

**Wallcreepers are often found near torrents, caves and scree. Birds are constantly on the move, clambering up near-vertical rock faces and flicking their wings as they search for insects.**

*It seems likely that the spectacular crimson coverts and white spots evolved as visual signals, this form of communication being more effective in mountainous terrain than sound.*

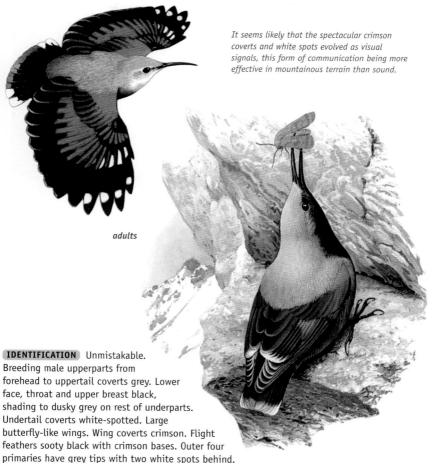

*adults*

**IDENTIFICATION** Unmistakable. Breeding male upperparts from forehead to uppertail coverts grey. Lower face, throat and upper breast black, shading to dusky grey on rest of underparts. Undertail coverts white-spotted. Large butterfly-like wings. Wing coverts crimson. Flight feathers sooty black with crimson bases. Outer four primaries have grey tips with two white spots behind. Tail black, tipped grey with a white spot on outertail feathers. Male moults between July and September. Tail and flight feathers then look blacker but face and upper breast lose black, becoming white, shading to grey. Legs black at all times. Bill black, needle-like, long and decurved. Female and juvenile similar to non-breeding male. **HABITAT** Rocky, broken, precipitous mountain terrain, 1,000–2,000m. **VOICE** Call short chirp; song comprises clear whistles in crescendo, rising in pitch.

# TREECREEPER
*CERTHIA FAMILIARIS*

**LENGTH** 12.5cm
**WINGSPAN** 17.5–21cm

The Treecreeper is hard to find in the woods because of its camouflaged plumage and high-pitched voice, which is beyond the hearing of many. It creeps close to the trunk on its short legs, supported on its tail feathers.

*adult*

**IDENTIFICATION** Sexes alike. At a distance adult appears brown above and silky white below. At close range shows rufous rump, long, white supercilium and white-mottled and streaked back. Complex pattern on wings comprises two pale-buff wingbars on coverts, buff band across secondaries and primaries, and white-spotted tertials. Tail is long and brown with dark shafts; feathers are stiff and pointed, and when spread the tail looks frayed. Bill quite long, gently decurved (rare in European passerines) and dark brown. Legs pale brown. Juvenile very similar to adult but upperparts appear spotted. *See* entry for Short-toed Treecreeper, which is almost identical, for details of separation of the two species. **HABITAT** Predominantly in mature broad-leaved trees, but also conifers. **VOICE** Call thin 'tsiew'; song high-pitched cadence lasting 2.5–3 seconds.

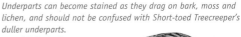

*Underparts can become stained as they drag on bark, moss and lichen, and should not be confused with Short-toed Treecreeper's duller underparts.*
LEFT: **Adult** singing.
BELOW: **adult**

12.5cm **LENGTH**
17–20.5cm **WINGSPAN**

# SHORT-TOED TREECREEPER
### *CERTHIA BRACHYDACTYLA*

The Short-toed Treecreeper is very similar to the Treecreeper; its most reliable field characteristic is its voice. Its calls are louder and less sibilant than its relative's and include a diagnostic, shrill, 'tseep'.

*adult*

*Attractive woodland bird; **adult** has delicately marked brown upperparts and white underparts.*

*Like Treecreeper, usually solitary outside the breeding season, but will associate with foraging tit flock.*

**IDENTIFICATION** Very similar to Treecreeper and often best distinguished by voice. Sexes alike. Adult is brown above and white below. Compared to Treecreeper, sustained observation should reveal these differences: (a) upperparts and wings are duller, browner and less obviously spotted; (b) dull brown rump; (c) shorter, duller supercilium often not showing in front of eye; (d) breast and rest of underparts washed grey or brown, most noticeably on the flanks; (e) bill usually looks longer and more slender, and bent at tip rather than gently decurved. Juvenile similar to adult but upperparts appear more spotted.
**HABITAT** Tall trees with rugged bark in parks, avenues, orchards, forest edge.
**VOICE** Call shrill 'zeet', and 'srriih'; song comprises short, loud phrase.

# RED-BACKED SHRIKE

*LANIUS COLLURIO*

**LENGTH** 17cm
**WINGSPAN** 24–27cm

**Red-backed Shrikes are summer visitors to Europe. Most of a shrike's prey is hunted using a 'wait-and-see' strategy from a perch with a good all-round view.**

*juvenile*

**IDENTIFICATION** Adult male has blue-grey crown and nape, chestnut back, blue-grey rump and black tail with white outer feathers. Underparts pinkish-white. Shows narrow, black band across forehead extending into broad, black mask through eye and across ear coverts. Flight feathers, tertials and greater coverts brown-black with chestnut margins. Bill black, distinctly hawk-like with hooked tip. Legs grey-black. Female has rufous-brown upperparts, reddish tail, pale-buff supercilium and cream underparts with brown crescent markings. Juvenile similar to female with close barring and black crescents on upperparts. **HABITAT** Sunny, open terrain with bushes and small trees for lookouts. **VOICE** Call harsh 'chack, chack'; song subdued, lengthy, with mimicry.

*female*

*male*

*male*

*At rest, frequently fans tail or swings it from side to side.*

*Now essentially extinct as breeding bird in Britain and northwest Europe, but may be seen on passage.*

18cm **LENGTH**
26–28cm **WINGSPAN**

# WOODCHAT SHRIKE

*LANIUS SENATOR*

Woodchat Shrikes prefer less open perches in trees than other shrikes, from which they drop or glide onto ground-prey or chase flying insects. Males have the best song of all European shrikes.

*juvenile*

*female*

**IDENTIFICATION** Small pied shrike with chestnut rear crown, nape and upper mantle in all adult plumages. Adult male has black forehead, which continues as broad, black patch through eye and ear coverts, and black wings and tail. Shows white outertail feathers, rump (conspicuous in flight), scapulars (forming two oval patches when perched) and underparts. Back grey. Bill short but strong, hook-tipped, black. Legs black. Female similar to male but colours duller and shows chestnut flecks in black forehead, white at base of bill, browner back and variable markings on breast. Juvenile has mostly grey or buff upperparts with pale whitish-buff scapulars, all barred with dark brown. Rump rufous and underparts dull white with many crescent-shaped bars. Whitish supercilium. Wings brownish-black with paler feather edges. Tail brownish-black with white edges.
**HABITAT** Woodland margins, old orchards, roadsides, maquis. **VOICE** Call 'kiwick, kiwick'; song is a rich sustained warble with mimicry.

*male*

*Adult birds are easily recognised by their black, white and chestnut plumage.*

# MASKED SHRIKE
*LANIUS NUBICUS*

**LENGTH** 17–18cm
**WINGSPAN** 24–26.5cm

The Masked Shrike has less of a hawk-like bill than other shrikes in Europe. It hunts more from the inside and lower branches of trees, and less from exposed perches.

**IDENTIFICATION** Small shrike, more slightly built than Woodchat Shrike, and with proportionately the longest tail of the region's shrikes. Male distinctively pied: generally black above and white below with reddish-orange flanks. Has white forehead and supercilium, white outertail feathers, white scapulars and broad, white bar across base of primaries. Bill slight, black. Legs black. Female similarly patterned to male but has greyer head, browner wings and less rusty underparts. Juvenile plumage scaly grey-brown; very hard to separate from young Woodchat Shrike but has longer tail and greyer upperparts. **HABITAT** Almost any wooded country, including citrus and olive groves. **VOICE** Calls hard 'tsr' and reedy 'keer'; song is a vigorous warble.

The Masked Shrike is a summer visitor to its breeding range, overwintering in Africa, south of the Sahara.

TOP AND ABOVE: *adult female*
BELOW: *adult male*

20cm **LENGTH**

32–34.5cm **WINGSPAN**

# LESSER GREY SHRIKE

*LANIUS MINOR*

The Lesser Grey Shrike has proportionately longer wings that allow it to chase prey rapidly, glide well, and hover and pounce like a Kestrel. It uses many perches in its breeding territory.

**IDENTIFICATION** Adult male has broad black band across forehead, over and through eyes and ear coverts. Rest of upperparts blue-grey. Male underparts white, with breast and flanks washed pink. Wings black with broad, white bar across base of primaries. Tail black with wide, white outer edges. Bill black, short and stubby. Legs brown. Female very similar to male but shows grey speckles on forehead, less pink below, and less blue above. Juvenile has black and white

*Juvenile has creamy-white underparts and a much smaller face mask than adult.*

*female*

patterns of adult on wings and tail but underparts creamy white and upperparts brownish-grey with fine, close, darker brown bars. Face mask reduced to broad, black eyestripe. Bill grey.
**HABITAT** Warm, open country with scattered or grouped bushes and trees. **VOICE** Calls variable; song is a soft, musical, chattering ramble with mimicry.

*male*

*Lesser Grey Shrikes generally perch conspicuously on wires and bushes.*

# GREAT GREY SHRIKE

*LANIUS EXCUBITOR*

**LENGTH** 24–25cm
**WINGSPAN** 30–34cm

Populations of Great Grey Shrikes are mainly resident from central Europe southwards, but northern birds are migrants, some travelling as far as southern Europe. The species is strongly territorial.

*adult*

*adult*

**IDENTIFICATION** The largest shrike. Northern European adult is tricoloured, with black face mask, wings and tail, grey upperparts and white underparts. Adult has white supercilium, white patch on scapulars, white-edged tail (which is long and graduated) and white, narrow bar across base of primaries. Bill quite long, hooked, black. Legs black. Sexes alike, but female has faint brown barring on breast in winter. Juvenile has brownish-grey upperparts and brownish-white underparts with faint, brown, wavy bars from throat to breast and flanks.
**HABITAT** Open country with plenty of bushes and trees.
**VOICE** Call harsh 'sheck, sheck'; song is a quiet, rambling warble with mimicry.

*1st winter*

24–25cm **LENGTH**
30–34cm **WINGSPAN**

# SOUTHERN GREY SHRIKE

*LANIUS MERIDIONALIS*

Formerly treated as a race of Great Grey Shrike, Southern Grey has now been elevated to species status. Birds from southern France and Iberia have pink-flushed underparts.

**IDENTIFICATION** All adult birds have greyish upperparts (tinged buff in birds from Iberia and southern France) and black face mask, wings and uppertail. Note the narrow white supercilium and whitish throat. Underparts are flushed pinkish-buff in birds from Iberia and southern France, grey in birds from North Africa and Middle East and pale grey in birds from Asia; latter have more extensive white on wing than other Southern Greys or Great Grey. Bill is long, hooked and black and legs are black. Sexes are similar. Juvenile has grey elements of plumage replaced by brownish-grey and grubbier looking underparts; faint barring is often seen on underparts. **HABITAT** Open country with plenty of bushes and trees. **VOICE** Call harsh 'sheck, sheck'; song is a quiet, rambling warble with mimicry.

*adult*

17–18cm **LENGTH**
26–27cm **WINGSPAN**

# ISABELLINE SHRIKE

*LANIUS ISABELLINUS*

*where found on migration*

Isabelline Shrikes breed across central Asia and winter in East Africa, southern Arabia and northwest India. Formerly treated as a race of Red-backed Shrike it is now recognised as a species.

**IDENTIFICATION** Distinctly pale shrike. Note contrast between grey-brown back and reddish-brown lower rump and tail. Adult male has mainly grey-buff upperparts and reddish-brown tail. Underparts whitish but with buff wash to breast and flanks. Head has black mask through eye. Female has more subdued plumage colours than male. First-winter bird (most likely in Europe) similar to female but scaly markings more extensive and present on face as well. **HABITAT** Open grassy areas with scrub. **VOICE** Calls include a harsh 'tchak'.

*adult*

# NUTCRACKER
## *NUCIFRAGA CARYOCATACTES*

**LENGTH** 32cm
**WINGSPAN** 52–58cm

The Nutcracker's distribution is dictated by its food supply; western birds are chiefly resident, but birds from further east are subject to irruptive movements when the conifer seed crop fails.

**IDENTIFICATION** Sexes alike. Adult body plumage chocolate-brown with teardrop-shaped white spot at tip of most feathers. Forehead and crown very dark brown, nasal bristles and lores creamy white. Wings brown-black, glossed bluish-green, with white spots on lesser and median coverts. Tail brownish-black with blue-green gloss above and feathers tipped white, becoming progressively wider from centre outwards; tail appears mostly dark from above but mostly white from below. Undertail coverts white in contrast to black base of tail and brown body. Bill long and black. Legs black. Juvenile paler than adult, with less well-defined white spots. **HABITAT** Cool forests of spruce or pine, in northern lowland and southern mountains. **VOICE** Utters a far-carrying 'kraak'; spring call 'kerr-kerr'; alarm call 'churr'.

adults

Each Nutcracker caches some 100,000 seeds in autumn, and needs 27,000 to survive the winter.

Hammers open cones with its bill, eats some seeds and buries many more.

34–35cm **LENGTH**
52–58cm **WINGSPAN**

# JAY
### *GARRULUS GLANDARIUS*

Jays are commonest in deciduous woodlands but are often inconspicuous except for their loud, raucous screech. Acorns are the Jay's staple winter diet.

*adult*

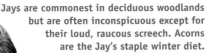

**IDENTIFICATION** A small crow, the most colourful in Europe. Sexes alike. Adult body pinkish-brown with white rump and undertail coverts, white forehead, crown streaked black, and broad, black moustachial stripe. Wings black with white at base of outermost secondaries forming short bar on closed wings; outer greater coverts, primary coverts and alula have shiny blue bars. Bill dark. Legs pale flesh-brown. Juvenile similar to adult, but plumage duller and crown less streaked. **HABITAT** Fairly dense cover of trees, usually broad-leaved, but also conifers. **VOICE** Loud, harsh, raucous calls, including 'skaaak skaaak' – far-carrying even in dense woodland.

*Most likely to be seen flying away from observer, showing rounded wings and striking black and white pattern of rump and tail.*

*adult*

# SIBERIAN JAY
*PERISOREUS INFAUSTUS*

**LENGTH** 30–31cm
**WINGSPAN** 40–46cm

The Siberian Jay is generally a sedentary resident and is very faithful to its chosen territory. It is a secretive bird in the breeding season, but sometimes becomes bold in winter, occasionally visiting feeding stations.

**IDENTIFICATION** Smallest member of the crow family in Europe, with proportionately longer tail than Jay and shorter, pointed bill. Adult has sooty-brown crown, nape and upper face. Dense pale-buff bristles at base of bill. Back and underparts brown-grey, becoming foxy red on rump, upper and lower tail coverts and belly. Wings sooty brown with foxy red coverts and bases to flight feathers. Bill and legs black. Sexes similar and juvenile similar to adult. **HABITAT** Natural, dense coniferous forest. **VOICE** Calls 'tchair', 'kook kook' and 'kij kij'; mewing like a Buzzard.

*Red in plumage is diagnostic for a bird of this size.*

*adult*

# AZURE-WINGED MAGPIE
*CYANOPICA CYANUS*

**LENGTH** 34–35cm
**WINGSPAN** 38–40cm

In the breeding season, April to June, the Azure-winged Magpie is secretive and keeps to tree cover. At other times it is noisy and bold.

**IDENTIFICATION** Small, elegant, long-tailed crow. Adult has forehead, crown and nape velvet black to a line below the eye. Back, rump and uppertail coverts grey-brown. Underparts off-white, with pale tinge of ashy colours on flanks and undertail coverts. Wings azure blue, with inner webs of tertials, greater coverts and primaries black. Tail noticeably graduated, blue above, dark grey below. Bill and legs black. Juvenile similar to adult but plumage duller. **HABITAT** Groups of trees, cork oak and olive groves, pine and eucalyptus plantations. **VOICE** Main call is a husky whistling 'zhreee', rising at end.

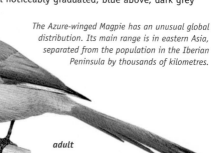

*The Azure-winged Magpie has an unusual global distribution. Its main range is in eastern Asia, separated from the population in the Iberian Peninsula by thousands of kilometres.*

*adult*

44–46cm **LENGTH**
52–60cm **WINGSPAN**

# MAGPIE
*PICA PICA*

Although the Magpie is predominantly
a bird of lightly wooded open country,
it has now moved into suburban and
urban habitats in several countries.

*adult*

ABOVE: *Long, graduated tail and black and
white plumage distinctive even at a distance.*
BELOW: *Flies with irregular short bursts of rapid wingbeats.*

*adult*

*adult*

**IDENTIFICATION** An unmistakable pied bird with a long, graduated tail. Sexes similar. Adult scapulars, belly and flanks white. Rest of plumage black with beautiful iridescence when seen closely in sunlight: purple on most of head and body, green on crown and scapulars, blue-green on wings, and brilliant bronze-green on tail with bands of several shades of purple near tip. Bill and legs black. Juvenile similar to adult but has shorter tail, duller plumage and less iridescence. **HABITAT** Mainly a lowland bird in lightly wooded country. **VOICE** Commonest call is a staccato chatter 'chacker chacker chacker chacker'.

# ALPINE CHOUGH
## *PYRRHOCORAX GRACULUS*

**LENGTH** 38cm
**WINGSPAN** 75–85cm

Alpine Choughs are masters of the air. They fly fast and with great skill, manoeuvring near cliffs and in fierce air currents. At popular ski resorts they often become tame, even taking food from visitors' hands.

**IDENTIFICATION** Adult has all-black plumage with a sheen: blue-green gloss, particularly on wings. Sexes alike. Bill pale yellow. Legs orange. May be distinguished from Chough by its yellow, shorter bill, duller plumage, longer tail, only four separated primaries in flight and straight leading edge to the wings. Juvenile similar to adult. **HABITAT** Strictly montane, ranging from tree-line to snow-line. **VOICE** Calls include a frequent 'chirrish'; in chorus often utters a piercing 'chreee'.

*A small flock in aerial display, calling the diagnostic 'chree', is a memorable sight.*

*adult*

39–40cm **LENGTH**
73–90cm **WINGSPAN**

# CHOUGH
### *PYRRHOCORAX PYRRHOCORAX*

**Choughs are excellent fliers: they can glide, soar on thermals and perform aerial manoeuvres, all to the accompaniment of many contact calls. They probe the ground with their bills for insect grubs.**

**IDENTIFICATION** Adult plumage all black; most parts have a blue gloss, although tail, tail coverts and flight feathers have a greener iridescence. Bill red and downcurved. Sexes alike. Juvenile duller than adult, with shorter, orangey bill. Adult Chough separable from adult Alpine Chough by length of bill, shorter tail, about as long as primary tips when bird is standing, five to six primary 'fingers' (in flight), and distinct call. **HABITAT** Inland crags or coastal cliffs (for nesting) near grassy swards (for feeding). **VOICE** Common call is a yelping 'cheeow' or 'kiaa'.

*adult*

*adult*

Glossy plumage is
entirely black.

*When a perched bird gives a call it often conspicuously flips its wings and tail to help advertise its presence.*

*Choughs are gregarious even in the breeding season, and small flocks can be seen flying along the cliffs.*

*adult*

# JACKDAW
*CORVUS MONEDULA*

**LENGTH** 33–34cm
**WINGSPAN** 67–74cm

Jackdaws often associate with Rooks on feeding grounds and their presence is often detected by hearing their 'kjack' contact calls. They are wary in the countryside, but quite approachable in towns and villages.

ABOVE: *adult*; BELOW: *juvenile*

**IDENTIFICATION** Sexes alike. At a distance adult appears black with grey nape and ear coverts. Close views reveal purple gloss on black crown, some blue gloss on wings and back, and greyish cast on underparts. Eyes of adult pale grey, very distinctive. Bill short and black. Legs black. Juvenile duller than adult, grey patch less contrasting; eyes brown, taking a year to become grey. **HABITAT** Groups of old trees, avenues in town or country; sea cliffs, mountain crags. **VOICE** Short, loud 'kjack' is the common contact note; many other short call notes.

One of the smallest members of the crow family in Europe.
BELOW: *adult*

The Jackdaw will choose almost any nest site so long as it is a hole – from sea cliffs to old mine shafts and church towers.

64cm **LENGTH**
130–150cm **WINGSPAN**

# RAVEN
### *CORVUS CORAX*

In Europe Ravens occur where they can find eyrie-style nest sites overlooking a large foraging area. Most Ravens are sedentary.

*adult*

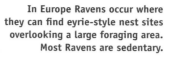

**IDENTIFICATION** The largest member of the crow family, one-third bigger than Rook and Crow, and as big as a Buzzard. Sexes similar. All-black, iridescent plumage; purple-blue on wings, reddish-purple on tail. Shaggy throat feathers and wedge shape to tip of tail are distinctive. Black bill is massive, especially deep upper mandible, markedly curved towards the tip. Legs black. Juvenile similar to adult.

**HABITAT** From coast to 3,000m, but not dense forest, dense settlement or cultivation.

**VOICE** Typical call is a deep, resonant 'karronk'; also utters a deep 'prruk' and 'toc-toc-toc'.

*The Raven's principal food is carrion, but it will also eat live small animals and seeds and fruit.*

*adult*

*Large, entirely black crow with resonant, deep 'prruk, prruk' call.*

*Long throat feathers give bearded appearance; this and heavy bill help distinguish Raven from Carrion Crow.*

371

# CARRION CROW
*CORVUS CORONE*

**LENGTH** 45–47cm
**WINGSPAN** 90–100cm

Until recently, Carrion and Hooded Crows were considered to be the same species, just subspecies separated by geographical range. In 2002 they were 'split' and elevated to separate species status.

**IDENTIFICATION** Has all-black plumage, bill and legs. Could be confused with juvenile Rook, which lacks adult Rook's whitish face. But note that species' proportionately longer bill. Sexes are similar and juvenile body plumage is brownish-black. **HABITAT** Farmland and open country with scattered trees. **VOICE** Call is an abrupt 'kawr', often three together.

*adult*

Carrion Crow can be confused with Rook and Raven, although latter is much bigger, has long throat feathers and noticeably wedge-shaped tail.

*Powerful, dagger-like bill can tear flesh with ease.*

*adult*

45–47cm **LENGTH**
90–100cm **WINGSPAN**

# HOODED CROW
### *CORVUS CORNIX*

The Hooded Crow is the northern and eastern counterpart of the Carrion Crow, its range extending to Ireland and northern Scotland. Its habits are identical to those of its cousin the Carrion Crow.

**IDENTIFICATION** Has ashy grey back of neck, mantle, back rump, scapulars, lower breast, belly, flanks, axillaries and undertail coverts. Rest of plumage is black. Bill and legs are black. Both sexes are alike. Juvenile is similar to adult but grey elements of plumage have buffish tinge. **HABITAT** Open country, moors and coasts, especially in winter. **VOICE** Call is an abrupt 'kawr', often three together.

*adult*

> Hooded Crow has grey back and undersides and grey on innerwing.

*adult*

# ROOK
## *CORVUS FRUGILEGUS*

The Rook is gregarious at all times; after the breeding season family groups join other families for feeding, roosting and migrating.

*juvenile*

**IDENTIFICATION** Adult all black except for whitish-grey skin around base of bill, from lower forehead, behind the gape, and on upper throat. Black is iridescent in sunlight with shades of greenish- and reddish-purple. Separable from Carrion Crow by whitish face, steep forehead, narrower bill, more fingered wingtips in flight, round-tipped tail, glossier plumage and loose thigh feathers. Juvenile has black nasal bristles and no bare grey skin. **HABITAT** Wherever tall trees border agricultural land. **VOICE** Commonest call is a prolonged 'kaah'.

*Face and chin are pale grey and unfeathered.*

*adult*

*adult*

*Long, loose thigh feathers give 'baggy trousers' effect.*

24cm **LENGTH**
44–47cm **WINGSPAN**

# GOLDEN ORIOLE
### *ORIOLUS ORIOLUS*

Golden Orioles are summer visitors to Europe. Although they are secretive and arboreal birds they are well known because of the male's far-carrying song.

*adult female*

*adult female*

*adult male*

**IDENTIFICATION** Adult male has bright-yellow head and body, black wings and tail. Head marked by black lores. Black-centred tail has yellow corners. Wings black with short yellow bar across tips of primary coverts. Eye crimson. Bill strong, dark pink. Legs dark grey. Female has yellowish-green body, greenish-brown

*The Golden Oriole's French name,* loriot, *well describes its 'lo-lo-loriot' song.*

wings and brownish-black tail with yellow corners. Underparts palest on chin to upper-breast; all underparts streaked dull brown. First-year male is streaked and has bright-yellow plumage replaced by dull olive-yellow. Some mature females appear almost as yellow as male but lores always grey. Juvenile like female but has dark-brown eye and slate-grey bill; takes two years to attain adult plumage. **HABITAT** Tree-loving but not a forest bird; parks, large gardens, copses, open woods. **VOICE** Call cat-like; alarm rattle; song is a melodious, flute-like whistle.

# STARLING

*STURNUS VULGARIS*

**LENGTH** 21.5cm
**WINGSPAN** 37–42cm

The Starling is gregarious throughout the year. Winter roosts in evergreens, reedbeds or on buildings commonly comprise 100,000 or more birds.

**IDENTIFICATION** Male in winter has glossy black plumage, with buff tips to feathers of upperparts, buff edges to wing feathers and white tips to feathers of underparts from throat to belly. Bill grey-brown with yellow base. Legs reddish-brown. Eyes brown. Male in summer loses buff and white feather tips, and due to wear the bird looks darker and very glossy, with green, purple, bronze and blue iridescence. Lemon-yellow bill. Female has broader spots in winter than male, keeps some spots all year and is less glossy. Bill has pinkish base in breeding season, eye has a paler ring on the iris. Juvenile looks like a different species with mouse-brown plumage, darker above than below. Shows whitish chin and grey-brown bill. Moults in autumn and attains first-winter plumage similar to adult; bill black. **HABITAT** Almost anywhere; very ready to live with man; needs holes to nest in, open ground to feed on. **VOICE** Calls include characteristic 'tsiew', 'tcherr'; song is a lively medley of whistles, gurgles and mimicry.

*immature, 1st autumn*

*Breeding-plumage male is very glossy and colourful, and beak has blue base.*

BELOW AND RIGHT: *winter adult*

21–23cm **LENGTH**
38–42cm **WINGSPAN**

# SPOTLESS STARLING
### *STURNUS UNICOLOR*

**In the western Mediterranean this starling fills the same niche as its commoner relative, feeding and breeding in a wide variety of habitats, including inner cities.**

**IDENTIFICATION** Male in summer has all-black plumage, glossed purple (not green as in Starling and without pale edges to wing feathers). Feathers of throat are long and bird looks bearded (more so than Starling). Bill pale yellow with bluish-black base. Legs pale pink. In early winter, shows pale tips to feathers on head, mantle and underparts; bill dark. Female similar to male but less glossy; has small, white spots on fresh undertail coverts and pale-yellow margins to larger wing feathers. Juvenile similar to, but darker than, juvenile Starling. First-winters have pale tips to body feathers. **HABITAT** Open woodland, near short grass for foraging; fields and marshes in winter. **VOICE** Similar to Starling, but song louder, especially introductory whistles.

ABOVE: *summer adult*

***Winter*** *bird shows pale tips to feathers.*

*Like its common cousin, the Spotless Starling often nests in holes in trees, or in buildings, using a foundation of grass and twigs, with a soft lining. Its diet is similar too: mainly invertebrates in spring and summer, and seeds and fruits at other times.*

***Summer adult*** *has bearded appearance.*

# ROSE-COLOURED STARLING

**LENGTH** 21cm
**WINGSPAN** 38–40cm

*STURNUS ROSEUS*

The Rose-coloured Starling breeds erratically in Eastern Europe. After breeding but before autumn migration, the birds form flocks that wander in search of food.

*summer male*

**IDENTIFICATION** Adult male's head, crest, neck and upper breast dark with purple sheen. Wings black with greenish sheen and tail and undertail coverts black. Mantle, back, lower breast and belly pink. Pink elements of plumage appear grubby in winter and black lacks sheen. Bill and legs pink. Female like male but plumage duller at all times. Juvenile has essentially pale sandy brown plumage, darkest on wings and tail. Bill yellow and legs pinkish-brown. **HABITAT** Typically arid grassland and semi-desert. **VOICE** Calls include a thin 'kri'; song varied and twittering.

*juvenile*

*summer male*

14–15cm **LENGTH**
24cm **WINGSPAN**

# HOUSE SPARROW
### *PASSER DOMESTICUS*

The House Sparrow is widespread throughout Europe, although it is almost entirely restricted to habitats close to human habitation. It is generally a sedentary resident.

*male*

**IDENTIFICATION** Male warm brown above and greyish below, with grey crown, black eyestripe, black bib with broken bottom edge, dull-white cheeks, grey rump, black-brown, square-ended tail and white wingbar. Bill black in breeding season, grey at other times. Legs pink or brown. Female lacks strong plumage pattern. At a distance appears dull brown above and dingy white below. Shows broad, pale-buff supercilium and lighter brown or buff edges to wing feathers. Bill grey, legs pink. Juvenile similar to female. **HABITAT** Almost invariably associated with human habitation. **VOICE** Calls include familiar 'cheep' or 'chirrp'; song is a succession of chirps.

*Adopts perky stance when perched, with chest puffed and tail cocked.*

> House Sparrows are gregarious, nesting in loose colonies and forming flocks for roosting, feeding and dust-bathing.

ABOVE: *female*; BELOW: *male*

# TREE SPARROW
*PASSER MONTANUS*

In Europe the Tree Sparrow is much less associated with settlements than the House Sparrow. It is particularly fond of lightly wooded farmland.

*In flight, shorter tail and faster flight action distinguish Tree Sparrow from House Sparrow.*

**IDENTIFICATION** Smaller and more trim than House Sparrow. Sexes alike. Adult distinguished from male House Sparrow by rich, dark-chestnut crown and nape, and whiter cheeks, which almost form a white collar contrasting noticeably with crown and black bib (smaller than House Sparrow's); the cheek shows a conspicuous black patch below and behind the eye. Back and rump yellowish-brown. Tail dark brown. Wings show two pale wingbars. Underparts whitish, palest on belly, and washed buff on flanks. Bill black. Legs pale brown. Juvenile as adult but duller. **HABITAT** Small woods, roadside trees, ivy-covered cliffs, parks, wooded suburbs. **VOICE** Distinctive, repeated 'chet' or 'teck' is characteristic of birds in flight.

*adults*

*Unlike House Sparrows, male and female Tree Sparrows share incubation of the eggs.*

15cm **LENGTH**
23–26cm **WINGSPAN**

# SPANISH SPARROW
### *PASSER HISPANIOLENSIS*

Spanish Sparrows breed colonially, and outside the breeding season the species is very gregarious. In Spain, in autumn, flocks of up to 4,000 form.

**IDENTIFICATION** Male has chestnut crown, nape and sides of neck. Black bib extends to unique arrowhead streaks on breast and flanks. White cheeks very noticeable. Short, white, broken supercilium. Mantle and rump grey. Wings brown with two pale wingbars, and tail dark brown. Bill black in breeding season, paler at other times. Legs light brown. Female and juvenile dull brown and dingy white below; almost indistinguishable from equivalent plumages of House Sparrow. **HABITAT** Cultivated land, settlements; also arid regions, and woods and thickets. **VOICE** Call distinct, contralto 'chup'; song similar to House Sparrow's but richer.

*male*

ABOVE: *female*; BELOW: *males*

# ROCK SPARROW

*PETRONIA PETRONIA*

**Rock Sparrows are sociable birds and form flocks of up to several hundred from late summer to spring.**

*Runs around on ground like a pipit rather than hopping and jumping like a House Sparrow.*

*adult*

**IDENTIFICATION** Adult is superficially like female House Sparrow, but has longer wings, shorter tail and heavier bill. Upperparts and wings dusty brown, heavily streaked with brown-black. Underparts buffish-white, streaked and spotted brown especially on flanks and undertail coverts. Tail dark brown with white terminal spots, which show clearly in flight. Both sexes have distinctive striped head pattern: creamy coloured central crown stripe, dark-brown lateral crown stripes, broad off-white supercilium and dusky ear coverts. Bill large, deep and greyish. Legs brownish-yellow. In spring male has bright-yellow patch on upper breast. Sexes otherwise similar. Juvenile similar to adult female. **HABITAT** Treeless terrain with sparse vegetation; sometimes vineyards, olive groves. **VOICE** Characteristic call is a nasal 'pey-ee'; song comprises a repetition of calls.

# SNOW FINCH

*MONTIFRINGILLA NIVALIS*

**During the summer months, Snow Finches are found between 2,000m and nearly 3,000m; in winter, however, they may be forced to descend to lower levels in adjacent valleys.**

*Similar to Snow Bunting, but has a quite different range.*

**IDENTIFICATION** Finch-like member of the sparrow family with considerable amount of white in plumage. Adult has blue-grey head, white underparts and brown mantle. Wings white with black tips, extremely striking in flight. Tail white with black central bar. Male has black bib and dark bill in summer but has yellow bill and loses bib in winter. Female similar to winter male. Juvenile similar to winter male but with dull bill. **HABITAT** Bare, stony sites, above the tree-line in summer. **VOICE** Sparrow-like song includes Chaffinch-like 'pink'.

*Snow Finches are birds of mountaintops and Alpine slopes; in Europe they are found in the Pyrenees, Alps and more locally in the Italian Abruzzi Mountains and in the Balkans.*

*adult*

12cm **LENGTH**
21–25cm **WINGSPAN**

# GOLDFINCH
## *CARDUELIS CARDUELIS*

*During the winter months especially, when alternative sources of food are in short supply, teasel seeds are very important for Goldfinches.*

**The Goldfinch feeds on seeds taken directly from plants, and birds can often be seen acrobatically extracting thistle seeds or swinging on alder or birch catkins.**

LEFT: *adult*; ABOVE: *juvenile*

**IDENTIFICATION** Adult unmistakable with golden-yellow panel along centre of black wing and head patterned vertically in bands; red from bill to eye, white behind eye, black crown and sides of neck. Sexes similar. Mantle, back, breast band and flanks pale rufous, rump whitish. Tail black. White spots to tips of flight and tail feathers. Bill noticeably pointed, pinkish with dark tip. Legs pale flesh. Juvenile reveals yellow on wings in flight but head and body plumage greyish-brown, spotted and streaked brown until autumn moult. **HABITAT** Orchards, parks, gardens, scrub, thickets, rough grassland, overgrown sites. **VOICE** Call a liquid 'tswitt-witt-witt'; song a characteristic, cheerful tinkling.

*The breeding territory is small, just around the nest, but the pair forages for food up to a kilometre away.*

adult

adult

383

# CHAFFINCH
*FRINGILLA COELEBS*

LENGTH 14.5cm
WINGSPAN 25–28cm

The Chaffinch is one of the commonest and most widespread of all birds in western Europe. It is gregarious outside the breeding season.

*male*

**IDENTIFICATION** Male very distinctive, with pink face, breast and belly. Crown, nape, upper mantle blue-grey; lower mantle chestnut brown. Greenish rump, white undertail coverts and black forehead. Tail black with white outer feathers. Wings black with pale fringes to flight feathers; shows broad, white wingbar across tips of greater coverts, and long, deep, white blaze from shoulder to scapulars on lesser and median coverts. Bill blue in breeding season but dull pinkish-grey at other times. Legs grey or brown. Female plumage pale olive-brown above and greyish-white below; has same diagnostic tail and wing patterns as male. Bill pinkish-grey and legs reddish-brown. Juvenile similar to female.

**HABITAT** Woods, forest, coniferous plantations; also in farmland, parks and gardens.

**VOICE** Call 'chink'; male's call in spring, 'wheet'; song is an accelerating phrase ending in a flourish.

*female*

BELOW: **Male's** *contrasting plumage highlighted by pink breast.*

14cm **LENGTH**
25–26cm **WINGSPAN**

# BRAMBLING
*FRINGILLA MONTIFRINGILLA*

*winter male*

In autumn all European Bramblings eventually migrate south and west, but many remain in the northeast of their wintering range as long as possible while stocks of beech-mast last.

*In flight, white rump is key identifying feature.*

**Breeding male's** black head and bright breast unmistakable.

**IDENTIFICATION** Identified at all times by buffish-orange breast and shoulder, diagnostic long, white rump and black, slightly forked tail. Breeding male has glossy black head and mantle, orange throat, breast and shoulders; rest of underparts white. Wings black with narrow white bar across tips of greater coverts and white patch below orange shoulder. Bill blue-black. Legs brownish-flesh. In winter, male's head and mantle mottled with brown; bill yellowish with black tip. Female has underparts and wing pattern of male but in washed-out colours. Head has dark-brown crown, greyish nape with brown lateral stripes, buff supercilium and ear-coverts, whitish chin and throat. Bill grey in summer, blue-black in winter. Juvenile as female. **HABITAT** Birch and mixed forest; woodland, and open ground in winter. **VOICE** Call a wheezy 'tsweep'; song a monotonous, repeated 'dwee'.

BELOW: *winter female*

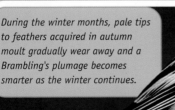

*winter male*

During the winter months, pale tips to feathers acquired in autumn moult gradually wear away and a Brambling's plumage becomes smarter as the winter continues.

# GREENFINCH
## *CARDUELIS CHLORIS*

The Greenfinch is widespread in Europe. It is mainly a lowland species closely allied to its habitat of trees and open ground, on which it forages for seeds. Small flocks form outside the breeding season.

**IDENTIFICATION** Male is striking olive-green and yellow, darker olive above and yellower below. Tail and flight feathers brown-black, with brilliant yellow fringes to primaries (forming bold patch on bottom edge of folded wing), and brilliant yellow on bases of outer four pairs of tail feathers. Underwing yellow. Yellow patterns very noticeable in flight. Tail short, distinctly forked. Bill stout, conical, pale flesh. Legs pale flesh. Female similar to male but duller overall, with indistinct streaks on crown and mantle. Juvenile even duller than female and more distinctly streaked above and below. **HABITAT** Densely leafed trees in woodland edge, orchards, parks, graveyards, gardens. **VOICE** Call loud nasal 'tsweee'; flight call rapid twitter; song strong, twittering trill.

*Adult male* (BELOW) *has brighter colouring than* *adult female* (RIGHT)*.*

*juvenile*

Winter flocks will stay at a food source until it is exhausted.

**12cm** LENGTH
**20–23cm** WINGSPAN

# SIKIN
## SISKIN
*CARDUELIS SPINUS*

*winter female*

Siskins are particularly fond of spruce, alder and birch seeds, which they extract with their tweezer-like bills. They feed mostly in the trees.

**IDENTIFICATION** Both sexes have black wings with a broad, yellow wingbar across tips of greater coverts and inner primaries. Adult male green above and yellow below, with diagnostic black forehead, crown and chin. Tail forked, black, edged along basal two-thirds with brilliant yellow. Belly and undertail coverts white, the latter streaked black. Tapered, pointed bill, yellowish. Legs dark brown. Female lacks male's black crown. Breast yellow, rest of underparts white, streaked black. Yellow on wings and tail patterned like male but less obvious. Juvenile similar to female but browner and more streaked. **HABITAT** Especially coniferous forest; alders, birches by streams; gardens in winter. **VOICE** Calls include 'dluee' and 'tsüü', often given in flight; song a sweet twitter with wheezy ending.

LEFT: *summer male*
BELOW: *winter male*

Peanuts at bird tables are particularly welcome in early spring, when the alder seed crop is exhausted.

# BULLFINCH
*PYRRHULA PYRRHULA*

LENGTH 15cm
WINGSPAN 25cm

Rather a shy and retiring species, the Bullfinch is heard more often than it is seen: its soft, piping calls carry a surprising distance through the undergrowth; birds often travel in pairs.

**IDENTIFICATION** A dumpy finch with a stubby, black bill and conspicuous white rump, seen in flight. Male has black cap, blue-grey nape and mantle, and pinkish-red underparts, except for white undertail feathering; hue of red underparts distinctly different from other birds found in same habitats. Wings black with broad white wingbar; tail black. Female has similar patterning to male but more sombre, muted colours, appearing pinkish-buff. Juvenile similar to female but lacks black cap. **HABITAT** Undergrowth near woodland edge, hedgerows and gardens. **VOICE** Call is a distinctive, low piping 'teu'.

ABOVE: *female*
LEFT: *male*

*male*

*White rump shows well in flight.*

11.5cm **LENGTH**
20–23cm **WINGSPAN**

# SERIN
### *SERINUS SERINUS*

Originally a Mediterranean species, the Serin spread north during the 19th century. Northern populations migrate south for the winter.

*male*

*Breeding birds defend small territories, may form neighbourhood groups and are often very tame; the density of these groups varies markedly from a few pairs to over a hundred pairs per square kilometre.*

**IDENTIFICATION** A tiny finch, as small as a Blue Tit. Male is streaky, greenish-brown above with bright-yellow head, breast and rump. Male's blackish-brown wings have pale fringes to wing coverts showing as pale wingbars. Tail deeply forked. Black eye looks beady on yellow face. Stubby grey bill. Legs brown. Female has same basic pattern as male, but browner above with duller yellow parts. Juvenile resembles dull female. Confusion with female or juvenile Siskin likely, but distinguished by small bill, narrow wingbars and uniformly streaked underparts. **HABITAT** Forest edge, clearings, parkland, orchards, vineyards, gardens.
**VOICE** Call a distinctive 'tirrilillit'; song a rapid succession of chirps, jingles and twitters.

*female*

# CITRIL FINCH
*SERINUS CITRINELLA*

**LENGTH** 12cm
**WINGSPAN** 23–24cm

**The Citril Finch is a high altitude species found in the mountain ranges of southern Europe during the summer months, some birds moving to lower elevations in winter.**

**IDENTIFICATION** Citril Finch adult is mainly yellow-green with slate-grey nape and sides to neck, yellow rump and unstreaked underparts. Tail and wings black, latter with yellowish-green wingbars. Bill greyish with dark tip. Legs brownish. Female similar to male but duller. Juvenile buffish-brown above, pale buff below, streaked on crown, mantle and underparts. **HABITAT** Woodland, especially spruce bordering alpine meadows at 700–3,000m. **VOICE** Call a metallic 'chwick'; flight call 'didididid'; song a fast tinkling twitter.

*male*

# CORSICAN FINCH
*SERINUS CORSICANA*

**LENGTH** 12cm
**WINGSPAN** 23–24cm

**Formerly regarded as a subspecies of Citril Finch, the Corsican Finch has been elevated to species status. It is resident on Corsica and Sardinia.**

**IDENTIFICATION** Corsican Finch adult is mainly yellow-green with streaked brown back, slate-grey nape and sides to neck, yellow rump and unstreaked underparts. Tail and wings black, latter with yellowish-green wingbars. Bill greyish with dark tip. Legs brownish. Female similar to male but duller. Juvenile buffish-brown above, pale buff below, streaked on crown, mantle and underparts. **HABITAT** Wide range of woodland and scrub. **VOICE** Call a metallic 'chwick'; flight call 'didididid'; song a fast tinkling twitter.

*male*

18cm **LENGTH**
29–33cm **WINGSPAN**

# HAWFINCH
### COCCOTHRAUSTES COCCOTHRAUSTES

**Hawfinches are easily overlooked due to their shy nature and habit of favouring dense foliage in tall trees in the breeding season. They are easier to find in winter when they sometimes feed on the ground.**

*Because of its huge bill, the Hawfinch is the only European bird that can successfully tackle hard-cased Hornbeam seeds, and it can also crack open cherry stones.*

*male*

**IDENTIFICATION** Large and unmistakable finch with distinctive profile, both when perched and in flight. Bill proportionately massive and triangular in outline. Bird looks top-heavy and large-headed when perched; in flight shows a considerable amount of white and looks short-tailed with proportionately large head and neck. Male has mainly orange-buff and pinkish-buff plumage. Shows black

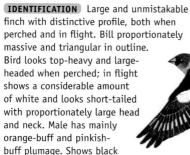

*male*

around base of bill and on bib. Mantle reddish-brown and wings dark but showing broad, white band on coverts. Undertail feathering and tip of tail white. Female similar but with duller colours. Juvenile has brownish plumage and spotted underparts. **HABITAT** Mixed woodlands, mainly deciduous. **VOICE** Loud, Robin-like 'tic' call.

*female*

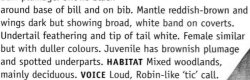

# LESSER REDPOLL

*CARDUELIS CABARET*

**LENGTH** 13–14cm
**WINGSPAN** 20–25cm

Lesser Redpolls are perhaps easiest to see in the winter when they gather in flocks, and the trees in which they feed have lost their leaves.

**IDENTIFICATION** Plumage variable but generally has brown, streaked upperparts, pale underparts streaked on flanks, and streaked rump; shows two white wingbars. Male has black chin, red forecrown and narrow band of white running from base of forecrown above eye; shows pinkish flush to breast, most apparent in breeding season. Female similar to male but shows less extensive red on forecrown, base of which is black not white, and lacks pink flush to breast. Bill short, triangular in profile, and yellowish with curved culmen in all birds. Juvenile similar to female but lacks red on forecrown. **HABITAT** Favours birch and alder woodland; will also nest in conifer plantations and forests. **VOICE** Trilling, unmusical song delivered in flight; utters fast 'chuchuchuh-uh' call.

*female*

*female*

*male*

*male*

14cm **LENGTH**
23cm **WINGSPAN**

# COMMON REDPOLL

### *CARDUELIS FLAMMEA*

Subtle plumage and vocal differences exist between Common Redpoll and its Lesser cousin, and the two do not interbreed where their ranges overlap.

*male*

**IDENTIFICATION** Plumage variable and overall similar to Lesser Redpoll but overall paler and greyer. Some pale birds are similar to Arctic but note Common's streaked rump and stouter bill. All birds show two white wingbars. Male has black chin, red forecrown and pink-flushed breast, most obvious in breeding season. Female has less extensive red on forecrown. Bill is short, triangular and yellowish with curved culmen. Juvenile lacks red on forecrown. **HABITAT** Birch forests in summer, birch, willows and alder in winter. **VOICE** Trilling, unmusical song delivered in flight; utters fast, rattling 'chuchuchuh-uh' call.

13–14cm **LENGTH**
21–27cm **WINGSPAN**

# ARCTIC REDPOLL

### *CARDUELIS HORNEMANNI*

Arctic Redpolls often only move south from their Arctic breeding grounds in the severest of winter weather. The diagnostic unstreaked rump is often hard to see.

**IDENTIFICATION** Similar to other redpolls but typically paler, in some races almost white. Rumps of adult birds unstreaked. Bill triangular and yellowish with straight, not curved, culmen. Male has pale buffish-brown upperparts and pale, white underparts with faintly streaked flanks. In breeding season may have pink flush on breast. Shows black bib and red forecrown. Female similar to male but darker. **HABITAT** Breeds on Arctic tundra; in winter, most remain in northern latitudes. **VOICE** Chattering flight call similar to Redpoll's but slower.

*adult male*

# LINNET
## *CARDUELIS CANNABINA*

The Linnet eats almost exclusively seeds, its favourites being the seeds of chickweed, persicaria, fat-hen and charlock. They often form large winter flocks.

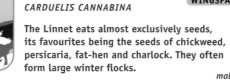

*male*

*male*

**IDENTIFICATION** Male has chestnut mantle, scapulars and wing coverts. Wings and tail dark brown with white edges to some flight and tail feathers, showing as indistinct wingbar on perched bird and as greyish patches in flight. Bill greyish-brown and head grey except for crimson forehead. Bill greyish. Legs dark brown. Female lacks male's crimson breast and forehead. Brown back streaked darker than on male and underparts streaked buff-brown. Like male, female shows distinctive whitish wing and tail patches. Juvenile similar to female but more heavily streaked, so shows less contrast between upperparts and underparts. Wing and tail patches indistinct.

*female*

**HABITAT** Scrub, heath, hedges, vineyards, maquis, uncultivated fields. **VOICE** Alarm call 'tsooeet'; flight call 'tihtihtihtit'; song a musical, soft warbling twitter.

*Breeding birds perch very openly on the tops of low bushes.*

*male*

14cm **LENGTH**
22–24cm **WINGSPAN**

# TWITE
### *CARDUELIS FLAVIROSTRIS*

Although Twites look very much like Linnets or redpolls, their choice of habitat and distinctive alarm and contact calls should help to identify them.

*juvenile*

*summer male*

*Pink rump prominent in flight; shows very little white on wings.*

**IDENTIFICATION** Adult is liable to be confused with female or juvenile Linnet but plumage is generally darker, more tawny above and more heavily streaked below; the ground colour is warm buff. Shows white wing patches and tail sides but these features less noticeable than on Linnet. Sexes similar but male has rose-pink rump, that of female being same colour as mantle. Both sexes have yellow bill in winter but grey bill in summer. Juvenile similar to winter adult. **HABITAT** Almost treeless countryside in cool and often rainy climate. **VOICE** Call nasal 'chweek'; constant twitter in flight; song hoarse and twanging.

*summer male*

# CROSSBILL
*LOXIA CURVIROSTRA*

**LENGTH** 17cm
**WINGSPAN** 27–30cm

The Crossbill is widespread throughout much of Europe wherever suitable habitats occur. Its bill is superbly adapted for extracting seeds from the cones of conifers, particularly spruce trees, and in this choice of food it has no bird competitors.

**IDENTIFICATION** Adult male has mainly bright-red plumage except for the dark wings. Adult female is green except for the dark wings. Juvenile has brown, heavily streaked plumage; sometimes shows faint wingbars but these much less conspicuous than on juvenile Two-barred Crossbill. **HABITAT** Conifer forests, mainly pine and spruce. **VOICE** Loud, persistent 'chip chip' flight call; song comprises trilling notes followed by Greenfinch-like calls.

LEFT: *female*
BELOW LEFT: *male*
BELOW: *male feeding*

*Dumpy finch with robust bill; mandible tips cross.*

16cm **LENGTH**
28–30cm **WINGSPAN**

# SCOTTISH CROSSBILL
*LOXIA SCOTICA*

The Scottish Crossbill is the only bird that is endemic to Britain: that is, it occurs nowhere else in the world.

**IDENTIFICATION** Out of range, could easily be confused with small-billed Parrot Crossbill or large-billed Crossbill. Bill is heavy with tips of mandibles overlapping. Adult male has bright-red plumage, except for darker wings. Adult female has green plumage except for darker wings. Juvenile has grey-brown, heavily streaked plumage with same bill shape as adult. **HABITAT** Conifer forests. **VOICE** Loud 'chip chip' flight call; song includes trilling and Greenfinch-like notes.

*male*

17.5cm **LENGTH**
32cm **WINGSPAN**

# PARROT CROSSBILL
*LOXIA PYTYOPSITTACUS*

Parrot Crossbills are usually sedentary but when the pine seed crop fails they sometimes irrupt in search of food. Small flocks sometimes reach east England.

**IDENTIFICATION** Superficially very similar to Crossbill. Generally shows larger and heavier bill, the mandible tips of which cross but cannot be seen to project in silhouette. Head and neck also appear proportionately larger. Male has red plumage with dark wings. Female has yellowish-green plumage with dark wings. Juvenile has grey-brown, streaked plumage. **HABITAT** Conifer forests, mainly pine. **VOICE** Utters 'chip chip' flight call, lower pitch than Crossbill's; song comprises Greenfinch-like elements, lower pitch than Crossbill's.

*Most bulky and heavy-billed crossbill.*

*adult male*

# TWO-BARRED CROSSBILL

**LOXIA LEUCOPTERA**

**LENGTH** 15cm
**WINGSPAN** 26–29cm

While supplies of larch seeds (the favoured food) last, Two-barred Crossbills are residents. But if the cone crop fails they are forced to irrupt in search of food.

**IDENTIFICATION** Adults of both sexes distinguished by relatively long, slender bill with overlapping mandible tips and two striking white wingbars. Male has pinkish-red plumage, while that of female is yellowish-green. Juvenile shows double wingbars but has grey-brown, streaked plumage and lacks adult's white tips to tertial feathers. **HABITAT** Conifer forests, especially larch. **VOICE** Rattling and buzzing song; utters chattering call in flight; occasionally toy trumpet call heard.

White wingbars impressive at rest and in flight.

The crop of larch seeds was particularly poor in 2008 and a large scale irruption of Two-barred Crossbills occurred in the summer. In August of that year, unprecedented numbers reached Scotland from across the North Sea. In the absence of conifers, many of these birds were forced to feed on the seeds of coastal plants, such as Thrift.

adult male

juvenile

13.5cm–15cm **LENGTH**
25cm **WINGSPAN**

# SCARLET ROSEFINCH
*CARPODACUS ERYTHRINUS*

Scarlet (or Common) Rosefinches are summer visitors to Europe. Although not especially shy, they are rather unobtrusive.

**IDENTIFICATION** Medium-sized finch with large, stubby bill; all ages and plumages show two pale wingbars. Mature adult male distinctive with red head, breast and rump; wings brown with wingbars tinged pink and underparts white. Immature male and adult male in winter have less intense colour. Female and juvenile have undistinguished brown plumage with underparts pale and streaked. **HABITAT** Scrub and forest edge. **VOICE** Male has distinctive, far-carrying, whistling song.

*Female (ABOVE) much duller than male (BELOW).*

The breeding range of the Scarlet Rosefinch spread west during the late 20th century, and it now nests in significant numbers as far west as southern Scandinavia.

*The **breeding male**'s smart colours are a fitting complement to his tuneful song, which contains elements reminiscent of the Golden Oriole.*

399

# PINE GROSBEAK
## PINICOLA ENUCLEATOR

**LENGTH** 18.5cm
**WINGSPAN** 31–35cm

Pine Grosbeaks are generally rather sedentary.
They feed on the ground, where they hop and
walk, and among branches, where their
progress can be rather cumbersome.

**IDENTIFICATION** Comparatively large,
dumpy finch with large head and stout
bill. Both sexes show two conspicuous
pale wingbars, those of male tinged pink.
Wings of both sexes appear dark grey and
show grey feathering on undertail and
lower belly. In flight, tail looks relatively
long. Adult male has pinkish-red
plumage, while that of adult female is
mainly greenish-yellow. First-year male
and female resemble dull version of adult
female. Juvenile plumage is dull grey-
brown. **HABITAT** Northern taiga forest.
**VOICE** Loud, fluty and yodelling song.

*Although unobtrusive, Pine Grosbeaks
are not shy and can often yield very
good views when found.*

*female*

*adult male*

400

18cm **LENGTH**
26–32cm **WINGSPAN**

# CORN BUNTING
### *EMBERIZA CALANDRA*

A locally common bird of farmland, the Corn Bunting occurs throughout most of mainland Europe as far north as the Baltic coast.

*adults*

**Flies short distances with legs dangling, on fluttering wings.**

**IDENTIFICATION** Large, dumpy bunting with rather plain plumage. Bill large and pinkish and dark eye proportionately large. Upperparts buffish-brown and heavily streaked. Underparts whitish and also heavily streaked, particularly on breast. Often flies on fluttering wings and with legs dangling. Sexes similar, and juvenile similar to adult. **HABITAT** Farmland with hedgerows. **VOICE** Song a unique, discordant jangling; flight call a low-pitched, loud 'kwit' or 'quilp kwit-it'.

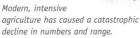

*Modern, intensive agriculture has caused a catastrophic decline in numbers and range.*

*adult*

The male's distinctive song is one of the most characteristic sounds of agricultural land in southern Europe.

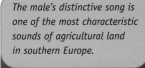

# YELLOWHAMMER
*EMBERIZA CITRINELLA*

During the breeding season, Yellowhammer males frequently announce their presence by singing from the top of a bush or an exposed branch.

*male*

**IDENTIFICATION** Male in summer is attractive, with mostly lemon-yellow plumage on head and underparts. Plumage often has suffusion of chestnut forming breast band and chestnut on wings, mantle and rump; bright, unstreaked rump striking in flight. In winter male's plumage is duller, the feathers having greyish-green tips. Female much duller than male in all plumages and with extensive streaking on head and breast in particular. **HABITAT** Farmland, heaths, scrub. **VOICE** Chirping song, often rendered in English as 'a little bit of bread and no cheese'; rasping call.

RIGHT: *female*

*Breeding **male** much more colourful than female and non-breeding birds.*

16cm **LENGTH**
22–25cm **WINGSPAN**

# CIRL BUNTING
### EMBERIZA CIRLUS

*male*

**Cirl Buntings are sometimes conspicuous in early spring, when the male sings his Lesser Whitethroat-like rattling song from a prominent perch.**

**IDENTIFICATION** Adult male has striking head pattern with black throat and black through eye. Underparts mainly yellow but shows greenish and chestnut breast band. Upperparts mostly chestnut but rump grey-green. Female lacks male's bold head markings and rest of plumage is washed-out version of his. Juvenile similar to female but plumage generally buffish-brown.

**HABITAT** At least partly wooded Mediterranean habitats, hedgerows, scrub and farmland. **VOICE** Male's song is a metallic rattle on one note.

LEFT: *Female distinguished by olive-green rump and buff breast with neat streaks.*

*male*

# BLACK-HEADED BUNTING

**LENGTH** 17cm
**WINGSPAN** 26–29cm

*EMBERIZA MELANOCEPHALA*

**Invariably associated with hot, dry regions, the Black-headed Bunting is common in lowland mainland areas in the eastern Mediterranean between May and August.**

**IDENTIFICATION** Comparatively large bunting with robust, grey bill. Male unmistakable with black head, bright-yellow underparts, yellow sides to neck and chestnut back; wings and tail dark. Female has much more subdued colours, head being greyish-brown. Underparts very pale dirty yellow, and back shows hint of male's chestnut colour. Juvenile superficially resembles Corn Bunting; has rather plain, buffish-brown plumage with streaking on crown and back. **HABITAT** Olive groves, orchards and maquis. **VOICE** Song comprises initial harsh phrases followed by series of notes with tinny ring; flight call a sharp 'tsit'.

*male*

*female*

*juvenile*

*Black-headed Buntings winter in south Asia. By contrast, most other summer migrants to Europe winter in Africa.*

16cm **LENGTH**
23–26cm **WINGSPAN**

# CINEREOUS BUNTING

### *EMBERIZA CINERACEA*

The Cinereous Bunting has an extremely limited global range with isolated populations scattered from Iran to western Turkey; it also breeds on the Greek island of Lesvos.

**IDENTIFICATION** Rather slim, elongated bunting. Adult male has yellowish head and grey-buff underparts. Upperparts are grey-brown overall with streaks on mantle. Note the two pale wingbars. Adult female is similar but plumage colours are much less intense. Juvenile is brown above, pale below and heavily streaked all over. **HABITAT** Stony slopes with short vegetation. **VOICE** Song a ringing 'tsi tsi tis tsee', similar to Cretzschmar's Bunting; call a sharp 'tzit'.

*male*  *singing male*

14cm **LENGTH**
22–24cm **WINGSPAN**

# YELLOW-BREASTED BUNTING

### *EMBERIZA AUREOLA*

The Yellow-breasted Bunting's main breeding range is central Asia; in Europe a few hundred pairs nest in Finland, where it is present from late May to August.

**IDENTIFICATION** Mature summer male has black face and chestnut cap, nape, back and breast band. Underparts and partial throat band yellow; shows white on undertail and two white wingbars. First-summer male has incomplete markings on head. Female has striped head with white throat and white stripe above and behind eye. Underparts pale yellow, and upperparts streaked brown; wingbars less conspicuous. Juvenile has buffish-brown plumage, broad pale super-cilium and dark brown streaked rump. **HABITAT** Flooded woodland and wetland scrub. **VOICE** Jingling song recalling that of Ortolan Bunting; call a sharp 'tsee'.

*female*  *male*

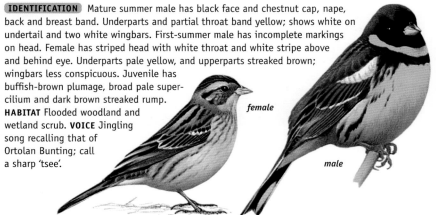

# LITTLE BUNTING
*EMBERIZA PUSILLA*

**LENGTH** 13cm
**WINGSPAN** 20–22cm

The smallest member of the bunting family in the region, the Little Bunting nests in Finland and northern Norway, present from May to August.

**IDENTIFICATION** Recalls non-breeding Reed Bunting but smaller; has finer bill with straight culmen. Breeding male has rusty-brown head with buff supercilium and black stripe above eye defining rusty crown stripe. Shows thin, dark stripe running from behind eye and around ear coverts; small pale spot conspicuous on otherwise rusty-brown ear coverts. Underparts white, streaked on breast and flanks, and upperparts streaked brown. Female, non-breeding male and juvenile similar to breeding male but with subdued colours. **HABITAT** Favours swampy forests during breeding season. **VOICE** Song a series of sharp phrases; call a metallic 'tik'.

*1st-autumn birds (ABOVE), like adults, have boldly striped plumage, striking rusty-brown ear coverts, and a well-marked head pattern.*

15–16cm **LENGTH**
18–21cm **WINGSPAN**

# REED BUNTING
### *EMBERIZA SCHOENICLUS*

*female*

During the breeding season, Reed Bunting males in particular often perch on prominent twigs or barbed wire fences, affording excellent views to the observer as they sing their tirelessly repetitive songs.

ABOVE AND LEFT: *The **male's** new feathers have buff tips, obscuring the black and white pattern, but these wear away over the winter to reveal his spring finery.*

**IDENTIFICATION** In breeding season male is distinctive, with black bill and black head. White on underparts extends around nape as narrow collar and as moustachial stripes to base of bill. Back brown with dark streaking and rump greyish. In non-breeding male, pale feather tips on head make black elements of plumage appear brownish. Female has stripy-headed appearance with black 'moustache' being prominent; plumage otherwise similar to that of male. Juvenile similar to female but with even less distinct markings on head. **HABITAT** Favours wetland habitats, but sometimes found in drier terrain. **VOICE** Song a short series of chinking phrases; call a thin 'seep'.

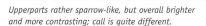

*Upperparts rather sparrow-like, but overall brighter and more contrasting; call is quite different.*

# RUSTIC BUNTING

**LENGTH** 15cm
**WINGSPAN** 21–25cm

*EMBERIZA RUSTICA*

During the breeding season, Rustic Buntings favour damp, boggy woodland with ground vegetation that often includes bog moss and bilberry. They are usually fairly tolerant of people.

**IDENTIFICATION** A well-marked bunting. In some plumages, superficially similar to Reed Bunting, but has proportionately longer bill with straight, not curved, culmen; in all plumages, has pale spots on otherwise dark ear coverts. Male in breeding plumage has bold black and white stripes on head, which has rather peaked appearance. Has rusty chestnut nape, back and breast band with chestnut streaks on flanks and white underparts. In breeding plumage, female similar to male but black on head replaced by brown. **HABITAT** Breeds in northern woodlands. **VOICE** Song a ringing 'see-see-see-see'; call a sharp 'tik'.

*immature*

*summer male*

The summer diet includes numerous adult and larval stages of aquatic and waterside insects, as well as fruits and seeds as the season progresses.

16cm **LENGTH**
22–27cm **WINGSPAN**

# ROCK BUNTING
*EMBERIZA CIA*

*male*

The Rock Bunting invariably favours stony or rocky ground – ideally on sunny, south-facing slopes. In much of its range it is sedentary and resident.

**IDENTIFICATION** Attractive bunting with triangular, silvery grey bill in all plumages. Male is a distinctive and attractive bird, with grey head boldly marked with black stripes. Underparts orange-brown and upperparts, including rump, reddish-brown. Female rather similar to male but plumage always washed-out and less distinct. Juvenile has brown, streaked plumage. **HABITAT** Sunny slopes with broken ground. **VOICE** Male has Dunnock-like song; calls include a sharp 'tsee'.

*Characteristically feeds on broken ground, searching for seeds and insects, but progress usually remarkably slow.*

*female*

*juvenile*

*Despite their colourful plumage, Rock Buntings can be tricky to spot; their plumage often matches the colour of their favoured rocky habitat, and their unobtrusive habits do not help in finding them.*

# CRETZSCHMAR'S BUNTING

*EMBERIZA CAESIA*

The species can be confused with Ortolan Bunting; the warmer, reddish plumage of Cretzschmar's, particularly on the underparts, throat and 'moustache' stripes, is the best feature for identification.

ABOVE: *female*; RIGHT: *male*

**IDENTIFICATION** A well marked, colourful bunting, superficially rather similar to Ortolan, with reddish bill and legs. Male has blue-grey head with reddish-orange 'moustache' stripes and throat; eyering buffish. Underparts reddish-orange and back and wings reddish-brown. Female similar to male but with more subdued colours and some streaking on head. Juvenile very similar to juvenile Ortolan but plumage has reddish, not sandy-olive, tone. **HABITAT** Dry, sunny slopes. **VOICE** Song a ringing 'tsee-tsee-tsee'; flight call a sharp 'chit'.

*male*

410

16cm **LENGTH**

23–28cm **WINGSPAN**

# ORTOLAN BUNTING

*EMBERIZA HORTULANA*

Ortolan Buntings are typically rather unobtrusive birds that feed on the ground. On migration they are often found in ploughed or harvested fields.

BELOW: *female*
BOTTOM: *male*

**IDENTIFICATION** Attractive bunting with rather subdued colours and pinkish bill and legs. Male has greenish-grey head with pale-yellowish eyering, 'moustache' markings and throat. Underparts orange-red and upperparts mostly reddish-brown. Female has less intense colours on head than male and streaking on breast, but otherwise similar. Juvenile has mostly sandy brown plumage. **HABITAT** Variety of habitats, including agricultural land and rocky slopes. **VOICE** Male has ringing 'see-see-see-see' song; 'chip' flight call.

411

# SNOW BUNTING

*PLECTROPHENAX NIVALIS*

BUNTINGS

**LENGTH** 16cm
**WINGSPAN** 32–38cm

**In Europe, the Snow Bunting nests commonly in Scandinavia and Iceland and is widespread in winter on the coast of northwest Europe. On the ground they run as if powered by clockwork.**

**IDENTIFICATION** Breeding-plumage male unmistakable, with striking black and white plumage and black bill. Breeding female has white plumage tinged with orange-buff wash and black elements of male's plumage replaced by brown. Bill dark. In autumn and winter, plumage of adults and juveniles rather variable but back and nape usually appear orange-brown. Often shows buffish-orange on cap and cheeks and as breast band. Underparts always white and bill yellow. In flight shows considerable amount of white on wings and tail in all plumages. **HABITAT** Breeds on Arctic tundra; in winter, on grassland, often coastal. **VOICE** Song a rapid trilling, sung either from perch or in flight; tinkling calls.

ABOVE: **1st winter**

ABOVE: Plumage of **winter birds** variable but bill always yellow. BELOW: **Breeding male** sings sweet, musical song during short display flight.

15.5cm **LENGTH**
26–28cm **WINGSPAN**

# LAPLAND BUNTING

*CALCARIUS LAPPONICUS*

**In Europe the Lapland Bunting breeds in northern Scandinavia. In winter, feeding flocks are unobtrusive.**

*winter male*

**IDENTIFICATION** Male in breeding season unmistakable. Head has striking black, white and chestnut markings and black-tipped yellow bill. Underparts white and back brown with bold streaks. Female in breeding season similar to male but has black on face replaced by worn-looking brown feathering. Both male and female non-breeding birds lose bold markings on head but usually retain hint of chestnut on nape; chestnut wing coverts bordered by two white wingbars are good features for identification. Juvenile recalls winter female but lacks chestnut on nape. Gait of Lapland Bunting is like Snow Bunting's: crouches low and runs rather quickly and jerkily like clockwork toy. **HABITAT** Nests on Arctic tundra; on migration seen on coasts; in winter favours open, often cultivated land, sometimes coasts. **VOICE** Calls include dry, quick rattle, 'tik-ik-ik-it' and liquid 'tew'; song is a rapid trill, sung either from perch or in flight.

ABOVE:
**1st winter** *On ground, crouches low and runs quickly and jerkily through stubble like clockwork toy.*

*breeding male*

*Male easy to see in breeding season because it likes to perch prominently.*

# SNOW GOOSE
*ANSER CAERULESCENS* **LENGTH** 70–75cm

Annual visitor to northwest Europe from
North America, mainly in winter; also
escapes from captivity. Seen in two
colour phases. Adult white phase is pure white
except for black primaries and greyish upperwing
primary coverts. Adult blue phase is a mixture of
blue-grey and white.

*adult*

# BAR-HEADED GOOSE
*ANSER INDICUS* **LENGTH** 70–80cm

Regular escape from captivity, seen amongst
flocks of wild geese. Adult has mainly pale
grey-brown plumage on body. Head white
except for two dark, transverse bars
on crown. Neck dark brown
with bold white stripe
down side. Bill and
legs orange-yellow.

*adult*

# RING-NECKED DUCK *AYTHYA COLLARIS* **LENGTH** 42cm

Annual visitor to northwest Europe from North America, mostly in winter.
Similar to Tufted Duck. Male has blackish head, neck, breast
and back; crown is peaked; greyish flanks separated
from black breast by white vertical stripe.
Female is brown with pale 'spectacle'
around eye.

*male*

# LESSER SCAUP *AYTHYA AFFINIS* **LENGTH** 42cm

Annual visitor to northwest Europe from North America, mostly in
winter. Similar to Greater Scaup but smaller; smaller bill has only
small black tip. Has peaked, not rounded, head.
Female and juvenile are grey-brown,
palest on flanks with
pale spot at base
of bill.

*male*

**414**

## SURF SCOTER *MELANITTA PERSPICILLATA* **LENGTH** 50cm

Vagrant to northwest Europe from North America, mostly in winter. Has large, flat-topped head; large bill continues slope of forehead. Male is black except for white patches on nape and forehead and diagnostic bill pattern. Female and juvenile are brown with pale patches on head.

*male*

## AMERICAN WIGEON
### *ANAS AMERICANA* **LENGTH** 50cm

Annual visitor to northwest Europe from North America, mainly in winter. Similar to Wigeon. Adult male has yellow crown, green mask, pinkish-grey mantle and pinkish-buff underparts. Female and juvenile have reddish-brown flanks with mottled brown back; greyish head has dark eye patch.

*male*

## BLUE-WINGED TEAL *ANAS DISCORS* **LENGTH** 39cm

Annual visitor to northwest Europe from North America. Male has blue-grey head and white crescent in front of eye; body plumage is mottled brown with dark spots. Female, eclipse male and juvenile are mottled grey-brown (recalling Teal) with white patch at base of bill.

*male*

## BLACK DUCK *ANAS RUBRIPES* **LENGTH** 57cm

Annual visitor to northwest Europe from North America. Large, robust dabbling duck. Recalls female Mallard. Male has chocolate-brown body with paler feather edges, and paler grey-brown head; legs are orange. Female and juvenile are similar but with olive bill and brown legs.

*male*

# GREEN-WINGED TEAL
*ANAS CAROLINENSIS* **LENGTH** 34–38cm

Annual visitor to western Europe from North America, mainly in winter. Tiny dabbling duck, similar to Teal. Male is similar to male Teal but with white vertical stripe at front of flanks. Female and juvenile have mottled brown plumage; indistinguishable from female Teal.

*male*

# WOOD DUCK
*AIX SPONSA* **LENGTH** 40–50cm

Frequent escape from wildfowl collections. Male unmistakable and showy, with red bill and green head showing white stripes. Deep red breast has vertical white stripe; flanks buff and back dark. Female similar to female Mandarin with white 'spectacle' around eye.

*male*

# STELLER'S EIDER *POLYSTICTA STELLERI* **LENGTH** 43–47cm

Present all year in north Norway; rare winter visitor to Baltic, typically among Eider flocks. Mature adult male has unmistakable combination of plumage and proportions. Female has dark brown plumage; bill size and head outline are similar to male.

*male*

# PIED-BILLED GREBE *PODILYMBUS PODICEPS* **LENGTH** 32–35cm

Rare vagrant to Europe from North America, mainly in winter. Small, dumpy grebe. Tail short with powder-puff of white undertail feathers. Adult is grey-brown, darker above than below. Bill is marked with striking black band in breeding season only.

*summer adult*

# WILSON'S STORM-PETREL
*OCEANITES OCEANICUS*  **LENGTH** 16–18cm

Antarctic breeder, found from Bay of Biscay to Isles of Scilly
in summer months. Similar to European Storm-petrel: mainly
sooty black with white rump. Yellow-webbed feet project
beyond square-ended tail in flight; this feature
is diagnostic.

*WILSON'S
STORM-PETREL
adult*

# MADEIRAN STORM-PETREL
*OCEANODROMA CASTRO*  **LENGTH** 20cm

Breeds on remote Madeiran islands, otherwise
seen at sea, north to Bay of Biscay. Very similar
to Wilson's and European Storm-petrels. Dark
upperwings show only faint pale band across
secondary coverts. Tail is
slightly forked.

*MADEIRAN
STORM-PETREL
adult*

*BLACK-BROWED
ALBATROSS adult*

# BLACK-BROWED ALBATROSS
*THALASSARCHE MELANOPHRIS*
**WINGSPAN** 220–240cm

Rare visitor to European Atlantic
waters from southern oceans. Glides
on stiffly held wings. Upperwings and
mantle are dark. Body white except
for black 'eyebrow' line above eye
and darkish tail feathers. Bill long
and yellowish.

# MACRONESIAN SHEARWATER
*PUFFINUS BAROLI*  **LENGTH** 27–28cm

Nests on island sea cliffs; otherwise
always at sea. Rarely seen north of
Spanish coast. Flight is fast and fluttering.
Smaller than similar Manx Shearwater with
proportionately shorter wings. Adult has white
underparts including underwing. Upperparts are
blackish-brown.

*MACRONESIAN
SHEARWATER
adult*

# AMERICAN BITTERN *BOTAURUS LENTIGINOSUS* LENGTH 70–80cm

Very rare vagrant to western Europe from North America. Similar to Bittern. Adult has brown, streaked plumage. White throat has reddish-brown streaks. Cap reddish-brown (blackish in Bittern). Has black flight feathers (brown in Bittern).

*adult*

# PALLID HARRIER
### *CIRCUS MACROURUS* LENGTH 44–46cm

Central Asian breeding species; winters in Africa. Migrant through eastern Europe, rare further west. Similar to Montagu's and Hen Harriers. Adult male is very pale grey with small black wingtips. Adult female is similar to female Montagu's Harrier.

*male*

*ANDALUSIAN HEMIPODE adult*

# ANDALUSIAN HEMIPODE
### *TURNIX SYLVATICA* LENGTH 15–16cm

A small, secretive, Quail-like bird; adult has rusty red breast and boldly black-spotted flanks. The crown is brown and finely barred and has a creamy stripe, and the upperparts are brown with darker brown bars and cream streaks. The female is more strikingly marked than the male with overall browner colouring. Formerly occurred in southern Spain, but it is most probably extinct now; it may still occur in North Africa.

*CREAM-COLOURED COURSER*     *adult*

# CREAM-COLOURED COURSER
### *CURSORIUS CURSOR* LENGTH 23cm

Breeds in North African and Middle Eastern deserts; rare vagrant elsewhere. Adult has pinkish-buff plumage, striking head pattern and dark underwing. Juvenile is similar but with scaly markings on upperparts and breast, and indistinct head pattern.

# SOCIABLE PLOVER
### *VANELLUS GREGARIUS* LENGTH 28cm

*SOCIABLE PLOVER adult*

Rare vagrant to Europe, mainly autumn and winter, from Asian breeding grounds. Breeding adult is grey-buff with striking head pattern and dark belly. Winter adult has white belly; head pattern less distinct. Juvenile recalls scaly-looking winter adult.

# WHITE-TAILED PLOVER
*VANELLUS LEUCURUS* **LENGTH** 28cm

Rare vagrant to Europe from Asia. Adult pinkish-buff, palest on face and belly with greyish-buff cap and red eyering; legs yellow, bill dark. Colours are less intense in winter than summer. White rump and tail striking in flight. Juvenile has scaly-looking mantle.

*adult*

*adult*

# SPUR-WINGED PLOVER
*VANELLUS SPINOSUS* **LENGTH** 25–27cm

Scarce breeder in southeast Europe and Middle East. Adult has mainly black and white underparts and buff wing coverts and back. Face and shoulders are white. In flight, mostly white underwing contrasts with black primary tips and belly.

# GREATER SAND PLOVER
*CHARADRIUS LESCHENAULTII* **LENGTH** 24cm

Migrant in eastern Mediterranean, rare vagrant elsewhere. Breeding adult is mainly sandy brown above and white below, with red chest band, white face and dark eye patch. Male is brighter than female. Winter adult recalls large-billed Kentish Plover.

*GREATER SAND PLOVER male*

# CASPIAN PLOVER
*CHARADRIUS ASIATICUS* **LENGTH** 19cm

Very rare Asian vagrant to Europe, mainly in spring. Breeding male has dark-grey cap, white face and throat, dark ear coverts, brown back, brick-red chest band and white underparts. Other plumages are duller with less well-defined chest band.

*CASPIAN PLOVER male*

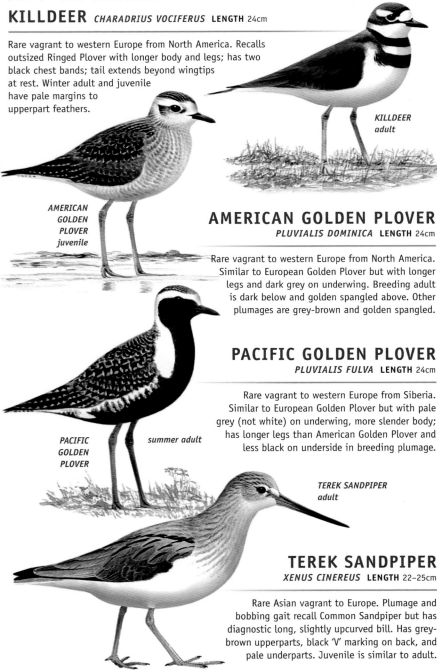

# KILLDEER *CHARADRIUS VOCIFERUS* LENGTH 24cm

Rare vagrant to western Europe from North America. Recalls outsized Ringed Plover with longer body and legs; has two black chest bands; tail extends beyond wingtips at rest. Winter adult and juvenile have pale margins to upperpart feathers.

KILLDEER
adult

AMERICAN
GOLDEN
PLOVER
juvenile

# AMERICAN GOLDEN PLOVER
## *PLUVIALIS DOMINICA* LENGTH 24cm

Rare vagrant to western Europe from North America. Similar to European Golden Plover but with longer legs and dark grey on underwing. Breeding adult is dark below and golden spangled above. Other plumages are grey-brown and golden spangled.

# PACIFIC GOLDEN PLOVER
## *PLUVIALIS FULVA* LENGTH 24cm

Rare vagrant to western Europe from Siberia. Similar to European Golden Plover but with pale grey (not white) on underwing, more slender body; has longer legs than American Golden Plover and less black on underside in breeding plumage.

PACIFIC
GOLDEN
PLOVER

summer adult

TEREK SANDPIPER
adult

# TEREK SANDPIPER
## *XENUS CINEREUS* LENGTH 22–25cm

Rare Asian vagrant to Europe. Plumage and bobbing gait recall Common Sandpiper but has diagnostic long, slightly upcurved bill. Has grey-brown upperparts, black 'V' marking on back, and pale underparts. Juvenile is similar to adult.

# SHARP-TAILED SANDPIPER

*CALIDRIS ACUMINATA* **LENGTH** 18cm

**SHARP-TAILED SANDPIPER**
*summer adult*

Rare vagrant to Europe from Siberia. All birds have brown upperparts, pale underparts, brown cap and ear coverts and broad, pale supercilium; breeding plumage adult has streaks on throat and arrow markings on flanks and undertail.

# RED-NECKED STINT

*CALIDRIS RUFICOLLIS* **LENGTH** 13–15cm

Very rare Asian vagrant to Europe. Similar to Little Stint with shorter bill and legs but longer wings and tail. Adult is grey above and white below; head is rufous in breeding season. Juvenile similar to winter adult but has reddish-brown on crown and mantle.

**RED-NECKED STINT**
*juvenile*

# LEAST SANDPIPER

*CALIDRIS MINUTILLA* **LENGTH** 12cm

Rare vagrant to Europe from North America. Similar to Little Stint but with yellow legs. Breeding adult is grey-brown above with chestnut on cap, ear coverts, back and mantle. Winter adult lacks chestnut. Juvenile is buffish-brown above with reddish-brown on back, crown and ear coverts.

**LEAST SANDPIPER**
*juvenile*

# SEMIPALMATED SANDPIPER

*CALIDRIS PUSILLA* **LENGTH** 14cm

Rare vagrant to Europe from North America. Similar to Little Stint but with broad-based, blob-tipped bill. Juvenile and first autumn (plumages most likely to be seen in Europe) are overall grey-brown above, with reddish-brown feathering on mantle and back, and whitish below.

**SEMIPALMATED SANDPIPER**
*juvenile*

# PECTORAL SANDPIPER
*CALIDRIS MELANOTOS* **LENGTH** 21cm

Regular vagrant from North America. Recalls
Dunlin but with longer neck and smaller
head. Juvenile (plumage most likely to
be seen in Europe) has buffish-brown
upperparts, neck and breast. Shows neat
division between streaks on breast and
white underparts.

*PECTORAL SANDPIPER juvenile*

**WHITE-RUMPED SANDPIPER**
*juvenile*

# WHITE-RUMPED SANDPIPER
*CALIDRIS FUSCICOLLIS* **LENGTH** 16cm

Vagrant from North America. Recalls winter-
plumage Dunlin with longer body; longer wings
extend beyond tail at rest. Bill has dull orange
at base to lower mandible; white rump seen
in flight. All birds are overall grey above
and white below. Juvenile's back
feathers have pale margins.

# BAIRD'S SANDPIPER
*CALIDRIS BAIRDII* **LENGTH** 15cm

Autumn vagrant from North America. Similar to
Dunlin but with shorter bill and elongated rear
end. Juvenile (plumage typically seen in Europe)
has grey-brown upperparts with scaly looking
back; neck and breast are grey-brown and
underparts are white.

*BAIRD'S SANDPIPER
juvenile*

*SPOTTED SANDPIPER juvenile*

# SPOTTED SANDPIPER
*ACTITIS MACULARIA* **LENGTH** 19cm

Vagrant from North America. Very similar
to Common Sandpiper but with shorter
tail. Breeding adult has grey-brown
upperparts and white underparts with
dark spots. Winter adult and juvenile
have well-marked wing coverts.

# SOLITARY SANDPIPER
*TRINGA SOLITARIA* **LENGTH** 20cm

Rare vagrant from North America. Similar to Green Sandpiper but smaller, with proportionately shorter legs and longer wings; in flight, reveals dark rump, not white. Upperparts dark olive-brown, speckled with white spots. Underparts are mainly white.

**SOLITARY SANDPIPER**

*juvenile*

*juvenile*

**BUFF-BREASTED SANDPIPER**

# BUFF-BREASTED SANDPIPER
*TRYNGITES SUBRUFICOLLIS* **LENGTH** 19cm

Annual vagrant from North America. Recalls small juvenile Ruff but distinguished by uniformly buff throat and underparts (white in Ruff), shorter, straighter bill and scaly appearance (especially in juvenile) to mantle and back. Legs are yellow in all birds.

*juvenile*

# WILSON'S PHALAROPE
*PHALAROPUS TRICOLOR* **LENGTH** 23cm

Vagrant from North America. Larger than other phalaropes, with longer bill and legs. Breeding adult has white underparts and throat with orange, red, black and grey on upperparts. Other plumages are pale grey above, white below; juvenile has dark feathers on back.

*LESSER YELLOWLEGS juvenile*

# LESSER YELLOWLEGS
*TRINGA FLAVIPES* **LENGTH** 24cm

Annual vagrant from North America. Recalls Wood Sandpiper but with long, bright yellow legs. Winter adult and juvenile (plumages typically seen in Europe) have grey-brown head, neck and upperparts, spangled on back; underparts are greyish-white.

# GREATER YELLOWLEGS
*TRINGA MELANOLEUCA* **LENGTH** 30cm

Rare vagrant from North America. Recalls Greenshank but legs are yellow. Winter adult and juvenile (plumages typically seen in Europe) have grey back and mantle with pale margins to feathers; juvenile has extensive white spotting on upperparts.

*GREATER
YELLOWLEGS
juvenile*

*STILT SANDPIPER
summer adult*

# STILT SANDPIPER
*CALIDRIS HIMANTOPUS* **LENGTH** 20cm

Rare vagrant from North America. Recalls a *Tringa* wader with longer legs; long bill has downcurved tip. Breeding adult has dark-streaked head and neck, black barring on underparts, and chestnut on crown and ear coverts. Other plumages are greyish above, whitish below.

*LONG-BILLED DOWITCHER
juvenile*

# LONG-BILLED DOWITCHER
*LIMNODROMUS SCOLOPACEUS* **LENGTH** 28–30cm

Rare vagrant from North America. Recalls outsized Snipe. Breeding adult plumage essentially reddish-brown with dark markings. Winter adult has grey-brown upperparts and whitish underparts; juvenile similar but shows chestnut margins to mantle and back feathers.

*UPLAND SANDPIPER
juvenile*

# UPLAND SANDPIPER
*BARTRAMIA LONGICAUDA* **LENGTH** 27cm

Rare vagrant from North America. Recalls tiny, short-billed Curlew with yellowish legs and long wings and tail. Adult upperparts mottled brown; head, neck and breast buffish with dark streaks. Juvenile is similar but back feathers have pale margins.

# IVORY GULL *PAGOPHILA EBURNEA* LENGTH 40–42cm

Rare Arctic vagrant to northern European coasts. Adult has pure white plumage. Bill bluish but grading to yellow towards tip, which is red. Legs and feet black. Juvenile and first-winter birds are white with variable amounts of black spotting and grey feathering on face.

*IVORY GULL juvenile*

*ROSS'S GULL juvenile*

*ROSS'S GULL winter adult*

# ROSS'S GULL
## *RHODOSTETHIA ROSEA* LENGTH 30–32cm

Rare Arctic vagrant to coasts. Small, long-winged gull with wedge-shaped tail and small bill. Winter adult (typical plumage seen in Europe) is pale grey and white on head and underparts. Subtle pink suffusion sometimes seen. Juvenile has dark zigzag on upperwings.

*PALLAS'S GULL summer adult*

# PALLAS'S GULL
## *LARUS ICHTHYAETUS* LENGTH 59cm

Scarce winter visitor to eastern Mediterranean; rare vagrant elsewhere. Large gull with massive bill. Breeding bird has black hood; reduced to dark smudge around eye in winter. Juvenile has more extensive dark markings on wings and dark-tipped pink bill.

# BONAPARTE'S GULL
## *LARUS PHILADELPHIA* LENGTH 29cm

Rare vagrant from North America. Similar to Little Gull but adult has black (not white) wingtips. Summer adult has black hood; winter adult has white head with dark smudges. First winter has dark diagonal band on inner upperwing and black trailing edge along entire wing.

*BONAPARTE'S GULL 1st winter*

# FRANKLIN'S GULL *LARUS PIPIXCAN* **LENGTH** 34cm

Rare vagrant from North America. Adult is grey above, white below, with red bill and legs. In flight, upperwing has white trailing edge. Has black hood in summer, but just black band on nape in winter. First winter recalls adult but back is darker and tail is black-tipped.

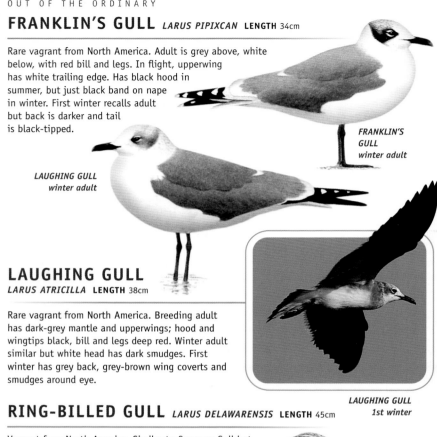

**FRANKLIN'S GULL**
*winter adult*

**LAUGHING GULL**
*winter adult*

# LAUGHING GULL

## *LARUS ATRICILLA* **LENGTH** 38cm

Rare vagrant from North America. Breeding adult has dark-grey mantle and upperwings; hood and wingtips black, bill and legs deep red. Winter adult similar but white head has dark smudges. First winter has grey back, grey-brown wing coverts and smudges around eye.

**LAUGHING GULL**
*1st winter*

# RING-BILLED GULL *LARUS DELAWARENSIS* **LENGTH** 45cm

Vagrant from North America. Similar to Common Gull but larger; its larger bill has a black band and its eye has yellow iris. Winter adult has brownish streaking on head and nape. First-winter bird has variably grey-brown upperparts with pale mantle and spotted head and neck.

*winter adult*

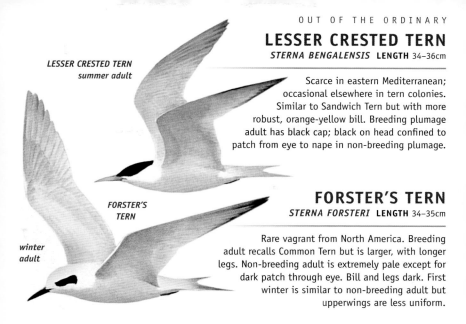

## LESSER CRESTED TERN
*STERNA BENGALENSIS* **LENGTH** 34–36cm

*LESSER CRESTED TERN*
*summer adult*

*FORSTER'S*
*TERN*

*winter*
*adult*

Scarce in eastern Mediterranean; occasional elsewhere in tern colonies. Similar to Sandwich Tern but with more robust, orange-yellow bill. Breeding plumage adult has black cap; black on head confined to patch from eye to nape in non-breeding plumage.

## FORSTER'S TERN
*STERNA FORSTERI* **LENGTH** 34–35cm

Rare vagrant from North America. Breeding adult recalls Common Tern but is larger, with longer legs. Non-breeding adult is extremely pale except for dark patch through eye. Bill and legs dark. First winter is similar to non-breeding adult but upperwings are less uniform.

# YELLOW-BILLED CUCKOO *COCCYZUS AMERICANUS* **LENGTH** 28–30cm

Rare vagrant from North America. Juvenile (plumage likely to be seen here) has grey-brown upperparts with chestnut on flight feathers. Underparts whitish. Has narrow yellow eyering. Underside of tail is grey with white tips. Bill dark but base of lower mandible yellowish.

*juvenile*

*COMMON*
*NIGHTHAWK*

*immature*
*male*

# COMMON NIGHTHAWK
*CHORDEILES MINOR* **LENGTH** 24–25cm

Rare vagrant from North America. Recalls European Nightjar but has shorter, forked (not rounded) tail and longer wings. Finely marked grey-brown plumage gives excellent camouflage against fallen leaves. White wing patch striking in flight. Adult male has white throat.

# OLIVE-BACKED PIPIT *ANTHUS HODGSONI* LENGTH 14–15cm

Rare vagrant from Asia. Recalls Tree Pipit. Olive-green upperparts have little streaking. Underparts have dark spots on breast and flanks; belly and undertail white. Supercilium is buff in front of eye, white behind eye. Has black and white marks on ear coverts.

*RICHARD'S PIPIT juvenile*

*OLIVE-BACKED PIPIT juvenile*

# RICHARD'S PIPIT

## *ANTHUS RICHARDI* LENGTH 18cm

Vagrant from Asia. Large pipit with long tail, legs and hind-claw. Has streaked brown upperparts. Underparts pale buff with warm wash and dark streaks on breast. Head has streaked crown, buff lores and broad supercilium, palest behind eye. Bill long and stout.

*RICHARD'S PIPIT juvenile*

*CITRINE WAGTAIL male*

# CITRINE WAGTAIL

## *MOTACILLA CITREOLA* LENGTH 17–18cm

Scarce passage migrant (E) and vagrant (W). Breeding male has lemon-yellow head and underparts and black collar. Back grey and wings dark with two white wingbars. Yellow is less intense in other adults. First-winter birds pale grey above, white below; white wingbars.

BELOW: *BLACK LARK male*

# BLACK LARK *MELANOCORYPHA*
## *YELTONIENSIS* LENGTH 18–20cm

Rare vagrant from Asia. Plump-bodied lark with a stout bill. Breeding male is mostly black except for silvery edges to feathers on back. Female and immature have similar proportions to male but mostly scaly-looking plumage except for dark wings.

# WHITE-THROATED ROBIN
*IRANIA GUTTURALIS* **LENGTH** 17–18cm

Scarce breeding species in southeast Europe. Plump-bodied, thrush-like bird. Male has grey upperparts, black face with white throat, white supercilium and orange-red underparts. Female and immature lack male's black on head; orange is restricted to flush on flanks.

*male*

*SIBERIAN RUBYTHROAT*
*male*

# SIBERIAN RUBYTHROAT
*LUSCINIA CALLIOPE* **LENGTH** 14cm

Rare vagrant from Asia. Adult male is mostly grey-brown, palest on underparts, with pale supercilium, white submoustachial stripe and ruby-red throat. Adult female lacks male's red throat. First-autumn bird is similar to respective sex adult with pale tips to wing coverts.

*RED-FLANKED BLUETAIL*
*male*

# RED-FLANKED BLUETAIL
*TARSIGER CYANURUS* **LENGTH** 13–14cm

Occasional breeder in Finland, rare vagrant elsewhere. Adult male has blue upperparts and tail. Has white throat; underparts otherwise pale, flushed orange-red on flanks. Female and first-autumn birds have blue tail but other blue elements of male's plumage buffish-brown.

*SIBERIAN STONECHAT*
*male*

# SIBERIAN STONECHAT
*SAXICOLA MAURA* **LENGTH** 12.5cm

Rare vagrant from Asia. Similar to Stonechat. Male is more strikingly black and white with orange-red flush to breast. Note pure white, unstreaked rump and white wing panel. Adult female and immatures are buffish-brown above, paler below, with very pale rump.

# DESERT WHEATEAR
*OENANTHE DESERTI* **LENGTH** 14–15cm

*DESERT
WHEATEAR*

*male*

Rare vagrant from Middle East and Asia.
All-black tail is diagnostic in all birds.
Male recalls black-throated form of
Black-eared Wheatear but black on
face and throat links with black
wings. Other elements of plumage
pale sandy brown except for
white rump.

*DESERT WHEATEAR
1st winter*

# SWAINSON'S THRUSH
*CATHARUS USTULATUS* **LENGTH** 18cm

*SWAINSON'S
THRUSH*

Rare vagrant from North America. All birds have conspicuous
buffish-yellow eyering. Juvenile (plumage seen in Europe) has
warm olive-brown upperparts, sometimes showing pale spots.
Underparts greyish-white with black spots on neck.
Legs pink in all birds.

*GREY-CHEEKED
THRUSH
juvenile*

*juvenile*

# GREY-CHEEKED THRUSH
*CATHARUS MINIMUS* **LENGTH** 18cm

Rare vagrant from North America. Similar to
Swainson's but lacks that species' buffish
eyering. Juvenile (plumage seen in Europe)
is grey-brown above, greyish-white below, with
dark spots on breast. Has buffish margins to
wing coverts and tertials. Legs are pink.

*VEERY
juvenile*

# VEERY *CATHARUS FUSCESCENS* **LENGTH** 17cm

Rare vagrant from North America. Recalls Nightingale
with warm-brown upperparts and tail; underparts
mostly greyish-white. Throat, sides of neck and
upper breast have pale buffish wash and
faint grey-brown spotting; note the
faint, pale wingbar.

# HERMIT THRUSH *CATHARUS GUTTATUS* LENGTH 17cm

Rare vagrant from North America. Recalls Thrush Nightingale with olive-brown head and back, reddish-brown lower rump and tail, and greyish-white underparts; shows dark spots on throat and upper breast; margins of primaries reddish-brown. Legs are pinkish.

**HERMIT THRUSH**
*juvenile*

**AMERICAN ROBIN**
*male*

# AMERICAN ROBIN
*TURDUS MIGRATORIUS* LENGTH 25cm

Rare vagrant from North America. Adult male has grey upperparts, white 'eyelids' and dark streaking on throat; breast and belly are red. Adult female is similar but red is much less intense. Juvenile similar to female but even duller, appearing browner on upperparts.

# DARK-THROATED THRUSH
*TURDUS RUFICOLLIS* LENGTH 25cm

Rare vagrant from Asia. Occurs as two races. Adult male always pale grey-brown above and white below; race *atrogularis* (most regular in Europe) has black breast; race *ruficollis* (Red-throated Thrush) has red breast. Females and juveniles duller than respective race males.

**DARK-THROATED THRUSH**
*male*

**EYEBROWED THRUSH**
*male*

# EYEBROWED THRUSH
*TURDUS OBSCURUS* LENGTH 23cm

Rare vagrant from Asia. Adult male has dark grey head with white supercilium, and white below eye and on throat. Has brown back and wings, and orange-red breast and flanks. Female and juvenile male are similar but colours are less intense.

# WHITE'S THRUSH *ZOOTHERA DAUMA* LENGTH 27cm

Rare vagrant from Asia. Recalls immature Mistle Thrush but overall appearance is more scaly. Adult's body feathers have numerous black crescent markings; wings buff-brown with pale feather margins. Juvenile's dark markings more rounded than crescent-shaped.

*adult*

*SIBERIAN THRUSH*

*male*

# SIBERIAN THRUSH
*ZOOTHERA SIBIRICA* LENGTH 22cm

Rare vagrant from Asia. Adult male is blue-black with white supercilium; paler flanks show dark crescent-shaped markings; belly white. Juvenile male similar but overall paler. Female similar to juvenile male but dark elements of plumage are warm brown.

# BLYTH'S REED WARBLER
*ACROCEPHALUS DUMETORUM* LENGTH 13cm

*BLYTH'S REED WARBLER adult*

Breeds from Finland eastwards; rare vagrant elsewhere. Medium-sized, slim warbler; similar to Reed and Marsh Warblers. Adult is grey-brown above, pale below; note short primaries and dark-tipped lower mandible of bill. Juvenile similar but upperparts warmer brown.

# PADDYFIELD WARBLER
*ACROCEPHALUS AGRICOLA* LENGTH 13cm

Breeds from eastern Romania eastwards; vagrant elsewhere. Recalls Reed Warbler but plumage shows more contrast. Pale brown above with reddish rump. Note dark eyestripe and white supercilium. Underparts pale. Juvenile's plumage shows less contrast than adult.

*PADDYFIELD WARBLER adult*

# YELLOW-BROWED WARBLER
### *PHYLLOSCOPUS INORNATUS* LENGTH 10cm

Regular autumn migrant from Asia. Tiny, active
warbler, between Goldcrest and Chiffchaff in size.
Has greyish-green upperparts and greyish-white
underparts. Note long, pale-yellow supercilium
and double pale-yellow wingbar.

*juvenile*

# PALLAS'S WARBLER
### *PHYLLOSCOPUS PROREGULUS* LENGTH 9cm

Autumn vagrant from Asia. Tiny, active warbler;
recalls Yellow-browed but smaller and more
striking. Has greenish-yellow upperparts and
greyish-white underparts. Note dark eyestripe,
yellowish supercilium and crown stripe, two pale
wingbars and yellow rump.

*juvenile*

# DUSKY WARBLER
### *PHYLLOSCOPUS FUSCATUS* LENGTH 11cm

Rare vagrant from Asia. Small, active warbler; similar to Chiffchaff
but legs pink, not blackish, and plumage darker. Has mostly
brownish upperparts and yellowish underparts. Note
the bold, dull yellowish supercilium, often
brightest in front of eye.

*juvenile*

# RADDE'S WARBLER
### *PHYLLOSCOPUS SCHWARZI* LENGTH 12cm

Rare autumn vagrant from Asia. Large, plump
warbler with short, thick bill and
proportionately large
head; movements slower
than similar warblers. Has brown
upperparts and yellowish-buff underparts.
Note broad, pale supercilium, palest behind
eye. Legs are pale.

*juvenile*

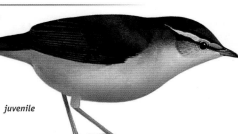

# BOOTED WARBLER *HIPPOLAIS CALIGATA* LENGTH 12cm

Rare autumn vagrant from Asia. Small and pale, similar
to *Phylloscopus* warblers, but more stocky with more
robust bill and pale lores. Adult has grey-buff
upperparts and pale underparts, washed
buff on flanks. Juvenile has
darker upperparts and
flanks than adult.

*juvenile*

# SYKES' WARBLER
*HIPPOLAIS RAMA* LENGTH 11–12cm

Rare autumn vagrant from Asia. Similar to Booted Warbler with
which it was formerly considered conspecific. Differs in
paler grey-buff upperparts, paler, less buff-washed
underparts, longer primary projection and
marginally longer bill. Juveniles
resemble adults.

*juvenile*

*DESERT WARBLER*
*adult, Middle*
*Eastern*

# DESERT WARBLER
*SYLVIA NANA* LENGTH 12cm

Rare vagrant from Middle East and
Africa. Small, extremely pale warbler. Generally
skulking but sometimes perches on top of bush like
Dartford Warbler. Has pale sandy buff upperparts
(greyest on Middle Eastern race) and white
underparts. Legs, bill and eye are yellow.

# AZURE TIT
*PARUS CYANUS* LENGTH 13cm

*AZURE TIT*
*adult*

Occasional in Finland; rare vagrant elsewhere. All birds have
largely white plumage. Head has narrow black stripe from eye to
join black nape band. Back pale blue-grey and wings blue with white
wingbar and white tips to secondary feathers. Tail blue with white tips.

# TRUMPETER FINCH
*BUCANETES GITHAGINEUS* **LENGTH** 12.5cm

Rare vagrant from Middle East and Africa. Small, compact finch with large, stubby bill; red in summer male but pinkish-buff in winter male and in female. Plumage is uniform buffish but male has pinkish flush to underparts and wings. Legs pinkish in both sexes.

*male*

# RED-EYED VIREO
*VIREO OLIVACEUS* **LENGTH** 12cm

Rare autumn vagrant from North America. Has red eye, stout bill, greenish-brown upperparts and striking head pattern: broad white supercilium and patch under eye, dark line through eye and dark margin to grey crown. Underparts are whitish. Legs are bluish.

*juvenile*

# AMERICAN REDSTART
*SETOPHAGA RUTICILLA* **LENGTH** 14cm

Rare autumn vagrant from North America. Has slaty black upperparts with red patches on sides of breast. Juvenile (most likely plumage seen in Europe) has grey-brown upperparts with orange-yellow on flanks and patches of yellow on wings and tail.

*juvenile*

# COMMON YELLOWTHROAT
*GEOTHLYPIS TRICHAS* **LENGTH** 12cm

Rare autumn vagrant from North America. Adult male has striking black mask, olive-brown upperparts and bright yellow throat and upper breast. Female and juvenile (latter is most likely plumage to be seen in Europe) lack black mask, having greyish lores and ear coverts.

*male*

# NORTHERN PARULA
*PARULA AMERICANA* **LENGTH** 11cm

Rare autumn vagrant from North America. Adult male has blue-grey upperparts, yellow throat and flush of orange on breast. Female and first winters (latter is most likely plumage seen in Europe) are similar but breast markings are less striking and flight feathers are fringed green.

NORTHERN
PARULA
*1st winter*

YELLOW-RUMPED
WARBLER
*1st winter*

# YELLOW-RUMPED WARBLER
*DENDROICA CORONATA* **LENGTH** 14cm

Rare autumn vagrant from North America. All birds have yellow rump. Breeding male is streaked blue-grey with two white wingbars. Female and first-winter birds (latter is most likely plumage seen in Europe) much duller with streaked warm-brown upperparts and two white wingbars.

# BLACKPOLL WARBLER
*DENDROICA STRIATA* **LENGTH** 14cm

Rare autumn vagrant from North America. All plumages show two striking white wingbars, and white spots on outertail feathers. Female and first-autumn birds (latter plumage is most likely in Europe) are heavily streaked and washed buffish-yellow. All birds have dark legs.

*1st winter*

# BLACK-AND-WHITE WARBLER
*MNIOTILTA VARIA* **LENGTH** 12cm

Rare autumn vagrant from North America. Plumage entirely black and white with prominent streaking. All plumages are similar except that first-autumn males have buffish wash to sides of neck and flanks and have greyish, not black, ear coverts.

*1st autumn*

## NORTHERN WATERTHRUSH *SEIURUS NOVEBORACENSIS*
**LENGTH** 14cm

Rare autumn vagrant from North America.
Superficially thrush-like warbler that bobs up
and down like a Dipper when feeding. Sexes are
similar and juvenile resembles adult; upperparts
are olive-brown and underparts are
off-white marked with black spots.

*1st winter*

## SCARLET TANAGER
*PIRANGA OLIVACEA* **LENGTH** 16cm

Rare vagrant from North America. Breeding male is
bright red with black wings and tail. Winter male
is olive-brown; female and first-winter male
(latter is most likely plumage to be seen
in Europe) are olive-yellow.

*1st winter*

## ROSE-BREASTED GROSBEAK
*PHEUCTICUS LUDOVICIANUS* **LENGTH** 20cm

Rare autumn vagrant from North America. Adult male is mainly
black above and white below with red flush on breast. Other
plumages have similar overall pattern but back is streaked
brown, with white wingbars, supercilium and moustachial
stripe; first-winter male has faint pink flush to breast.

*ROSE-BREASTED
GROSBEAK
1st winter*

## BALTIMORE ORIOLE
*ICTERUS GALBULA* **LENGTH** 18cm

Rare autumn vagrant
from North America.
Adult male has black
head, breast and upperparts, and orange rump and underparts.
Female and juvenile (latter is mostly likely plumage in Europe)
are brown instead of black and dull orange-buff rather than orange.

*BALTIMORE ORIOLE
1st winter*

**Abrasion** Wear and tear on feathers, which can change a bird's appearance dramatically. Pale parts wear more easily than dark; for example, white spots on gulls' wingtips wear off to leave a uniform dark colour.

**Barring** Narrow bands or stripes on a bird's plumage.

**Basal knob** Swelling seen at the base of the bill in some species of wildfowl.

**Boreal** Referring to northerly latitudes – those immediately south of the Arctic.

**Calls** Sounds uttered by birds other than song. In some non-passerines these may fulfill the same role as song, but they usually serve contact and alarm functions.

**Carpal** Area of feathers at wrist joint of wings, contrastingly marked in some birds of prey.

**Carr** Type of woodland; occurs in damp situations and normally comprises alder.

**Cere** Naked wax-like membrane at base of bill.

**Courtship** In order to mate and rear young successfully, pairs of most species must first break down their natural instinct to keep their distance, must reduce aggression and maintain a firm relationship, or pair bond; this is created and reinforced by courtship behaviour.

**Coverts** The name given to a group of feathers covering a particular part of a bird's body. Thus ear coverts cover the ear, undertail coverts are found on the undertail area and underwing coverts are found lining the inner part of the underwing. Those feathers on the upperwing not concerned with flight are also referred to as coverts; they are arranged in zones which are, from the leading edge backwards, referred to as greater, median and lesser coverts; those covering the bases of the primary feathers are called primary coverts.

**Culmen** Upper ridge of the bill.

**Display** Behaviour designed to demonstrate a bird's presence.

**Diurnal** Active during the day.

**Eclipse** A dull plumage, notable of male duck, acquired after breeding to reduce conspicuousness (ducks moult all their flight feathers and lose the power of flight for a short period while 'in eclipse').

**Extralimital** Outside the normal range.

**Feral** Precise definition means 'wild', but is used to describe a species or individuals once domesticated or captive but since released or escaped and living wild.

**Flank** Side of breast and belly.

**Gape** The opening or the corners of the mouth; 'to gape' is to hold the bill wide open.

**Garrigue** Sparsely vegetated habitat characteristic of arid, stony terrain in the Mediterranean region.

**Gliding** Effortless and usually level flight where wingbeats are not involved.

**Hirundines** Swallows and martins, members of the family Hirundinidae.

**Immature** Strictly speaking, it means not old enough to breed. But with birds this usually refers to a plumage state that precedes full adult plumage. Confusingly, some birds, such as eagles, are able to breed in immature plumage. Others, like the Fulmar, may not breed for several years even though visually indistinguishable from an adult.

**Irruption** The sudden large-scale movement of birds out of one area and their arrival into another; generally occurs in response to food shortage.

**Jizz** Field characteristics that are unique to a species.

**Juvenile** A bird in its first set of feathers, or juvenile plumage.

**Lek** Communal display ground.

**Lores** Region of feathers between the eye and the bill.

**Malar stripe** A marking originating at the base of the lower mandible of the bill.

**Mandible** One half of the bill.

**Maquis** Shrub-dominated vegetation typical of many parts of the Mediterranean region.

**Migration** Regular, seasonal movements of a species from breeding grounds to winter quarters; it is more or less predictable. Irregular movements caused by, for example, hard weather or food shortage also occur (*see* Fieldfare). Young birds invariably spread away from breeding areas in autumn – this type of movement is termed dispersal.

**Mimicry** Vocal mimicry is copying other sounds, natural or man-made; the precise reason for it is unknown.

**Mobbing** Small birds that discover a roosting owl or bird of prey, or sometimes a mammalian predator or snake, will flutter around or dive at it with loud calls, attracting other species to join in. The purpose is uncertain.

**Moult** Shedding and replacement of feathers or plumage in a regular sequence, which may or may not affect the appearance of the bird. Many species have feathers with dull tips that crumble away in spring to reveal brighter colours beneath. This is sometimes referred to as moulting by abrasion.

**Nest** Usually thought of as a structure to hold eggs. Some birds, however, dispense with nests and lay their eggs on the ground or on a ledge.

**Nocturnal** Active at night.

**Partial migrant** A species where only some individuals migrate.

**Passage** Refers to migrants and migration – a bird 'on passage' is en route to its winter or summer grounds. A 'passage migrant' is a species that appears in the spring and/or autumn but does not breed or spend the winter.

**Passerine** One of a large order of birds called the Passiformes, all members of which can perch (although many other birds can perch as well).

**Pelagic** Found on the open sea.

**Plumage** The whole set of feathers covering a bird. Also used to describe different combinations of colour and pattern according to sex, season or age (for example, summer plumage, adult plumage, etc.).

**Predator** An animal that eats other animals. Among birdwatchers the term is often used to describe an avian predator of other birds.

**Primaries** Outer flight feathers.

**Preening** Using the bill to clean and adjust the feathers.

**Puszta** East European grassy plain.

**Raptor** Bird of prey.

**Resident** A species that remains in a given area all year round.

**Roost** Rest or 'sleep', or the place where a bird or birds do this.

**Scapulars** Region of feathers between the mantle and the wing coverts.

**Scrape** Nest site of some wader species, where a small depression is made in the soil or gravelly substrate.

**Secondaries** Flight feathers in the middle of the wing.

**Sedentary** A non-migratory, non-dispersive species.

**Soaring** Effortless flight by broad-winged birds rising on heat thermals and updraughts.

**Song** Voice of a bird in a recognisable pattern for its species, be it an irregular flow or a repetitive phrase; intended to identify the individual and its species, to proclaim ownership of territory and/or attract a mate. Other vocal sounds are usually termed 'calls'.

**Species** A 'kind' of organism, basically isolated from others by its inability to cross-breed and produce fertile young. A subspecies is a recognisably different group (because of size or colour) within a species in a defined area. Apart from subspecies the remarkable feature of each bird species is the lack of variation within it, in terms of size, colour, pattern, voice, behaviour, food and nest; many other factors remain remarkably constant.

**Speculum** Coloured patch on a duck's wing, often used in display.

**Steppe** Treeless, grassy habitat associated mainly with Russia and eastern Europe.

**Supercilium** Stripe above the eye.

**Taiga** Forest type found at northerly latitudes, just before the tree-line is reached; often comprises spruce and birch.

**Territory** An area (or 'home range') occupied by a bird (or a pair), and which is defended against other individuals of the same species.

**Tertials** Inner flight feathers.

**Thermalling** Method of flight employed by broad-winged birds, including raptors and storks, where lift is provided by uprising currents of warm or hot air.

**Tundra** Northern, treeless habitat; normally characterised by the presence of permafrost.

**Vagrant** Usually a migrant that appears outside its normal range. During spring migration, southerly winds often induce migrants to overshoot. On autumn migration inexperienced juveniles are sometimes blown off course by strong winds or engage in 'reverse migration' (flying in the wrong direction).

**Vermiculation** Feather pattern where numerous worm-like lines create a close-packed pattern.

All photographs in this book were supplied by **Nature Photographers Ltd.**

All photographs were taken by **Paul Sterry** with the exception of those listed below; these can be identified by using a combination of page number and subject.

**Frank Blackburn:** 256 Lesser Spotted Woodpecker. **Mark Bolton:** 207 Roseate Tern (three images); 281 Alpine Accentor; 307 Fan-tailed Warbler; 398 Two-barred Crossbill. **Laurie Campbell:** 54 Black-throated Diver; 88 Golden Eagle. **Kevin Carlson:** 298 Rock Thrush. **Andrew Cleave:** 56 Black-necked Grebe; 131 Little Crake. **Peter Craig-Cooper:** 85 Lammergeier adult; 136 Crested Coot. **Ernie Janes:** 13 Snow Bunting flock; 93 Long-legged Buzzard; 106 Goshawk; 107 Sparrowhawk male; 120 Red Grouse female; 161 Sanderling flying; 162 Knot flock; 171 Turnstone flying; 228 Long-eared Owl. **Keith Lugg:** 111 Merlin juvenile. **Andrew Merrick:** 108 Levant Sparrowhawk male flying; 195 Yellow-legged Gull flying. **Jonathan Meyrav:** 316 Olive-tree Warbler. **Hugh Miles:** 124 Capercaillie female. **Philip Newman:** 100 Hen Harrier male and female; 120 Red Grouse male; 123 Black Grouse male and female; 397 Scottish Crossbill. **David Osborn:** 69 Gannet colony; 78 Cattle Egret; 95 Osprey (both images); 111 Merlin male; 116 Sanderling adult summer; 171 Turnstone adult breeding; 206 Caspian Tern standing; 417 Black-browed Albatross. **Bill Paton:** 128 Grey Partridge. **Richard Revels:** 89 White-tailed Eagle adult flying; 197 Great Black-backed Gull standing; 203 Little Tern adult flying (top image); 204 Sandwich Tern nesting adults; 210 Puffin flying; 211 Razorbill flying; 212 Guillemot flying. **Peter Roberts:** 184 Pomarine Skua. **James Sutherland:** 181 Jack Snipe. **Roger Tidman:** 47 Goldeneye flying; 50 Smew flying; 53 Red-throated Diver flying; 74 Bittern flying; 79 Great White Egret flying (bottom image); 85 Lammergeier juvenile; 89 White-tailed Eagle adult standing and juvenile flying; 92 Spanish Imperial Eagle juvenile; 93 Rough-legged Buzzard; 97 Short-toed Eagle perched; 98 Booted Eagle; 99 Bonelli's Eagle adult and juvenile; 101 Montagu's Harrier male perched, male flying, female flying; 102 Marsh Harrier male (two images); 109 Lanner Falcon; 112 Kestrel male flying; 115 Gyr Falcon; 126 Red-legged Partridge; 137 Coot flying; 141 Little Bustard female; 142 Great Bustard; 157 Temminck's Stint flying; 170 Ruff flying; 172 Whimbrel wing-stretching; 175 Bar-tailed Godwit adult summer; 178 Woodcock; 183 Arctic Skua dark phase flying; 190 Audouin's Gull flying; 191 Slender-billed Gull adult flying; 204 Sandwich Tern non-breeding flying; 205 Gull-billed Tern adult standing and flying; 226 Great Grey Owl; 239 Pallid Swift; 240 Little Swift; 258 Shore Lark; 263 Lesser Short-toed Lark; 266 Sand Martin; 318 Melodious Warbler (two images); 323 Subalpine Warbler female; 324 Western Orphean Warbler adult; 327 Garden Warbler; 351 Bearded Tit; 382 Rock Sparrow; 383 Goldfinch juvenile; 389 Serin; 400 Pine Grosbeak; 413 Lapland Bunting; 435 Trumpeter Finch. **Derek Washington:** 208 Common Tern standing.